About the Cover

The cover reproduces "Culture Contains the Seed of Resistance that Blossoms into the Flower of Liberation," a mural located on the east side of Balmy Alley in San Francisco, CA. Miranda Bergman and O'Brien Thiele. Copyright 1984.

Service Learning for Civic Engagement Series
Series Editor: Gerald Eisman

Available:

Race, Poverty, and Social Justice
Multidisciplinary Perspectives Through Service Learning
Edited by José Calderón

Gender Identity, Equity, and Violence
Multidisciplinary Perspectives Through Service Learning
Edited by Geraldine B. Stahly

Promoting Health and Wellness in Underserved Communities
Multidisciplinary Perspectives Through Service Learning
Edited by Anabel Pelham and Elizabeth Sills

Research, Advocacy, and Political Engagement
Multidisciplinary Perspectives Through Service Learning
Edited by Sally Cahill Tannenbaum

SOCIAL RESPONSIBILITY AND SUSTAINABILITY

SOCIAL RESPONSIBILITY AND SUSTAINABILITY

Multidisciplinary Perspectives
Through Service Learning

Edited by Tracy McDonald

Foreword by Robert A. Corrigan

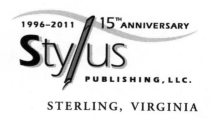

1996–2011 15TH ANNIVERSARY

Sty us
PUBLISHING, LLC.

STERLING, VIRGINIA

Published by Stylus Publishing, LLC
22883 Quicksilver Drive
Sterling, Virginia 20166-2102

Library of Congress Cataloging-in-Publication Data
Social responsibility and sustainability : multidisciplinary
perspectives through service learning / edited by Tracy
McDonald ; foreword by Robert A. Corrigan.—1st ed.
   p.   cm.— (Service learning for civic engagement series)
Includes bibliographical references and index.
ISBN 978-1-57922-417-2 (cloth : alk. paper)
ISBN 978-1-57922-418-9 (pbk. : alk. paper)
ISBN 978-1-57922-725-8 (library networkable e-edition : alk.
paper)
ISBN 978-1-57922-726-5 (consumer e-edition : alk. paper)
   1. Service learning—United States.   2. Civics—Study and
teaching (Higher)—United States.   3. Science—Study and
teaching (Higher)—United States.   4. Education, Higher—
Social aspects—United States.   5. College-school
cooperation—United States.   I. McDonald, Tracy, 1956–
LC220.5.S633   2012
378.1'03—dc23   2011018161

ISBN: 978-1-57922-417-2 (cloth)
ISBN: 978-1-57922-418-9 (paper)
ISBN: 978-1-57922-725-8 (library networkable e-edition)
ISBN: 978-1-57922-726-5 (consumer e-edition)

Printed in the United States of America

All first editions printed on acid-free paper
that meets the American National Standards Institute
Z39-48 Standard.

Bulk Purchases

Quantity discounts are available for use in workshops
and for staff development.
Call 1-800-232-0223

First Edition, 2011

10   9   8   7   6   5   4   3   2   1

CONTENTS

ACKNOWLEDGMENTS   *ix*

FOREWORD   *xi*
Robert A. Corrigan

ABOUT THIS SERIES   *xv*
Gerald S. Eisman

ACTIVITY/METHODOLOGY TABLE   *xvii*

CONTRIBUTORS   *xxi*

INTRODUCTION   *xxiii*
Tracy McDonald

SECTION ONE: ENVIRONMENTAL AWARENESS

1. RECONNECTING TO LAND, PEOPLE, AND COMMUNITY   *3*
   Ecological Lessons From the Puebla-Alberta Community
   Service Exchange
   Hans-Dittmar Mündel and Karsten Mündel

2. INTEGRATING SUSTAINABILITY AND SERVICE
   LEARNING INTO THE SCIENCE CURRICULUM   *21*
   Susan Sutheimer and Jesse Pyles

3. SUSTAINABILITY EDUCATION THROUGH AN
   INTERDISCIPLINARY AND SERVICE-LEARNING
   APPROACH   *35*
   Alison K. Varty, Shane C. Lishawa, and Nancy C. Tuchman

SECTION TWO: INCREASING CIVIC ENGAGEMENT

4. WHAT'S THE MATTER WITH AMERICAN DEMOCRACY?   *61*
   Responding by Embracing Civic Engagement and Sustainability
   Scott G. McNall

5. SUSTAINABILITY STARTS AT HOME   78
   A Hybrid Service-Learning Model for Teaching Environmental
   Sustainability
   J. Marshall Eames and Jeremy Brooks

6. LEARNING BY DOING ACROSS DISCIPLINES   116
   Activism, Environmental Awareness, and Civic Engagement
   Cheryl Swift and sal johnston

7. FROM WOLVES TO WIND POWER   135
   Fostering Student Understanding of Science, Stewardship, and
   Civic Engagement
   Karen Whitehead and Mary Kay Helling

8. MULTICULTURALISM AND SUSTAINABILITY
   EDUCATION   146
   Engagement With Urban School Communities via Food and
   Learning Gardens
   Dilafruz R. Williams

SECTION THREE: SUSTAINABILITY CONCEPTS IN
BUSINESS AND ECONOMICS

9. BUILDING BRIDGES AND SOCIAL CAPITAL THROUGH
   SERVICE LEARNING   165
   A Blueprint Model
   Curtis L. DeBerg

10. SUSTAINABLE DESIGN PRACTICES FOR THE SOCIAL
    ENTREPRENEURIAL BUSINESS   187
    Connie Ulasewicz

11. TEACHING SUSTAINABLE RURAL ECONOMIC
    DEVELOPMENT USING SERVICE-LEARNING PEDAGOGY   202
    Beth Wilson

INDEX   227

ACKNOWLEDGMENTS

We would like to give special thanks to colleagues within and external to the California State University who serve on the advisory board for the monograph series. Debra David, Barbara Holland, Kathy O'Byrne, Seth Pollack, and Maureen Rubin continue to provide invaluable advice on the development of the current volumes and the dimensions the series will explore in the future.

This volume would not be possible without the stories of inspired work of the thousands of dedicated faculty and lecturers working in the California State University system.

This material is based upon work supported by the Corporation for National and Community Service under Learn and Serve America Grant No. 03LHHCA003. Opinions or points of view expressed in this document are those of the authors and do not necessarily reflect the official position of the corporation or the Learn and Serve America Program.

FOREWORD

Perhaps once in a generation a movement comes along to redefine—even transform—higher education. I can point to the GI Bill of 1944, which opened the gates to a much broader population than had ever before enjoyed the opportunity to receive higher education. The civil rights struggle and the later antiwar movement galvanized students and faculty across the nation. Many of us participated directly in these movements; many more worked then, and in the years that followed, to overhaul what we perceived as an outmoded university curriculum as we struggled to open up the university to new ideas; new teaching strategies; and, most of all, underrepresented populations.

To this list, I would now add community service learning. I consider this movement in higher education as exciting as anything I have experienced as an educator. Service learning, and its central role in our goals of campuswide civic engagement and ethical education, may be the most significant development on our campuses since the curricular reforms of the 1960s. In fact, I believe that it will prove to be *the* higher education legacy of the early 21st century, and that it will have a lifelong impact on our students.

Since service learning began to take formal hold throughout the nation in the early 1990s, it has come to be seen as much more than community volunteerism linked with academic study. It is a vehicle for character and citizenship development—in short, for all that we most value in a liberal education. Through thoughtfully structured service-learning experiences, students can test and apply the values of a healthy democracy to some of the most complex and challenging issues of our time.

In recent years, higher education has begun more deliberately to pursue a historic mission: what I might call moral education—our responsibility both to our students and to society. The American Association of Colleges and Universities (1995) terms this "core commitments," and calls on us to educate our students "for personal and social responsibility." This is the highest aim of liberal education. It is the culmination of our mission to service; to preparing our students with the skills and desire to contribute positively to our democratic society and to the greater world; to fostering a campus climate where speech is open, but where we can disagree—even passionately—without venom or hatred; and to ensuring that our students find in the classroom a safe and receptive environment in which to express, test, and challenge varying views.

A true liberal education encompasses far more than the breadth of knowledge and exposure to fields other than one's major that typically shape general education programs. That is certainly necessary, but liberal education transcends subject matter. Liberal education addresses both mind and heart. It is a set of experiences that give our students the tools they will need to think about complex issues and to deal with them as informed, ethical citizens. Liberal education helps our students deal with ambiguity and contradictions, helps them evaluate competing arguments and perspectives so that they will not have to fall back on the comfort—and distortion—of a binary, good/bad, worldview.

Complexity characterizes our key social missions, as we seek to foster in our students respect and understanding of other cultures and viewpoints together with the skills they will need to move positively and effectively in a diverse and global society. I am most emphatically *not* talking about indoctrinating our students—presenting our values and asking them to take them as their own. Rather, I am talking about teaching our students *why* and *how* to think and reason about ethical and moral issues—not presenting them with answers, but developing their skills in finding their own way.

Liberal education prepares our students to act—and to do so in the context of values that take in the needs and concerns of others. Viewed in this context, the value of civically focused service learning is clear. It places our students in the arenas where ethics and efficacy need to join, where disciplinary boundaries are often irrelevant and integrative learning occurs naturally, and where students can gain a profound experience of their capacity—and responsibility—to effect positive change. As an antidote to cynicism and passivity, it is hard to top service learning.

Looking at the society into which they are graduating, our students might be excused for being cynical. From the front page to the business page to the sports section, headlines repeatedly reflect the ethical lapses of our society. This profound lack of integrity—the failure of a moral value system—is not restricted to one political party, to one religious group, to one ethnic group or one gender group. It cuts across our society. In giving a final message to graduating students, I have asked them to seek one goal: to say "No"—say *no* to greed; say *no* to opportunism; say *no* to dishonesty—and decide that integrity—their own moral compass—is what really matters.

If we accept that aim—and I believe we do—then service learning deserves a proud and prominent place in our curriculum. This series provides less a roadmap than a spur to creative course development for all faculty and administrators eager to adapt a powerful educational tool to a particular institution's nature, community, and student population.

Robert A. Corrigan
President, San Francisco State University
October 6, 2006

ABOUT THIS SERIES

Final Words About the Series on Service Learning and Civic Engagement

This volume, *Social Responsibility and Sustainability*, is the last in our series on service learning and civic engagement. The concept for the series grew out of discussions at the California State University (CSU) Office of the Chancellor in 2005–2006 about the evolving field of community service learning and paralleled similar discussions that were led by Campus Compact and others across the nation.

Practitioners who had achieved a level of recognition of the potency of service learning as pedagogy for introducing students to the world around them wished to turn their attention to how to enrich the pedagogy with methods and outcomes that had a deeper impact on the public good. That direction was called *civic engagement* and focused on how service learning, conducted with proper rigor, was the most potent method for developing the motivation, values, knowledge, and skills for students to make a difference in addressing community needs.

It is interesting to reflect on how far we have come since 2006. When administrators of the CSU Office of Community Service Learning proposed civic engagement as the focus for the 23-campus systemwide network of service-learning offices, the proposal was met with considerable resistance. As one director summed up his feelings, "Campus Compact has abandoned us, and now so have you!" As it turned out, the movement toward civic engagement swept across the academic landscape. Reflecting its new role, the CSU office was renamed the Center for Community Engagement, as are scores of university programs across the country, including the center run by that very same director.

In the process, civic engagement has been enriched by new methods ranging from community-based research to social entrepreneurship, all of which are based on the same fundamental principles of shared power, reciprocity, and mutual benefit that underlie exemplary service learning. The field of service learning has grown considerably, and it continues to do so. It is now recognized by the Association of American Colleges and Universities as one of five high-impact teaching practices, along with first-year seminars, learning communities, undergraduate research, and capstone experiences.

There is little doubt that we could continue to add to the series with monograph themes addressing other social issues. But it is now time to reflect on where we have been and where the movement is headed, and how the academy can best serve the communities of our nation and the world. The editors and contributors to these volumes are proud to be part of this great ongoing enterprise.

Gerald S. Eisman
Series Editor
December 2010

Activity/Methodology Table: *Social Responsibility and Sustainability*

Chapter	Discipline	Service Activity	Methodology	Applications	Type of Partner	Size of Class
Chapter 1: Mündel and Mündel	Religious studies, global and development studies	Students contributed to local organizations and schools in rural Alberta and rural Mexico	Action research Fieldwork Focus groups Mixed-method surveys	Community service learning Community development Environmental education	Various local organizations and businesses	10–25 students
Chapter 2: Sutheimer and Pyles	Chemistry, biology, sustainability	Direct service projects ranging from tree plantings to educational presentations	Single short project Fieldwork	Land-use management Public education and outreach Campus and community sustainability	Campuses, conservation groups, social service agencies, local school and public audiences	10–30 students
Chapter 3: Varty, Lishawa, and Tuchman	Interdisciplinary	Students planned, constructed, and staffed a campus biodiesel laboratory and developed related community outreach projects	Community-based research Laboratory research Curriculum development Capacity building	Education Small-business planning Environmental science Campus sustainability Renewable energy	Local high schools City of Chicago Parks District The Field Museum Local restaurants Chicago 49th Ward Green Corps	24 students

(continues)

**Activity/Methodology Table: *Social Responsibility and Sustainability*
Continued**

Chapter	Discipline	Service Activity	Methodology	Applications	Type of Partner	Size of Class
Chapter 4: McNall	Sociology	Sustainability and economic development	Qualitative	Public policy, behavior, energy use, sustainability	Universities, businesses, corporations focused on sustainability	20–30
Chapter 5: Eames and Brooks	Interdisciplinary	Students conducted research projects to help the neighboring community develop a sustainability plan	Qualitative and quantitative community-based research	Community development, sustainability, behavioral change, public policy	Edgewater Community Council, local businesses, local residents, local politicians	3 sections of about 30 students over two semesters
Chapter 6: Swift and Johnston	Environmental science	River cleanup, participation in food waste study	Survey research, fieldwork	Environmental science, environmental studies, sociology, anthropology	Community-based environmental groups, Bon Appétit	31 students

Chapter	Discipline	Service Activity	Methodology	Applications	Type of Partner	Size of Class
Chapter 7: Whitehead and Helling	Natural resource development, management, policy	Community-based research on selected environmental issue (wind power) and development of policy recommendation to state agency	Policy analysis Participant observation Problem-based learning Interviews	Natural resource development and management Public policy	Higher education institutions Department of Game, Fish, and Parks U.S. Fish and Wildlife Service National Park Service Yellowstone Association Institute Public Utilities Commission	20 students
Chapter 8: Williams	Environmental education, garden-based education	Service learning at K–12 school learning gardens	Autoethnography, reflective journals	Higher education–school partnerships K–12 curricular integration Growing food	K–12 public schools, Nonprofit food-based organizations	Several classes, each with 15–25 students, master's culminating research projects and theses

(continues)

**Activity/Methodology Table: *Social Responsibility and Sustainability*
Continued**

Chapter	Discipline	Service Activity	Methodology	Applications	Type of Partner	Size of Class
Chapter 9: DeBerg	Business education, entrepreneurship, social enterprise	University business students are consultants and mentors to teenage entrepreneurs	Experiential learning Project management Event planning	Community service learning Higher education–school partnerships	High schools Private sector advisors, evaluators, financial supporters	15–30 university students per semester
Chapter 10: Ulasewicz	Graduate studies in business and family and consumer sciences	Community-engaged scholarship	Case study reflection (written and oral, individual and group)	Sustainability Business design Social entrepreneurship	Nonprofit, socially responsible community-based and global business organizations	More than 20
Chapter 11: Wilson	Economics	Community-based research in various community and economic development fields	Survey research Firm background research Secondary source research Economic impact studies	Economic development Business development Environmental sustainability	City and county government, community development organizations, small business development organizations	15–20 students

CONTRIBUTORS

Jeremy Brooks (chapter 5) was an instructor in the natural science department at Loyola University Chicago, where he taught environmental sustainability. He is currently a postdoctoral fellow in the Beckman Institute at the University of Illinois Urbana-Champaign. (jsbrooks26@gmail.com)

Curtis L. DeBerg (chapter 9) is professor of business at California State University, Chico. (cdeberg@csuchico.edu)

J. Marshall Eames (chapter 5) is the director of University Environmental Sustainability at Loyola University Chicago. (jeames@luc.edu)

Mary Kay Helling (chapter 7) is associate vice president of Academic Affairs at South Dakota State University. (mary.helling@sdstate.edu)

sal johnston (chapter 6) is associate professor of sociology, Whittier College, California. (sjohnston@whittier.edu)

Shane C. Lishawa (chapter 3) is a research associate at the Center for Urban Environmental Research and Policy at Loyola University Chicago. (slishawa@luc.edu)

Tracy McDonald (volume editor) is professor of management at California State University, Chico. (moonchuckle@sbcglobal.net)

Scott G. McNall (chapter 4) is professor of sociology and served as the founding executive director of the Institute for Sustainable Development at California State University, Chico. (smcnall@csuchico.edu)

Hans-Dittmar Mündel (chapter 1) is professor of religious studies at the Augustana Campus, University of Alberta, Canada. (hans-dittmar.mundel@ualberta.ca)

Karsten Mündel (chapter 1) is assistant professor of global and development studies at the Augustana Campus, University of Alberta, Canada. (kmundel@ualberta.ca)

Jesse Pyles (chapter 2) is sustainability coordinator at Unity College in Maine. (jpyles@unity.edu)

Susan Sutheimer (chapter 2) is an environmental chemist and professor of chemistry at Green Mountain College in Vermont. (sutheimers@greenmtn.edu)

Cheryl Swift (chapter 6) is James Irvine Foundation professor of biology at Whittier College, California. (cswift@whittier.edu)

Nancy C. Tuchman (chapter 3) is professor of biology and director of the Center for Urban Environmental Research and Policy at Loyola University Chicago. (ntuchma@luc.edu)

Connie Ulasewicz (chapter 10) is an associate professor in the consumer and family studies/dietetics department at San Francisco State University, California. (cbu@sfsu.edu)

Alison K. Varty (chapter 3) is a biology instructor at the College of the Siskiyous, California. (varty@siskiyous.edu)

Karen Whitehead (chapter 7) is provost and vice president emerita for Academic Affairs, South Dakota School of Mines and Technology. (karen.whitehead@sdsmt.edu)

Dilafruz R. Williams (chapter 8) is professor of educational leadership and policy at Portland State University, Oregon. (williamsdi@pdx.edu)

Beth Wilson (chapter 11) is department chair and professor of economics at Humboldt State University, California. (beth.wilson@humboldt.edu)

INTRODUCTION

Tracy McDonald

Several years ago, I made the decision to rededicate my teaching and research to focus on sustainability. As the world faced its multitude of crises, there was one that struck me: the proposition that humans, for the most part, were triggering climate change. Predictions regarding the effects of the melting of the polar ice caps on sea levels became more commonplace. We saw pictures of starving polar bears hanging on to chunks of broken ice to avoid drowning in the Arctic seas. Evidence was increasing that life, as we knew it, was in jeopardy.

I recall one of those perfect, blue-skied spring days in my hometown of Chico, the sort of day that can make you believe that there is nothing wrong in the world. My students were excited because spring break was coming. Looking at their young faces so expectant and beautifully innocent, I reflected on the complexities of their future. Out of nowhere came, what was for me, a deep realization. No matter how staggering the crises we were facing as world citizens, none was more important than the issue of climate change. If we did not collectively make concerted and rapid changes, all other problems, no matter what their magnitude, would eventually become irrelevant. The planet could survive without us. This moment was an epiphany of sorts. From that point on, I devoted the large part of my work toward creating change in my own College of Business and became passionately involved in campus and community-wide, sustainability-focused efforts. This monograph contains the work of university faculty members who have also been moved, in one way or another, to make sustainability the focus of their work and to use service learning as one method of teaching sustainability to their students. I am sure each has a deeply personal story as to how they came to that place.

A few words must be said regarding how we conceive of the term *sustainability*. I will borrow from the World Commission on Environment and Development's (1987) definition of *sustainable development*: ". . . meeting the needs of the present without compromising the ability of future generations to meet their own needs" (p. 54). This definition is general enough that it can be applied as easily to work exploring sustainability in the sciences as to work in business. Though we view sustainability as interdependently encompassing the ecological, economic, and human aspects of our existence, we have chosen to focus more narrowly on environmental sustainability. Issues such as human rights, the rights of labor, corporate power, and effects on the economy are interwoven with environmental sustainability in many of the chapters. However, this more encompassing interpretation of sustainability is too large to tackle in a volume of this length. Further, we define the term *community* loosely. In one chapter, you might read about students co-creating change with a community located just down the street from campus. In another, students may fly to a different country and become part of a foreign community composed of individuals they have yet to meet. In some cases, highly educated scientists or politicians may form a community with whom students work, while in others students create change with disadvantaged children living on the margins of affluent society. Ultimately, we recognize that we live in a world community and that for the effective action to occur, we must all work together.

Public opinion regarding climate change is not encouraging. In fact, Americans view climate change as less of a threat than they did some years ago (Newport, 2010). Gallop polls show that almost half of Americans think the seriousness of climate change is exaggerated (compared to 31% in 2005), fewer Americans believe climate change will occur or pose a serious threat in their lifetimes (28%) compared to 2005 (35%), and the percentage of Americans believing that climate change is due to natural versus human-created causes has increased (34% in 2005 compared to 46% today). A study from the Pew Research Center for the People & the Press (2009) shows that Americans do not see climate change as having as high a priority as the economic downturn and health care.

These changes in public opinion make it imperative that our students possess a thorough understanding of the gravity of climate change and that we provide them with empowering opportunities so that they leave the university confident in their abilities to make a difference. Certainly, students are called in many worthy directions and not all students will be called in the name of preserving our planet. But, the work contained in this volume and similar work occurring worldwide, show us that we can be confident that there will emerge a cadre of students who will hold sustainability as a core value and who will be equipped with the skills and abilities to become responsible and vibrant members of their communities. These are the graduates who will model sustainability by living sustainably, who will engage in political activism, who will teach others about sustainability in the myriad ways that that knowledge can be passed on, who will create products and new ways of doing things that are less destructive to our planet. These graduates will likely embody sustainability in ways we cannot even fathom. According to McKibbon (2010), addressing climate change has become more urgent than ever, and he views civic engagement as the most effective way of addressing the crisis. The authors of these chapters have already begun this work.

Work in this area is formidable. One cannot address the issue of sustainability without an interdisciplinary approach. As we all know, working across the disciplines is time-consuming and demanding, but the fruits of such work can result in unique pedagogies, blossoming friendships, and unparalleled growth on the part of students, instructors, and community members. The diversity of approaches represented here is rather amazing. Creating community gardens, working side by side with peasants in Mexico, helping stakeholders find common ground on environmental issues, and writing proposals to obtain funding for the benefit of a community are just a few of the ways students have become engaged in creating a more sustainable world. A few of our authors have been working in this area for more than two decades. They are the pioneers who walked the path before us so that the work is more clearly defined for the rest of us. Each chapter represents a unique approach to promoting civic engagement as a means to creating a more sustainable world. Shining through the words of each contributor is a deep commitment to both sustainability and to their students and their communities. It has been a humbling and intimate honor to work with each individual. During my 27-year career, I have never been so impressed by the dedication, involvement, creativity, and hard work that characterize each author and his or her work. This work is a gift to all.

This book is divided into three sections. The first is "Environmental Awareness." In order for students to meaningfully engage themselves with their communities, they must first become aware of the ecological aspects of sustainability and perhaps, more importantly, the interdependence of the ecosystem with human and with institutional decisions and behavior. For change to occur there must be awareness that a problem exists. In these chapters, we will see the development of awareness in two ways: first, students themselves learning about the issues surrounding sustainability and, second, sharing that awareness with the community.

Our lead chapter is "Reconnecting to Land, People, and Community: Ecological Lessons From the Puebla-Alberta Community Service Exchange," by father-and-son team Mündel and Mündel. A key premise of their work is that for a community to be healthy, its ecological, economic, and social spheres must be in balance. In this interdisciplinary exchange program with the Universidad de las Americas, Puebla (UDLAP), students work side by side with people of the land. Rural villages near Puebla, Mexico, and rural Alberta, Canada, serve as learning laboratories for students, faculty, and villagers. All involved become more aware of the factors affecting environmental health and the key threats to healthy community. Combined with community service, students engage in reflection and analysis. Participants leave the program empowered with the knowledge that they can be agents of positive change. Mündel and Mündel show us the fruits of taking students outside the classroom to an unfamiliar setting so that they begin to challenge their assumptions and stereotypes. Students' engagement with a seemingly foreign community allows them to master material in a personally meaningful way. We see that becoming aware of sustainability is a three-way process involving students, faculty, and community partners.

Chapter 2, Sutheimer and Pyles's "Integrating Sustainability and Service Learning Into the Science Curriculum," begins with the observation that it is unusual for science classes to have significant service-learning components. Since science classes tend to be large and heavy on content and since in a rural setting it is difficult to find community partners, the authors propose a unique solution: "Simple Short Projects (SSPs)" that take place over just a few class periods. A major characteristic of SSPs is that the student is viewed as an educator who creates an awareness of the importance of sustainability in the community. These projects can be a challenge because the instructor must be creative and flexible to logically integrate the projects in sequence of course topics while taking into account the time frame of the community partner. Civic engagement in the sciences, the authors contend, is key to educating students and the general public about critical environmental issues. Through these SSPs, the authors report that students begin to experience the imperative of social responsibility. From Sutheimer and Pyles, we learn that we need not take on a massive project to integrate service learning into our courses. The authors show us that with creativity and flexibility, we can include civic engagement in almost any course.

In chapter 3, "Sustainability Education Through an Interdisciplinary and Service-Learning Approach," Varty presents the Solutions to Environmental Problems (STEP) program wherein students address environmental issues by actively working as self-directed work teams with community organizations. There are several STEP courses offered, each with a different focus. Varty describes STEP: Biodiesel, which focuses on the environmental, social, economic, and political impact of the use of fossil fuels. Lectures and discussions and a laboratory section in which students learn to make biodiesel fuel provide the classroom experience. The service-learning component is a project, designed by the student team, to suit the needs of a community mentor with whom the team has partnered. Varty provides an impressive array of projects. She has observed lasting effects on students, faculty, the university, and community and in the area of sustainability. A major contribution of Varty's work is that she shows us the feasibility and power of using student-directed teams, and she provides an excellent example of how a variety of unique projects can effectively be used to satisfy a common set of course goals.

The second section of the book, "Increasing Civic Engagement," explores the means by which we can foster commitment to community service. As the authors of this section demonstrate, if our students are to become active participants in society, we must provide them with opportunities that engage them and allow them to experience their capacity to effect change. They must learn that responsibility to society comes with that capacity.

In chapter 4, "What's the Matter With American Democracy? Responding by Embracing Civic Engagement and Sustainability," McNall discusses the role American colleges and universities play in guiding students to become active and educated citizens. A major premise of this chapter is that civic engagement opportunities create students who are willing to voluntarily take actions that can improve the state of the world. His chapter describes the process at his own university. California State University, Chico, followed in creating a culture of both civic engagement and sustainability. A significant focus of the chapter is the importance of well-articulated and democratically created core values and goals in the creation of transformative learning experiences. McNall points out how an infrastructure committed to sustainability and a mechanism for communicating across disciplinary and divisional lines are essential in creating such change. Shepherding his university's journey as executive director of the Institute of Sustainable Development, McNall witnessed the growth of programs of study, student organizations, and community partnerships aimed at creating a more sustainable world. McNall provides a compelling example of how one university distinguished itself for its leadership in sustainable development.

"Sustainability Starts at Home: A Hybrid Service-Learning Model for Teaching Environmental Sustainability" is the title of our fifth chapter, which is authored by Eames and Brooks. Both their university and its surrounding community had undergone processes leading to major transformations that resulted in both players' coming to fully embrace sustainability. The context was ripe for civic engagement opportunities. This chapter focuses on an interdisciplinary, science-based course, Environmental Sustainability. The goal of the course is for students to come to realize, through group research projects, how the biosphere functions and what steps can be taken to reduce human-created adverse environmental impacts. Students worked with outside partners to find solutions for community problems related to this goal. The authors provide many examples of projects, describing the work students carried out with local business owners, advocacy groups, governmental agencies, and a diverse host of other decision makers. The level of detail the authors provide is particularly valuable. Instructors wishing to develop a course emphasizing sustainability and civic engagement will find this chapter to be a well-marked roadmap.

Swift and johnston illustrate how service learning may be incorporated at the freshman level through integrating courses from other disciplines. The sixth chapter is entitled "Learning by Doing Across Disciplines: Activism, Environmental Awareness, and Civic Engagement." Here, the authors describe how they linked a freshman-level writing course to an introductory environmental management course to create an interdisciplinary community among students and faculty. Social justice and participative democracy were important learning themes. A major goal of the course was that students become aware of how their daily activities impact the environment. During the service-learning portion of the course, students explored resource consumption within their community. The unique contribution of this chapter is that it demonstrates service learning as a means to teach sustainability is effective, even at the freshman level. The authors offer a compelling data analysis that supports the effectiveness of their approach, and they provide evidence that the use of service-learning communities is superior to more traditional teaching approaches.

Chapter 7, Whitehead and Helling's "From Wolves to Wind Power: Fostering Student Understanding of Science, Stewardship, and Civic Engagement," specifically explores the arena of politics. The authors describe how a small group of faculty members and administrators representing all institutions of higher learning in South Dakota convened a conference to discuss the role of democracy in the stewardship of public lands. One outcome of the conference was the interdisciplinary course offered here as the seventh chapter. The course, representing six disciplines, required students to work in small groups and take a stand on an environmentally related topic of their choice. With the intention of developing more engaged citizens, the course challenged students to explore their own attitudes toward stewardship. They interacted with individuals representing such entities as the Department of Game, Fish and Parks; Partners for Fish and Wildlife; U.S. Fish and Wildlife Services; and a South Dakota legislator. Student groups conducted research on their topic and contacted state representatives. The capstone of the course was a presentation to policy makers in the state capitol. One learning outcome was the realization that environmental issues are more complex than they may seem at the surface. Whitehead and Helling conclude that working in an interdisciplinary fashion with stakeholders representing varying views brought out the strengths of students and faculty alike. This chapter stands out in that it demonstrates the potential power students have in changing policies through concerted research, communication, and effort.

In the eighth chapter, Williams describes a partnership between public schools and her students at Portland State University. Her chapter, entitled "Multiculturalism and Sustainability Education: Engagement With Urban School Communities via Food and Learning Gardens," describes a civic engagement project she uses in several of her courses. Through this experience, Williams's mostly White, middle-class students come to understand sustainability by exploring how race and class are related to matters of food in the form of ecological injustice. Since her students have not had direct exposure to those who live in segregated communities where poverty, food security, and lack of health care are conditions of everyday life, she partners her students with pre-K–8 children who live in low-income, racially diverse communities. The medium of instruction is "learning gardens," a community project wherein Williams's students work with public school youth and together build gardens and grow food. Through this experience, students come to appreciate the interdependence of individual, community, and ecological health. They see that they have responsibility for Earth and its inhabitants and realize that sustainability of communities is a prerequisite for sustainability of the planet. The unique contribution Williams makes is clarifying the connection between sustainability and poverty, and demonstrating how an experience of working in the community with those from disadvantaged backgrounds gives students a sense of agency in changing the world.

The last section of the book, "Sustainability Concepts in Business and Economics," explores how we can prepare students to encourage and be a part of sustainable business practice. The inherent meaning of the term *sustainability* is the same across disciplines, yet each discipline seems to place its own stamp on the meaning of the term. Thus, in business the term *triple bottom line* is used to describe a business that makes efforts to operate in a manner that makes a profit in a way that does not degrade the environment and respects the people and cultures that have a stake in the operation of the business. Our last three chapters address sustainability within the business context. This section is important because business is the largest contributor to CO_2 gasses.

In chapter 9, "Building Bridges and Social Capital Through Service Learning: A Blueprint Model," DeBerg makes the case that the traditional business model in which profit is the driving force is outdated and that business schools should adopt a larger worldview in which concepts such as social capital, civic engagement, social responsibility, and sustainability are important drivers of successful business. He goes on to present his own model depicting the relationship and differences among these various terms. Service learning is the best means by which these nonfinancial aspects can be taught, he holds. The chapter continues with examples of various means by which business schools can incorporate sustainability into their curricula. In the remaining sections of the chapter, DeBerg focuses on his own work in engaging students with service learning. Serving as the faculty advisor of Students for the Advancement of Global Entrepreneurship (SAGE), DeBerg has coached university business students who help high school students create social entrepreneurial ventures. These ventures, which provide a service to the community, demonstrate that making money and being socially responsible are not mutually incompatible. DeBerg's unique contribution is his cohesive and well-thought-out analysis of how business can and should be seen through a larger lens. This chapter should stimulate and inspire instructors teaching both within and outside the realm of business and create interdisciplinary collaborations in the area of sustainability.

Like DeBerg's chapter, Ulasewicz's "Sustainable Design Practices for the Social Entrepreneurial Business" addresses civic engagement as pedagogy for teaching sustainability and social entrepreneurship. Chapter 10, however, explores a very specific aspect of social entrepreneurship: the design of sustainable products and services. Ulasewicz, in collaboration with a business school colleague, created a course on social entrepreneurship. The aim was to bring together analytically oriented business students and creativity-oriented design students in the hope of creating a synergy based on the two orientations. A major focus of the course was the recognition that creating and consuming clothing uses resources, some of which are nonrenewable. Guest speakers from local organizations visited the class and their organizational practices served as cases through which students explored sustainability and social entrepreneurship. Students provided their expertise to help these and other social-entrepreneurial ventures operate more sustainably. Reflections, in the students' own words, testify to the power of the civic engagement experience. The unique contribution of this chapter is in how Ulasewicz shows us that a variation of the sometimes dry case method of instruction can result in probing analysis and deep questioning by students. In addition, we see how the pairing of students from two diverse majors combined with a service-learning experience often resulted in personal transformation on the part of students.

The final chapter, Wilson's "Teaching Sustainable Rural Economic Development Using Service-Learning Pedagogy," describes the incorporation of service learning into a course entitled Sustainable Rural Economic Development. The key focus of the course is finding the right balance between natural resource extraction and maintaining these same resources for other types of economic activity. In addition, Wilson's course examines the challenge of conducting economic activities in a manner that preserves the rural quality of life in Humboldt County, California. In the course, students worked with economic development practitioners, governmental agencies, or nonprofit organizations. She required that projects result in general benefits for the community while serving community economic development. Students, together with their site sponsors, developed plans that articulated learning and service objectives and expectations. The reviews by students and sponsors that Wilson provides attest to the value of the experience. She concludes that the depth of understanding and synthesis of ideas she observed would not be possible without the service-learning component. Wilson's chapter explores an issue that is of great import to the entire planet: How can we balance the use of land with environmental sustainability?

We hope that these chapters inspire you to create new challenges and opportunities for your students, whether in the form of new course development or modification and reworking of existing courses. We hope you are stimulated to approach colleagues in different departments and grow professionally as a result of the demands and joys of interdisciplinary work. Community is increasingly important as our world seems to be growing larger and more impersonal. We hope that you look to the community outside of your university and form alliances that are a benefit to you, your students, and the community you are part of. Fostering passion and excitement so that students come to realize their own power in making a difference in the world has been a common theme in each of these chapters. Like the authors represented in this volume, you too have the potential for changing your students' lives. And by changing their lives, you are changing the world. For an instructor, is there any greater measure of success?

November 7, 2010
Portland, Oregon

References

McKibben, B. (2010). *Earth: Making a life on a tough new planet.* New York: Times Books.

Newport, F. (2010). *Americans' global warming concerns continue to drop: Multiple indicators show less concern, more feelings that global warming is exaggerated,* March, 2010. Retrieved November 1, 2010, from http://www.gallup.com/poll/126560/Americans-Global-Warming-Concerns-Continue-Drop.aspx#1

Pew Research Center for the People & the Press (January 2009). *Economy, jobs trump all other policy priorities in 2009.* Retrieved November 1, 2010, from http://people-press.org/report/485/economy-top-policy-priority

World Commission on Environment and Development. (1987). *Our common future.* Oxford: Oxford University Press.

SECTION ONE

ENVIRONMENTAL AWARENESS

RECONNECTING TO LAND, PEOPLE, AND COMMUNITY

Ecological Lessons From the Puebla-Alberta Community Service Exchange

Hans-Dittmar Mündel and Karsten Mündel

E ducators in the area of sustainability often teach or develop programs out of a deep concern for the state of our planet and its people. Though not out of a lack of commitment, many educational efforts in the area of sustainability could make a greater contribution to learning than they do. Some of the reasons for this are

1. lack of sufficient focus on ecological issues (Selby, 2006);
2. the failure to address social and environmental limits of growth economics (Daly, 1996); and
3. the alienation students often feel toward their own education (Nathan, 2005).

Along with our colleagues at Augustana Campus, University of Alberta, we have developed a program that teaches sustainability in a manner that addresses these issues. Our program is an international community service-learning exchange that fully immerses students and faculty in rural communities in Morelos or Puebla, Mexico, and Alberta, Canada. We have found that students participating in the Puebla-Alberta Community Service Exchange (PACSE) become experientially aware of the ecological issues facing rural communities. They start to question the assumptions growth economics are based on, and they become self-motivated and self-directed learners.

In this chapter we explore how we teach ecological sustainability through PACSE, a five-month, full-credit program that has evolved over the past 15 years. Our central thesis is that university administrators wishing to reverse environmental degradation must help students and professors to reconnect to real communities, the people who live in these communities, and the land these individuals inhabit. We first offer a brief exploration of the theoretical and philosophical underpinnings of our program. We then describe how our program moves beyond the walls of the classroom and the confines of our individual disciplines into rural communities. The end result is a valuable immersion experience that has led to deep academic reflection and questioning of assumptions that were once taken for granted. Finally, we share what we discovered about student ecological learning in PACSE and explore the challenges of staffing a place-based program.

From Farming to Freire: A Theoretical Framework

We built this international community service-learning exchange on the three key pillars of education at Augustana Campus: the importance of community, the environmental crisis we are facing, and a philosophy of transformation based on challenging assumptions. First, we wanted to design a program that allows students and faculty to experience and reflect on the gifts of and threats to rural communities. Augustana is in Camrose, a prairie town in Alberta, Canada, that services the surrounding rural areas. Initially, through the work of individual instructors, Augustana was committed to supporting our local environment and now continues to uphold that commitment at the institutional level. We believe our research and teaching should connect us to and serve our local community.

As Wendell Berry (1977) pointed out, the ecological crisis is a crisis of agriculture, of character, and of culture. If we want to teach ecological sustainability, we have to witness and experience the stress our land and our rural communities are under and how that stress affects agriculture, an endeavor that falls under the production models of industry. To see the ecological crisis as a crisis of character means that we help our students discover the connection between gaining insight and taking action. To explore the ecological crisis as a crisis of culture requires that we listen to the oral histories of rural folk and examine the changes that are happening to their culture as their communities are pulled into the vortex of a global consumer culture.

This approach engages rural people, their communities, and the specific pieces of land upon which they have an impact.

Augustana's academic dean, Roger Epp, has dedicated much of his academic career to resisting the economic, political, and cultural trends that are "writing off the rural West" (Epp & Whitson, 2001). Many faculty members at Augustana are "at home in the rural" (Epp, 2008) and want to transmit a sense of place to their students. We can best do this by extending education beyond the walls of our campus, which in our case is rural Alberta. We address the first pillar of education at Augustana by grounding our program in the ecological, social, and economic spheres right at home in our own community. Thus, Alberta is one of the two locations of our exchange program.

The second pillar is in the nature of the environmental crisis itself. In focusing on what happens to humans in an industrial growth economy, Erich Fromm (1968) asked, "*Must we produce sick people in order to have a healthy economy* [italics in original]?" (p. 2). Extending Fromm's rhetoric, we question whether we have to make the land and communities sick so that our economy can grow. David Korten (1995) said it is "[the] continued quest for economic growth as the organizing principle of public policy" that accelerates "the breakdown of the ecosystem's regenerative capacities and the social fabric that sustains human community" (p. 11). For us, the nature of the crisis meant that we had to find ways for learners and teachers to experience and transcend the core paradox of the inverse relation of the health of our growth economy and the ecological state of communities. Immersion through living and working in two very different rural communities helps us experience this key paradox and invites reflection and critical analysis. Witnessing that despair is a fact of life for many rural Mexicans is a surprise for many of our students. Being faced with the depth of the ecological crisis facing these rural communities is a wakeup call that helps free our students from the paralysis often seen in society at large.

The third pillar, a philosophy of transformation, forces students to challenge the common assumption that economic growth is a positive driver of society. Our focus is on providing students with the opportunity to become part of, rather than observers of, rural communities. This sort of experience- and community-based education often results in a disconnect between what students have learned as members of a prosperous society and what they see during their brief periods as members of rural communities that have been directly affected by the values of the dominant economic and political interests of society and motivates them to search for alternatives. The challenge we present to our students and to ourselves is not just to move physically beyond the walls of the university, but also to ground our epistemologies and pedagogies so they focus on the rural and often marginalized sectors of societies. Our work draws heavily on Freire (1970/2000), Fals-Borda and Rahman (1991), and Maguire (1987). We also use a critical pedagogy of place (Gruenewald, 2003) that brings together critical pedagogy's concern for social justice with environmental sustainability. The foundation of our work is the interplay among the social, economic, and ecological spheres (Caton & Larsh, 2000). We ask our students to think of themselves, as well as of human institutions, as part of the ecological realm.

In sum, our rural context (in which we experience what is happening to land, people, and community), the nature of the environmental crisis (which is rooted in our growth economy), and our philosophy of transformative, place-based education pushed us to develop a community service exchange beyond the walls of classrooms and disciplines.

Moving Beyond the Walls

How did we make the move? Our vision demanded that we find villages where students could experience and reflect upon what helps or hinders rural communities in becoming sustainable. Hans-Dittmar Mündel found a Mexican partner at the Universidad Autonóma del Estado de Morelos (UAEM, the public university of the state of Morelos) who was a community developer and an educator trained by Paulo Freire.

First, we conducted a pilot project in Mexico (with 10 Canadian and 10 Mexican students) for six weeks that included three weeks of homestays and work placements in the village of Amatlàn, arranged by our Mexican partner, Arturo Ornelas Lizardi. Second, we conducted three weeks of reflection and analysis at a camp in Cuernavaca, Morelos, in 1995. After highly favorable evaluations by students, faculty, and staff, we started an interdisciplinary program for a full academic year, beginning the fall semester in rural Alberta and spending the winter semester in rural Mexico, focusing on sustainable rural development based on a transformative learning methodology.

The objectives for the integrative program were

1. Understand the philosophy, principles, and processes of community development.
2. Analyze the factors that influenced—positively as well as negatively—the sustainable development of rural communities in Alberta and the state of Morelos.
3. Develop leadership for social action among the participants.
4. Develop abilities to work effectively in intercultural contexts.
5. Attain functional fluency in English and Spanish.

To meet these objectives, we formed a partnership with Canada World Youth (CWY), a nongovernmental youth exchange organization committed to experiential place-based education.[1] This organization was responsible for most of the operational logistics of our program, including finding host communities and families to provide a temporary home for our students, identifying potential volunteer work opportunities, and assisting students in taking leadership for the explicitly educational days. CWY provided a full-time program coordinator for 10 months each year for these tasks. The Mexican partner university also provided a coordinator for 10 months. The work placements, in which students spent about 400 hours in each phase of the program, were negotiated by a staff member or by the students themselves. (Now in the five-month version of the program, students spend 200 hours per phase.[2]) Students work not to "make the village more sustainable," but to be in solidarity with the rural people and to learn from new experiences. Of course, they learn a great deal about ecological sustainability and often do contribute to environmental projects already taking place.

Augustana and UAEM took care of the academic aspects of the program. Hans-Dittmar was able to modify rural development courses that were on the books at Augustana to provide the community service credit as well as credit for a development seminar (two-course equivalent) in each phase. Typically, one to three academics from a wide range of disciplines from each institution participated with differing levels of involvement depending on their availability and interest in venturing into experiential place-based education.[3]

In 2007, after leadership had shifted from father to son, the program was reorganized. Currently, it is completely managed by the two academic institutions and is five months long. The exchange commences in rural Mexico in August and moves to rural Alberta at the beginning of October.[4] Our current Mexican partner is Universidad de las Americas, Puebla (UDLAP). Most of the elements of the exchange remain, albeit in an abbreviated form, given the time constraints.

Program Components

The program is based on a cohort of students from both universities with the goal of including an equal number of students from each country. This cohort goes through a Mexican and an Albertan phase. Before immersing the students in their villages, faculty and coordinating staff conduct orientation camps. The camps introduce students to the experiential approach we use and encourage them to reflect on how immersion in particular places creates unique learning opportunities. Students discover their own roles in transformative education; that is, they must be active in learning from their daily experiences and in teaching each other. They become oriented to the culture of the rural area they are about to enter, as well as to the realities of working as a cross-cultural class and in small cross-cultural research and education groups. They discover the first frustrations and joys of working and communicating in two languages and cultures. Given the possibility of significant linguistic challenges, the sessions at these camps are taught bilingually and incorporate techniques such as drama and drawing that are less based on a specific language. Students learn they can communicate well even if they are not fluent in each other's language.

After the orientation camp, faculty, coordinating staff, and students go to the particular rural community for another week of on-site orientation. Some faculty members on the interdisciplinary team return home after one or two weeks into the start of their fall semester. However, they virtually accompany the students via online submissions and queries whenever the students can use a computer in an Internet café, in a volunteer placement, or in a neighboring market town. At least one faculty member stays in the rural community with the students to act as academic and cultural guide and logistics coordinator. Immersion learning requires a staff presence because we recognize that learning happens around the clock and is not limited to formal sessions.

In the community, students live in counterpart pairs (normally a cross-cultural one) with host families, work three days a week in their work placements, and then spend two educational days on academic reflection and analysis with the support of the resident faculty member. On most weekends, participants join in the activities of their extended families. The students are encouraged to integrate themselves into the chores and celebrations of their family as much as possible as a way of discovering the gifts and challenges of life in their particular community. They are discouraged from escaping unfamiliarity by fleeing to the distractions of their normal lives, since avoiding the discomfort of being disoriented—of going through culture shock—would avoid the potential of finding a new, more ecological orientation to their lives.

The experience of community provided by actually living with *campesinos* (peasant farmers) and with rural Alberta families is complemented by work placements in community organizations ranging from farms to schools and from municipal governments to local newspapers. For the purpose of this chapter, our focus is on placements that were ecologically based. Some of our students developed *hortalizas* (organic vegetable gardens) at primary and secondary schools where they volunteered and also at individual homes. They assisted families in creating composting toilets and in building energy-efficient stoves that reduced the use of firewood by two thirds. Farming with campesinos allowed participants to discover the joy and sweat of physical work. Other students conducted environmental awareness workshops for rural youth using drama, village cleanup, and other interactive means. Through research and public awareness events, students participated in local struggles to preserve *semillas criollas* (indigenous heritage seeds) from the incursion of genetically modified seeds from agricultural products giant Monsanto. They were involved in a variety of water projects, since water shortage is a perennial concern in the villages around Tepoztlán, Morelos. In Canada, students have been involved in volunteer experiences such as water-quality testing, working as support staff in a café that uses locally sourced organic food, and cleaning and planting to preserve natural spaces. Others have worked on traditional or organic farms, at a local auction market, in a Hutterite colony (a religious group that lives and works communally in rural areas, originally from Moravia, now the Czech Republic), or in family and community support services (wherever volunteers were needed to do publicity, conduct surveys, or run programs). These placements have provided important experiences for students to reflect on the ecological sustainability of rural communities. However, when Canadian students ask what they should tell their parents and friends about what they are going to do in the Mexican phase, we do not mention any of these projects, since they perpetuate the notion that northerners have to teach people in the south to make their lives more sustainable. Instead we tell them to say they are going to live with campesinos to learn from them about land and community.[5]

Learning to Read Our World and Words: Our Teaching Modalities

The counterpart pairs, host families, and work placements in two rural villages provide the experiences we reflect upon and analyze during our two educational days a week. In the language of Paulo Freire (1970/2000), we are learning to read our world and the written words of scholars. The written assignments, small groups, and individual research projects help students deepen their ability to read their village in its particularities. We start with the students' experiences of a particular aspect of village life. One experience may be shared with the rest of the group through narration, drama, photography, and drawing. Then, using a variety of techniques, students are asked to reflect on the key issues. As we proceed to analysis, students try to uncover as many causes as they can, at ever deeper levels, of what they have observed. They may uncover local and global forces that are causing, for example, the migration of workers from Santa Lucia to the United States (usually as undocumented workers). Next, they explore the social, economic, and ecological consequences of this phenomenon. What is happening to the land? What is happening to the community? At some point, the students usually uncover a central paradox. For example, a parent migrates to the United States to improve the life of his or her family. As a result, the presence of the parent is replaced by money or consumer goods that the family can now afford. However, the social and ecological sustainability of the family and community decreases. More specifically, by shifting from subsistence to a cash economy, families produce far greater amounts of waste that must be disposed of and cause a greater environmental load. A good example is the shift from juices made from local agricultural produce to soft drinks and other bottled beverages. In the first instance, making juice results in compostable material or food for animals. In the second instance, not only do the beverage containers need to be disposed of, but the negative health impact of drinks high in sugar is significant. Ultimately, the challenge to the students is not to solve an environmental or economic problem, but to identify and transcend the paradox. To do this, we encourage students, in their personal writings, to try to find parallel motivations and paradoxes in their own lives. Only then can they see the depth of what we are facing in our interrelated ecological, social, and economic crises.

We also use many techniques such as *dinámicas* (dynamics) from the popular education tradition in Latin America.[6] The tree of life exercise, one such technique, serves as an integrative, rapid diagnostic tool. In small groups, students are asked to draw a tree of the community. The soil in which the tree is rooted represents all the environmental resources as well as negative impacts the community and its economic activities have on the land, air, and water. We rarely have great artists in the groups, so labeling is used in combination with images. The roots, whether strong or weak, deep or wide, represent the various economic activities of the community. The trunk of the tree shows who does or does not have voice and power in decision making that affects the community. The branches show the various social dimensions and services of the community. The crown of the tree and its leaves represent the culture, tradition, and values that nourish this community and shape the direction of its growth. The global forces that shape the nature of the growth of the community are often represented in the sky as clouds or hailstorms or wind, and again are labeled. As students examine and interpret each other's drawings, with the instructors posing questions as well, they begin to understand the depth to which aspects of community and global forces are interrelated.

For a tree of life to be diagnostic it has to graphically represent strengths and challenges of the community. For example, it could have some very weak or shallow economic roots, since a particular economic activity such as resource extraction is very vulnerable or short-lived. The trunk could have deep gashes, since many people are voiceless in the community. Some branches could be broken, since there may be nothing for youth to do. In ecological terms, it is significant that the growth and development or underdevelopment of the community is all connected visibly to the soil level, that is, the environment. Regardless of whether in the next step the students identify loss of fertile soil, scarcity of water, or migration to the United States as the key issue facing the sustainability of their host community, they will discover a vital connection to the ecology of the place as they research this central issue.

The opportunity to deepen and hone one's skills in reflection and analysis comes, in part, through immersion in two very different cultures. Experiencing and comparing life in rural Mexico and rural Canada is almost guaranteed to confront students with the problematic relationships between economic growth and ecological sustainability. In the Mexican (and in some Albertan) villages, many discover that limited access to advanced technologies in the household or in the fields and the scarcity of consumer goods do not adversely affect the quality of villagers' lives. Most students observe more hospitality, more community connection, more celebration, and more passion for life in these less-developed communities than in developed rural Alberta or industrial Mexico, with all its advanced technologies. Put simply, our students discover that beyond a certain minimal level of convenience, growth in consumer goods has no direct relationship to growth in happiness. What our students experience viscerally, ecological economist Mark Anielski (2007) analyzes in a scholarly way.

We also challenge students to identify concrete realities of village life, such as access to clean drinking water or incursions on community food sovereignty, which present significant threats to individual and community health whether or not the members appear happy. On the one hand, students discover it is possible to live very fulfilling lives without all the trappings of the global consumer culture. On the other hand, they learn to identify ongoing inequalities that should be redressed. The dual approach helps them to avoid falling into a cultural relativism that in effect maintains the ecologically destructive and socially unjust status quo. We try to leave our students with two questions: What are the material conditions for living sustainably? Whom does ongoing economic growth benefit, if it is rapidly degrading the environment and decreasing the health and happiness of people and their communities?

Assessing Student Work That Links Experience With Research

After we describe our program, a common question for our colleagues is, "How do you grade that?" Before discussing our assignments that apply to the whole integrative program with its aim of helping students identify what helps or hinders the sustainability of communities, it may be useful to highlight the particular outcomes of ecological learning that our teaching and specific assignments achieve. Student work reveals that the vast majority of the students have learned to

1. Understand the intimate interrelationship of environmental health with the political-economic and sociocultural aspects of communities.
2. Use integrative diagnostic tools to identify key threats and supports to maintaining healthy communities.
3. Identify global forces affecting the environmental (social and economic) health of communities.
4. Practice community-based research methods to gain a deeper understanding of one key area affecting the sustainability of one Mexican and one Canadian rural community.
5. Discover that working toward ecological sustainability involves personal and social transformation.

We have created a series of assignments that allows students significant flexibility to showcase their particular learning and that also allows us to assess their learning. The largest challenge is creating assignments that enable students to move beyond merely describing the intense experiences they have had to engaging them in analyzing their experiences in light of existing theories. We use biweekly reflections, portfolios, research groups, podcasting, and individual research papers to assist in the tasks of reflection and analysis.

Biweekly written reflections, a key assignment, incorporates a technique of asking *why* five times to get at the root cause of an issue. The first step is to describe an experience or situation, such as going for water with a host mother at 5:30 in the morning. The next step would be to ask why the host mother needed to get up at 5:30 and to identify water shortage as a cause. Through a series of subsequent *whys*, the student can show how the golf course, built upstream from the community 10 years ago by corporate interests from Mexico City and Spain, is taking most of the water. The goal of this assignment is to start the process of analyzing the daily experiences of the students' immersion. Initially, this is a difficult task to complete (often starting with a vivid description with no reflection or analysis), but by the time they have completed this process 8 or 10 times, students show the insights they have gained from their community engagement.

We also use portfolios as a way of summarizing a type of learning contract based on objectives to be met. We have organized the exchange into semidistinct learning areas that match the program objectives. (Each year the program objectives undergo slight modifications to deal with new contexts.) We ask the students to identify specific learning objectives they would like to achieve in each of the areas. As the ecological learning outcomes listed on p. 13 indicate, the range of student learning in attitudes and skills is significant.

At the end of each phase, students are expected to submit several proofs of achieving each one of their personal objectives. A proof can be a description of an interaction, a video blog, or some combination of creative and analytical work. For students who may not achieve their objectives, our assessment of their work is based on the quality of their explanation either of an alternative objective they did achieve or of why they did not achieve the original objective. A key purpose of having students prepare portfolios is to activate their own agency in learning. We instructors established the structures that facilitate learning, but there is significant space for students to decide what they want to learn and deliberately set out to do.

A final aspect of assessing student learning is through their work in small research groups. The intercultural cohort is divided into research groups that try to answer a specific question related to the particularities of the host community. By teaching participatory forms of research, students ask a series of questions about whose knowledge counts. They are often empowered as they realize that farmers and students can and do produce and use knowledge on a daily basis. An example of a question the participants pursue involving themselves and the *campesinos* could be: What have the environmental impacts been on your host community from the shift to mechanized agriculture in Mexico? The research groups also provide a way for the academic staff to have a series of discussions with students about the epistemological aspects of the current ecological crisis.

More recently, we have started teaching students how to present their research to the community in the form of video podcasts. Podcasting popularizes the knowledge when it appears on YouTube (http://www.augustana.ualberta.ca/programs/lab/international/PACSE/multimedia/), but more importantly, it is a way to check with the community about the conclusions the students have reached. Rather than writing a paper about people in a far-off land, students produce short videos they show to the very people the videos are about. These podcasts complement students' individual research papers, which draw on and deepen the research they conducted with their research group.

From Program to Courses and Credits

For an effective place-based and transformative learning event, the program and its vision comes first. If we had designed PACSE around discrete courses, we would have missed the integrative and holistic form of learning that is the key to our success. However, programs ultimately need to be divided into courses for the sake of evaluations and credits. As mentioned previously, Hans-Dittmar was able to modify three integrated rural development courses that were already on the books at Augustana into two seminars and two community service-learning courses and allow for an immersion Spanish course to be counted. Any undergraduate student in arts or sciences was invited to learn beyond the walls. The student could count some of the courses as part of his or her liberal arts core requirements in social sciences, integrative studies, and cultural studies; the rest could be taken as so-called option credits. Over the years, students from across the country have taken the Augustana courses and transferred them to their institutions for full credit.

The pressure for a major and minor in development studies grew at Augustana through the demands of students and faculty in the Mexico exchanges. Gradually an interdisciplinary global and development studies degree was developed, led by faculty from programs in sociology, biology, environmental studies, religious studies, political studies, philosophy, and economics. Currently, PACSE remains open to students from any major, faculty, or discipline.

The Mexican partner universities had their own challenges in assigning courses and credit. UAEM simply enrolled its students in Augustana's rural development courses and later revalidated their year to count toward their majors. Karsten Mündel negotiated with UDLAP so that students could enroll in some courses in their home institution and others at the host institution. Both Mexican institutions also count the community service component as part of the social service requirement. Mexican federal law requires all university students to fulfill a social service requirement to receive their degrees.

What We Have Learned

Our Students

Through interviews, conversations, and surveys evaluating student learning, the quality of student assignments, and instructor observations, we are convinced that the PACSE, for all the logistical and personnel challenges it presents, is one of the most powerful educational experiences students can have during their entire university career. Not only do students say it changed their lives, they actually embody that change by becoming more ecologically sensitive and socially responsible. We can see it on campus after their return and in their professional and volunteer lives after graduation, since we maintain contact with many of them. Transformative education does its work.

What we as academics have learned is that Mexican villages in particular are great ecological teachers for our students. When a Mexican host mother says, "Mi casa es tu casa" (My house is your house), the students discover this truth during the exchange. They really connect to a family, its community, and its land. It is in this connection, this love for a particular place that ecological living begins.

Faculty Experts Become Listeners and Learners

An integrative program beyond the walls of the university for full academic credit is an anomaly, although to us it is crucial for the task of transforming ecologically destructive patterns.[7] So what are some of the lessons we learned as academics involved in a transdisciplinary program between two culturally different universities in which campesinos and thrift store managers can become teachers and the text becomes the community?

Finding academic partners in Mexico and Canada at home in the rural is key to developing a successful rural community-service exchange. Over the years we have encountered many academics from both countries who like to visit the rural as scenic or rustic, and who may do field research, but are not necessarily at home there. At home means to develop the humility to be willing to learn from rural people. This usually includes a willingness to accept their hospitality, share their food and drink, and attend their celebrations and funerals. In Mexican villages suspicion is widespread of government and university folks who tend to come into campesino communities as so-called experts telling the locals how to solve their agricultural or health problems without ever getting to know them and their realities. In rural

Canada, the attitude, at least publicly expressed, seems to be the reverse. "You are the experts," residents may say, though privately they may feel that those university folks know nothing about how their world works. We were fortunate in having an academic and a rural community organizer, Arturo Ornelas Lizardi, as our first Mexican academic partner. We learned a lot from him, as he did from Paulo Freire, in how to approach and engage the inhabitants of Mexican villages.

Academic partners also need to pass on and cultivate the same humility and openness to our cohort of students. Through the transformative educational experiences described in this chapter, students came to develop vital relationships to land and people, and to the production of knowledge. Students became responsible for their own learning. Teachers also became learners.

A challenge in building capacity among new instructors is to communicate the nature of immersion learning. As a concept, immersion learning is generally associated with second-language acquisition, but there is increasing reference to practica and co-op–type placements for other areas of learning (e.g., Zink, Halaas, Finstad, & Brooks, 2008). For us, an important advantage of using an immersion model is that it encourages students to become fully engaged in the learning experience. While learners still have agency about how, if, and what they learn, the immersion model has significantly increased the likelihood that they will form meaningful relationships with the people and land in a rural community.

New instructors are not accustomed to how students interact with their professors in an immersion learning context. Contact between professors and students is not structured by class or office hours either in camp settings or in the villages. Since the students are having experiences and are learning around the clock, and to the extent that faculty members are in the community, they will come and talk about a variety of issues. Some of the best learning occurs as we are sitting at the *zócalo* (central plaza) or on the steps of the village church discussing everything from challenges with the host family, counterparts, and consumerism to personal relationships and career choices. Even research questions and how to proceed with the next focus group or set of interviews are clarified at informal times. These conversations are part of the support as students work on personal and social transformation toward a more ecologically sound life and lifestyle. Even the instructors, who intersect with the exchange only on certain days, should make informal, discretionary time part of their plan, rather than arriving for a formal session and rushing away afterward.

To balance the first clumsy steps in experience-based education of academics new to the program, we are now developing the notion of *core instructors* who have or develop the necessary transformative education skills. At least one skilled instructor stays in the Mexican community and connects regularly with the students in rural Alberta. The core instructor manages the reflection and analysis of place-based learning and may use members of the interdisciplinary team from two cultures in a variety of ways, including the transmission of particular theories or data at relevant points in the exchange. In this way a relative continuity of educational approach can be assured.

Conclusion

Over the past 15 years, we have moved students and faculty beyond the walls of the academy to learn how to reconnect to land, people, and community. We see this immersion learning of PACSE as a key way to achieve ecological education that explicates the paradox of economic growth at the expense of ecological health but also shows that another world is possible. Communities and students can understand the structures and phenomena that contribute to this paradox and can take active steps to reverse this trend. While we had to be brief in addressing the crucial questions of implementation, they point to a deeper issue: Do our universities have to change significantly if they, and not just individual instructors/researchers, are to tackle the most crucial task before us: restoring our economy, politics, and society to focus on preserving the land and communities where we live?

Notes

1. CWY has over 20 years of experience, mostly with younger students (ages 17 to 21). Its members are committed to working toward sustainable rural communities, and it had the funding and experience to prepare communities to receive students and to find work placements as well as host families. Without the support of CWY through money and personnel, the program could not have been launched and sustained for its first 9 years.

2. For a more thorough history of this phase, see Mündel (2002).

3. Faculty members are drawn from a diverse set of disciplines, including development studies, environmental science, religious studies, education, nursing, agriculture, women's studies, sociology, and economics. Even if a specific discipline is not represented by a faculty member in a given year, we often host guest lecturers from across the disciplines represented by the participating academic institutions.

4. The main reason to shift to a five-month model was decreasing student enrollments. For students who were not global and development studies majors, losing a full academic year was difficult to explain to parents.

5. We can learn a lot, for example, from the village of Amatlán, where humans have thrived for about 4,000 years. They must be doing something right in terms of sustainability.

6. *Popular education* refers to the people's education. It comes from the work of adult literacy and conscientization (e.g., Hope & Timmel, 1988a, 1988b).

7. Augustana was, and may still be, the only member of the Association of Universities and Colleges in Canada that offered a full academic year, and now a five-month program, in the field. And while Augustana has received national and provincial awards for this program and its excellence in international education, a few others follow this approach. It is easier by far for faculty to take students overseas and teach them in classes there, maybe complemented with some fieldwork, than to learn in an immersion setting. We also do not know of any cross-cultural cohorts that spend time in both countries together. Exchanges are often simply that we send our students to their university, and they send theirs to ours.

References

Anielski, M. (2007). *The economics of happiness: Building genuine wealth*. Gabriola, British Columbia, Canada: New Society Publishers.

Berry, W. (1977). *The unsettling of America: Culture & agriculture*. San Francisco, CA: Sierra Club Books.

Caton, L., & Larsh, S. (2000). An idea whose time has come: A decade of healthy community activity in Ontario. In Ontario Healthy Communities Coalition (Ed.), *Inspiring change: Healthy cities and communities in Ontario* (pp. 5–22). Toronto, Canada: Author.

Daly, H. E. (1996). *Beyond growth: The economics of sustainable development*. Boston, MA: Beacon Press.

Epp, R. (2008). A university at home in the rural. In R. Epp (Ed.), *We are all treaty people: Prairie essays* (pp. 189–202). Edmonton, Canada: University of Alberta Press.

Epp, R., & Whitson, D. (Eds.). (2001). *Writing off the rural West: Globalization, governments and the transformation of rural communities*. Edmonton, Canada: University of Alberta Press.

Fals-Borda, O., & Rahman, M. A. (1991). *Action and knowledge: Breaking the monopoly with participatory action research*. New York, NY: Apex Press.

Freire, P. (2000). *Pedagogy of the oppressed*. New York, NY: Continuum. (Original work published 1970).

Fromm, E. (1968). *The revolution of hope: Toward a humanized technology*. New York, NY: Harper & Row.

Gruenewald, D. A. (2003). The best of both worlds: A critical pedagogy of place. *Educational Researcher, 32*(4), 3–12.

Hope, A., & Timmel, S. (1988a). *Training for transformation: A handbook for community workers* (Vol. 1). Gweru, Zimbabwe: Mambo Press.

Hope, A., & Timmel, S. (1988b). *Training for transformation: A handbook for community workers* (Vol. 2). Gweru, Zimbabwe: Mambo Press.

Korten, D. C. (1995). *When corporations rule the world*. West Hartford, CT: Kumarian Press.

Maguire, P. (1987). *Doing participatory research: A feminist approach*. Amherst, MA: Center for International Education, School of Education, University of Massachusetts.

Mündel, K. (2002). *Examining the impact of university international programs on active citizenship: The case of student praxical participation in the Mexico-Canada rural development exchange*. Unpublished thesis, University of Toronto, Canada.

Nathan, R. (2005). *My freshman year: What a professor learned by becoming a student*. Ithaca, NY: Cornell University Press.

Selby, D. (2006). The firm and shaky ground of education for sustainable development. *Journal of Geography in Higher Education, 30*(2), 351–365.

Zink, T., Halaas, G. W., Finstad, D., & Brooks, K. D. (2008). The Rural Physician Associate Program: The value of immersion learning for third-year medical students. *Journal of Rural Health, 24*(4), 353–359.

2

INTEGRATING SUSTAINABILITY AND SERVICE LEARNING INTO THE SCIENCE CURRICULUM

Susan Sutheimer and Jesse Pyles

T he language of the sustainability movement in higher education is largely one of the sciences. Climate change, energy use, mercury pollution, ozone depletion, acid rain, and polymer recycling are fundamentally chemical situations. Problems with watersheds, deforestation, land use, and invasive species are understood and modeled through the application of biological principles. It follows that making sustainability meaningful to the masses requires a working understanding of fundamental science. Unfortunately, science education is perceived as intimidating by many students and much of the general public. One means of making science more accessible to students is to increase their ability to communicate difficult principles and to fuse the link between science and sustainability. Service learning provides an excellent vehicle to achieve this goal.

At Green Mountain College, science-based service-learning projects generally have three desired outcomes. First, they provide students with an opportunity to learn fundamental science by engaging in meaningful projects. Second, they encourage students to communicate science to the public through oral presentations or through their actions. Finally, they provide community partners with valuable services related to sustainability. To illustrate how these outcomes are met, we introduce the challenges associated with service learning in the sciences, demonstrate how "simple short projects" (SSPs) help science faculty successfully integrate community service learning into courses that are already dense with conceptually challenging material, and describe methods we have used so that the SSPs constitute a valuable experience for students learning about sustainability.

Institutional Context

Green Mountain College is a private liberal arts institution in rural Vermont. College administrators view the environment as the unifying theme for the institution's liberal arts foundation and the basis for its culture. All students, regardless of their major, investigate issues of environmental sustainability through the 30-credit environmental liberal arts (ELA) curriculum. Core courses such as Images of Nature, Voices of Community, and A Delicate Balance, along with discipline-specific courses, deliver a traditional slate of requirements having a sustainability focus that uniquely prepares students to investigate some of the most pressing environmental issues of our time. Environmentally focused majors such as environmental studies and natural resource management supplement traditional majors in unique interdisciplinary curricula.

Green Mountain's commitment to sustainability education extends beyond the classroom. The college has promoted the development of renewable energy in the region through its support of Cow Power, energy created from burning methane from cow manure on Vermont dairy farms, and an organic farm the college runs through an innovative sustainable agriculture program. Green Mountain was the first Vermont institution of higher education to sign the American College and University Presidents' Climate Commitment, a pledge to become climate neutral, and the Association for the Advancement of Sustainability in Higher Education recognized the college's efforts with the Campus Sustainability Leadership Award in 2007. Because of our strong environmental focus, service-learning projects that promote sustainability objectives on or off campus are strongly encouraged by the administration.

Opportunity and Challenge

Students and most of the general public are undereducated with respect to science. Few adults, young or old, fully understand the science that underlies pollution, waste, ecological restoration, energy, ozone depletion, acid rain, nuclear power, and global climate change. Additionally, there is a significant gap between what scientists know and how that knowledge is conveyed to the general public to enhance people's ability to make decisions about environmental policies. Service learning is one way students can communicate the science behind sustainability-related topics to their communities. Science students involved in service-learning courses can begin to see themselves as uniquely positioned leaders in sustainability efforts, as educators and as agents of change.

Unfortunately, actively engaging science students in service learning is relatively rare, especially compared to efforts in other disciplines. Chemistry, physics, and biology faculty are reluctant to try service learning. Reasons for this unwillingness include the real or perceived importance of covering a large amount of conceptually challenging material during each term, the daunting problem of large class sizes, difficulty in finding community partners, problems with student transportation and funding, and the often accepted fallacy that education in the hard sciences stops at the doors of the college classroom. Forging service-learning partnerships can take a great deal of time, requiring the commitment to joint meetings with community representatives and the detailed mechanics of designing projects. The numerous problems associated with using service learning in the sciences are reflected in a corresponding lack of publications: *The Journal of Chemical Education* lists only 10 articles on service learning since 1999—an average of only 1 each year (Sutheimer, 2008), and the acclaimed 21-volume series *Service-Learning in the Disciplines* (Zlotkowski, 1996–2006) contains a volume on biology but none on chemistry or physics. Science department faculty at Green Mountain College have tried to overcome some of these problems by developing innovative, but sometimes unconventional, service-learning projects.

The SSP

The SSP was created primarily to address the concern that little time exists for extensive service learning, since science courses cover a predetermined, large number of challenging, discipline-specific, time-consuming topics each term. SSPs are service-learning projects that might involve just a few classroom periods, a single laboratory session, or a laboratory session and one or a few class periods. Like any service-learning project, the SSP addresses the course goals and is relevant to course topics. Large classes can be broken into groups for SSPs, or smaller, more advanced classes can participate as a single group. The SSP relieves some of the problems of finding community partners, as partners are more willing to engage an entire class for short periods of time rather than the long periods that often characterize service learning in other disciplines (Sutheimer, 2008). At Green Mountain College, an additional difficulty is finding community partners because of its rural location, compared to institutions located in more metropolitan settings. We have used SSPs successfully for several years in a variety of science disciplines, including chemistry, biology, environmental science, and math.

Because relatively short amounts of class and lab time are used for SSPs, instructors are more likely to consider including service-learning projects in their curricula, and environmental organizations and nonprofits are more likely to call upon science faculty for community-based projects. Green Mountain has a reputation for being willing to adjust course activities to accommodate community needs; therefore, if projects are short in duration and simple in design, they are more likely to find a place in the science curriculum as well as in the community partner's schedule.

One example of a very successful SSP was a partnership between students in an environmental science course and the local chapter of the Nature Conservancy. One of the course goals was to illustrate how a buffer zone (the vegetated, protective area between a stream and cultivated farmland) enhanced the ecology of the area by preventing erosion and avoiding polluted water running off the fields into the stream. As part of creating a buffer zone, students planted tree saplings on Nature Conservancy property that abutted a local river. By working in the field at this compromised site, students were able to clearly make the connection between the need for reforestation and creation of the buffer zone. Nature Conservancy members were willing to schedule the tree planting at the class's normal lab time and provided the saplings and planting tools. Breaking down the planting groups into lab-section-size cohorts helped to accommodate the transportation and tool needs of the large class. As with other SSPs, the project was narrow in focus and of short duration, only two hours of class and five hours of lab time. Meanwhile, it met the needs of a grateful community organization by providing the labor needed to plant hundreds of saplings. Similar to more traditional service-learning projects, a reflective process following the field activity stressed the benefits to student and partner and sought connections to other parts of the course in which restoration was an important focus.

Another example from an organic chemistry class illustrates how a routine lab experiment can morph into an SSP. The lab curriculum for this course emphasized the chemistry of natural products, the extraction of useful substances from natural products, and transformations of natural products into useful chemicals. Among the goals of the course were to familiarize the students with how to extract natural dyes from plants and to link the chemistry of the dyeing process to the hands-on lab experience.

To begin, the instructor pointed the students to wildflowers that could be used for dyes and that were available on the campus grounds. The students harvested the plants, extracted the dyes by boiling the plants in water, prepared (mordanted) swatches of wool, and then dyed the wool swatches. The lab procedure the students performed was useful as an instructional tool but, as is true with most chemistry labs, lacked any societal significance. When someone suggested dyeing Onesies (one-piece infant bodysuits) for a local charity, the exercise instantly became a service-learning project. A local family service agency was happy to become the recipient of the students' work. Fourteen students dyed 28 Onesies using extracts of a variety of flowers, roots, and fruits. The students then donated the Onesies at a special class presentation arranged by the instructor and the service agency. During the presentation, the agency representative described its mission and the needs of the community. Students were excited that the revised lab, now a service-learning SSP, had a meaningful social purpose in addition to its original instructional purpose. Reflecting on this brief experience, one student said, "It was cool to be dyeing something for a reason," and another remarked, "It also felt more purposeful than most of the other labs we have performed in the past."

These examples show that service learning challenges faculty to design SSP projects that teach the material, engage students, and provide a valuable service to the community. It requires faculty to be flexible enough with their course structure to accommodate a onetime event or immediate community service opportunity for their students. Service learning dares us to understand the "need for flexibility and responsiveness to the unique attributes of the partners" (McCline & Eisman, 2008, p. 96). Willingness to be creative and flexible is characteristic of a good teacher, and such a teacher is likely to overcome the arguments against bringing service learning to science students.

Reflection and SSPs

Reflection is an important part of any service-learning project. Because SSPs are short, the reflection process is generally brief, concise, and focused. Methods for reflections include guided discussions, essays, online responses to a series of relevant questions, small-group discussions, and keeping journals. In the Onesies project, we used a guided discussion to illustrate how the project was valuable to the community organization as well as to student learning, and how knowledge of chemistry can contribute to a student's response to civic responsibility. The need to connect the service-learning project to goals is critical, and making these connections may require the instructor to reframe some of the course objectives. One could argue, for instance, that the Onesies project met the goal of a chemistry class for hands-on experience with natural products, but if the course goals did not include a social responsibility component, no good reason existed for the service-learning element. On the other hand, the mission statement of the college, and for most educational institutions, has a service/social responsibility component. The creative faculty member might then instruct students to reflect on how their project meets the goals of the institution as well as those of the class.

Service-learning reflection can also be an important tool for advancing sustainability initiatives on campus. Reflection may be the only structured opportunity for a diverse cross-section of students to give feedback on sustainability projects, especially where campus sustainability efforts are not part of the academic offering. Written and verbal feedback can provide campus leaders with important information about student attitudes and behaviors toward sustainability programs, about what works and what does not, and about sustainability topics that most excite students. Properly managed, this information can be used effectively to encourage student involvement in future sustainability endeavors. For example, a chemistry class studying the composition of plastics might do an SSP to educate the local community about recycling. Reflections on the experience could help the sustainability program at the college make changes in outreach materials about recycling to increase recycling rates for campus visitors.

Reflection presents another opportunity for the science instructor: challenging students to take the next step in the scientific process by asking questions that are experimentally verifiable. Is harvesting dyes from natural areas a sustainable process? Why are manufactured dyes, which cause more pollution, primarily used in the clothing industry rather than natural dyes? Could the chemistry of the dyeing process be altered to make the wastes biodegradable? Questions such as these challenge students to move beyond basic science—to think on new levels of scientific inquiry that enhances cognitive development.

The Campus as Community Partner

Periodically, our service-learning projects use the college itself as the community partner. While some service-learning practitioners may find the college partnership problematic, we maintain that the community does not necessarily start outside the gates of the institution, and that using the college as a partner eliminates some of the problems involved with transportation, risk management, permissions, logistics, and identifying community partners in rural areas. Indeed, using the campus community as partner can provide a living laboratory uniquely suited for applying science education to multidisciplinary sustainability issues. Additionally, as we will see, on-campus sustainability initiatives can spill over to stimulate future service outreach to the external community.

The Great Garlic Mustard Pull is an annual Earth Day event coordinated by either the Forest Ecology and Management class or the Biology II class at Green Mountain College. This daylong event is an open invitation to the entire college community, either as individuals or as a class, to pull the invasive, nonnative garlic mustard plant from a forested, riparian area of the campus. Student supervisors, working in shifts, provide information about the invasive species problem to all participants, guide the pullers to assigned areas, keep count of the number of plants that are removed, and compost the dislodged plants. This project illustrates a relatively simple sustainability project but one that allows students to see the practical benefits of fundamental science. These projects also give our students a brief opportunity to become project managers and allow them to share their scientific knowledge with the campus community. In three years, the project collected many hundreds of pounds of garlic mustard and virtually eliminated it from the campus.

The Great Garlic Mustard Pull has also propagated other sustainability-related SSPs in a variety of disciplines. Classes in environmental education, biology, environmental ethics, environmental chemistry, and other sustainability-focused courses are commonly involved in pulling garlic mustard during this event. In some cases, the entire class pulls mustard for a single class period, while in other cases, individual students might participate as part of an assignment. We have seen interesting examples on the part of faculty members in focusing student work on their own class topics. For example, an environmental education teacher may connect the project to methods of organizing hands-on field experiences, and the environmental ethics teacher might stress the influence of human activity on the natural landscape. Whatever the focus, a service-learning project that produces more service-learning projects is an exciting outcome of this sustainability-based science endeavor.

Another opportunity related to sustainability science was developed in our Public Policy and the Environment course among students who had already taken part in the Great Garlic Mustard Pull. Students in this class routinely research and submit an environmental policy to the college administration for possible adoption collegewide. These policies may be about topics such as smoking on campus or socially responsible investing by the institution. In cooperation with the Forest Ecology and Management class that sponsored the Great Garlic Mustard Pull, the students in the Public Policy and the Environment course proposed a policy on the control of invasive plant species on college properties. (Since complete eradication of invasive plants is often not feasible, their control and management is a reasonable alternative.) Eventually, their draft became the guiding policy for the management of invasive species on the college's 155-acre campus. It also became the incentive for another outcome of the Great Garlic Mustard Pull: the student-led development of the Invasive Species Management Plan for Green Mountain College. This plan included sustained funding for a natural areas crew of summer student workers whose job is to control invasive plants.

Designing service-learning projects like the Great Garlic Mustard Pull that have such broad implications and applicability are not generally the objective of the service-learning project designer. Nonetheless, this example illustrates how the reach of a project can become more extensive and self-propagating than initially anticipated. In a similar example, a class at Green Mountain developed a service-learning project that encouraged residents of the village of Poultney to change one lightbulb in their homes to an energy-saving compact fluorescent bulb. Working with the local hardware store, town management, and the chamber of commerce, students developed informational kiosks, knocked on doors, and gave presentations on the advantages of compact fluorescent bulbs. At the end of the project, nearly 99% of the homes in the village changed at least one lightbulb. This service-learning project was later emulated by neighboring towns and by other schools throughout the nation. Moreover, the class won statewide recognition for its community efforts.

The Student as Educator

Naditz (2008) pointed out that students can and have become active sustainability teachers on many college campuses. In his discussion of sustainability activities in new student orientation programs, he said that students who are enthusiastic about campus sustainability can have a big impact by sharing their enthusiasm with others. Service learning can provide the additional structure for students to become teachers of science as well as of sustainability. One example from our class involved a request from a local organization to be part of the Poultney Earth Fair. The afternoon event was designed to highlight the affordability of environmentally friendly consumer choices for the general public. The fair provided an opportunity for introductory science students to present hands-on science demonstrations of their choosing. Because the event was organized rather late in the academic year (April), this SSP required a last-minute syllabus change. The unanticipated change enhanced the course by allowing the students to learn by doing, helped out a local organization, and communicated the science of sustainability.

The structure of the earth fair service-learning project was relatively simple: Since the class was large, students were divided into working groups. During one class period each group chose its demonstration topic, the general layout for an informational poster, and ideas about hands-on presentations. The groups were instructed to focus on course topics and the science behind their projects.

One group chose green cleaning products as its topic. The students found information online about various homemade products, such as vinegar and water for cleaning windows, and developed a trifold poster on green cleaning. Additionally, they designed a method allowing visitors to their booth to clean a greasy mirror with the vinegar solution. Each student staffed the group's booth for two hours, explaining to the public why the homemade solution cleaned grease off glass and how its use could lessen effects on the environment compared to a commercial window-cleaning product. Most of the research and design on these projects were homework assignments with periodic updates during class periods. This structure minimized the impact on class time, yet from students' reflections we learned they were overwhelmingly appreciative of the opportunity to pass on their knowledge of science and the environment to the general public.

Passing on knowledge about the environment was central to another SSP conducted during a second-semester introductory chemistry course. Students offered a brief session on environmental explosions to middle school students during the annual Eco Expo sponsored by the local Natural Resources Conservation District for fifth and sixth graders to learn about the environment through demonstrations and hands-on activities. Chemistry students in small groups chose and researched their own demonstrations (low-energy, simple, and safe explosions) and were required to relate the relationship of the explosions to the environment and the theory behind the explosive processes to the onlookers. To accomplish this, the chemistry students needed to understand and interrelate gas laws (how gases are related with respect to temperature, volume, and pressure), entropy (why everything tends to become more random), energetics (what energy changes are involved), incomplete combustion (what happens when things burn with less than sufficient oxygen), and the serious pollution problems of airborne micrometer-size particulates. All these concepts needed to be mastered by the chemistry students and then simplified, since the notion of unseen, unfelt, and odor-free gases is a difficult concept for young students to comprehend. Our students stressed communicating the science of gases to the younger students by showing that explosions were simply chemical reactions that make gases expand rapidly. The chemistry students demonstrated, among others, the production of carbon dioxide (a greenhouse gas) from baking soda and vinegar, dust explosions, and the production of diesel engine–emitted particles. Since each demonstration emphasized an aspect of gases in the environment, the middle school students came away learning good basic science and the connection of basic science to the real world. All students—college and middle school—enjoyed the experience tremendously. In a reflective discussion following the project, our students were amazed at how much they learned about gases, explosions, and related environmental problems by teaching those concepts to others.

Irv Levy (Kay & Levy, 2009) and his students at Gordon College provide another great example of service learning in which students become science educators. They created an outreach program called Green Organic Literacy Forum (GOLum), which was designed to spread the word about green chemistry, the design of chemical processes to reduce or eliminate negative environmental impacts. The processes seek to reduce waste products, use nontoxic components, and have lower energy use. Students from Levy's organic chemistry class present hands-on demonstrations and information about green chemistry at local high school chemistry classes, after-school programs at the elementary level, and museums and national meetings (see http://www.gordon.edu/page.cfm?iPageID= 1004&iCategoryID= 73). They have produced a green chemistry video, sponsored a green chemistry lecture series on campus, presented their work at national science meetings, and designed a green chemistry curriculum that empowers middle and high school students and teachers to do outreach. GOLum is one of the premier outreach programs in chemistry education, teaching basic green chemistry to thousands of individuals of various ages and providing a model for all the sciences in the design of service-learning projects in which students are educators as well as agents of change.

Evaluation and Assessment

We highly recommend developing an assessment process at the outset of designing SSPs. As soon as the basic outline of the project is created, a survey or other mechanism should be designed for comparing the goals for the project with its outcomes. Working with the outreach office of the institution or the science department to design standard assessment procedures for service learning can be very helpful, ensure consistency, and save time.

We used four approaches to assess the value of SSP service-learning projects. First, the reflection component of the project often reveals qualitative information on the value of the experience. For instance, a reflection question on the environmental explosions service-learning project simply asked, "Did you learn anything from this experience?" As previously mentioned, students were enthusiastic about the science and sustainability concepts they learned. They realized the value of hands-on demonstrations when teaching middle school students, as well as the reality of Murphy's

Law: If anything can go wrong, it will. Students also often suggested ways to make projects a better learning experience for middle school students by encouraging them to guess what would happen, or by interacting more dynamically with them.

Second, we asked students several survey-type questions such as, "How valuable was this experience to your learning about our community?" or "How would you change this experience to make it more meaningful?" The Student Assessment of Learning Gains (SALG) instrument has been helpful to us (see http://salgsite.org). The SALG website asks students to rate how each component of a course helped them learn and to rate their gains toward achieving course goals. It is easily modified for specific applications and is free for instructors in all disciplines.

Third, we always seek input from our community partners. Because the projects are short, relatively tightly structured, and have considerable input from the partners, students invariably receive praise for their work. Verbal feedback and regular engagement with longstanding partners has created a free flow of honest communication about what does and does not work well and has been valuable in redesigning projects to fit the needs of the students, the course, and the community partner. Positive feedback is also made available to the college's public relations group for subsequent publication and distribution to the college community, alumni, and the public at large.

Evaluating service-learning projects should reflect the relative time involved; SSPs are usually a small fraction of the student's overall grade. When doing educational outreach, students can be graded on the clarity of their explanations, their willingness to interact with the public, and their basic knowledge. Other options include students' grading each other on their contributions to group effectiveness. Faculty can grade based on the quality of reflective essays, journals, or involvement in discussions.

Fourth, by following the employment trajectory of our graduates, we found that students who teach the basic tenets of environmental sustainability continue to incorporate them throughout their professional careers. Several of our graduates who were participants in service-learning projects are now educators at natural history museums, local farm and food programs, and nonprofit organizations that promote sustainability. Others have positions in the fields of solar energy, organic farming, and biodiesel manufacturing.

Future Prospects

Opportunities for service-learning projects vary with the needs of community partners and class scheduling. Since we have developed a reputation for flexibility, we expect community partners will continue to communicate their immediate and short-term needs, and that we will be able to respond by creating meaningful SSPs that strengthen these relationships. Some projects, such as the Poultney Earth Fair or the Onesies project, are now annual events. The Great Garlic Mustard Pull has become a victim of its own success and is being transformed into a project for controlling other invasive species. We plan to expand our contribution to community sustainability events, such as the Eco Expo and the Poultney Earth Fair, in which the students are educators. We will continue our regular events (e.g., town–gown meetings or community mixers) that invite community participation in service learning. During these events, new channels of communication can be opened between prospective partners and faculty members. Members of the community can express their needs and discuss possible ways to interact with students or develop projects. We continually look for new ideas, new subject areas, and new connections to the community.

Two new special projects are now under consideration. First, we plan to introduce green chemistry projects that involve informational sessions along with hands-on demonstrations at public venues such as museums and schools. Green Team students will develop and provide green experiences as part of their laboratory curriculum. Green chemistry is a concept that is easily understood, and Kay and Levy (2009) have shown it to be adaptable to outreach programs. Second, a new upper-level green chemistry course will have a major component dedicated to a service-learning project for the sustainable use of waste products from the college's new biomass plant. The plant, which burns wood chips sustainably harvested from the local area, will provide most of the heat and 20% of the electricity for the college. As a leader in the sustainability movement, Green Mountain College will thus provide leadership not only in reducing our carbon footprint but also in demonstrating environmentally benign uses of waste ash.

Additionally, through presentations at conferences, workshops, and publications in science and sustainability education journals, we plan to continue our efforts to help science faculty nationwide engage in environmental sustainability and socially responsible service-learning activities in their communities no matter the size or type of their institution.

Conclusion

Service learning in the sciences is an important key to educating students and the general public about critical environmental issues. Using creativity in designing projects and flexibility in implementing them, colleges and universities can bring service learning into the science classroom. By working with internal and external community partners, the students continue to reap the many benefits of the pedagogy. SSPs are not unlike more conventional programs where students gain hands-on experience with science, act as educators, begin to understand the basics of civic responsibility, and have an impact on the community in positive ways. Additionally, the use of SSPs decreases faculty concern over the amount of time required to cover the standard science curriculum. Short projects allow faculty to use service learning in situations where most science faculty would not have previously considered the possibility. Most importantly, our assessments indicate that service-learning programs enhance students' knowledge of scientific principles, improve their recognition of the value of community-based science education, and help them communicate the science of sustainability.

References

Kay, R. D., & Levy, I. J. (2009). Student motivated endeavors advancing green organic literacy. In P. T. Anastas, I. J. Levy, & K. E. Parent (Eds.), *Green chemistry education: Changing the course of chemistry* (pp. 155–166). New York, NY: Oxford University Press.

McCline, R. L., & Eisman, G. S. (2008). Selected case examples of service learning in business. In S. C. Tannenbaum (Ed.), *Research, advocacy, and political engagement: Multidisciplinary perspectives through service learning* (pp. 82–100). Sterling, VA: Stylus.

Naditz, A. (2008). Make love, not CO_2. *Sustainability: The Journal of Record, 1*(6), 381–386.

Sutheimer, S. (2008). Strategies to simplify service-learning efforts in chemistry. *Journal of Chemical Education, 85*(2), 231–233.

Zlotkowski, E. (Ed.). (1996–2006). *Service-learning in the disciplines* (Vols. 1–21). Washington, DC: American Association for Higher Education.

3

SUSTAINABILITY EDUCATION THROUGH AN INTERDISCIPLINARY AND SERVICE-LEARNING APPROACH

Alison K. Varty, Shane C. Lishawa, and Nancy C. Tuchman

The future of civilization is at risk because of environmental degradation resulting from climate change, loss of biodiversity, a severely altered nitrogen cycle, and pollution (Rockström et al., 2009). For society to sustain itself, humans must find solutions to these pressing problems. As trainers of future teachers, journalists, economists, business professionals, engineers, scientists, and politicians, those of us in higher education can play a role in solving these problems.

Unfortunately, the traditional narrow disciplinary approach to teaching in institutions of higher education may not be adequate to educate future environmental leaders (Cortese, 2003; Orr, 2003). Political, social, and ecological spheres interact in such a complex manner that solutions to environmental problems must come from individuals who understand their interplay. Lester Brown (2008), president of the Earth Policy Institute, stresses this point by stating the need for "political leaders who can see the big picture,

In addition to helping design, implement, and evaluate the learning experiences described in this chapter, the following colleagues from Loyola University Chicago and Northeastern Illinois University participated in workshops to discuss the format and content of the manuscript, wrote essays that informed content, and contributed to editing the manuscript: Elizabeth Coffman, Marshall Eames, Pamela Geddes, Patrick Green, Martina Schmeling, Christopher Skrable, Zachary Waickman, and Michael Welch.

who understand the relationship between the economy and its environmental support systems. And since the principal advisors to government are economists, we need economists who can think like ecologists" (p. 8). We believe it is essential that courses and programs of study aiming to train students to solve environmental problems be interdisciplinary.

Training students across disciplines to solve environmental problems also requires breaking down boundaries between theory and practice. In addition to providing foundational knowledge about environmental problems, colleges and universities need to provide students with more hands-on experience in addressing these problems (Orr, 1994; Senge, 2000). Because colleges and universities are nested in communities that face real environmental challenges, community-based service-learning experiences are a good means to accomplish this objective. Service learning is well documented in increasing student civic engagement and inspiring the conviction that individual and community actions can make a difference (Eyler, Giles, & Braxton, 1997). Service learning helps students identify issues of national and local importance (Astin & Sax, 1998; Eyler et al.), and develop life skills such as leadership and self-confidence (Astin & Sax). Thus, in addition to effecting positive environmental change, environmentally focused service-learning experiences may contribute to students' lifelong roles as environmental leaders.

The goal of this chapter is to share with faculty members at other institutions our experiences designing and conducting an interdisciplinary service-learning course focused on environmental sustainability at Loyola University Chicago (LUC). The interdisciplinary course, Solutions to Environmental Problems (STEP): Biodiesel, aimed to educate students about the environmental, social, economic, and political problems related to burning fossil fuels. The curriculum included the causes of climate change, acid rain, and air pollution, and how biofuels (alternative fuels made from renewable organic matter) address these issues. STEP: Biodiesel also gave students the opportunity to actively address these problems through biodiesel production and service-learning projects. STEP: Biodiesel was the first in a series of courses addressing pressing sustainability issues on Loyola's campus and in the local community. In this chapter, we describe the course design and its implementation and the impact the course has had on students, faculty members, the university, and the community. We conclude with an exploration of the challenges we faced in the process.

Loyola University Chicago

LUC is a private Catholic university with about 15,000 students at three Chicago-area campuses and two foreign academic centers (Beijing and Rome). In keeping with its Jesuit Catholic heritage, LUC has traditionally emphasized a rigorous academic curriculum, freedom of inquiry, and the need to generate knowledge in the service of humanity. LUC promises to prepare its students for extraordinary lives of achievement, scholarship, engagement, and service (see http://www.luc.edu/mission/).

In agreement with LUC's mission, there is a strong curricular focus on service learning and civic engagement. Twenty percent of LUC undergraduate students participate in one or more forms of experiential learning each semester, over half of which are service-learning classes. Much of LUC's curricular engagement with the broader community is coordinated by the Center for Experiential Learning (CEL), an interdisciplinary, academic center founded in fall 2007 to encourage and support the development of experiential and transformational learning opportunities for students across the curriculum. The CEL staff works with individual academic departments and schools to promote academic internship programs, service-learning courses, and undergraduate research opportunities.

The STEP Program

The faculty members involved in designing the STEP program at LUC are committed to training environmental leaders through interdisciplinary and service-learning experiences; this conviction guided the program's development. The development of STEP was also driven by our desire to give energized LUC students a voice in sustainability initiatives and to create a productive outlet for them to effect change on campus and in the community.

STEP is a program of LUC's Center for Urban Environmental Research & Policy (CUERP), an interdisciplinary academic center focusing on research, teaching, and outreach exploring humans' interactions with the urban environment. CUERP received funding from the U.S. Environmental Protection Agency (EPA) to launch the STEP program. The grant also included funds to build the LUC Biodiesel Laboratory. Thus, the first STEP courses, including STEP: Biodiesel, had a renewable energy theme. CUERP hired a full-time instructor to coordinate the STEP program. The essential qualifications for the STEP course coordinator include the ability to lead faculty from multiple disciplines; stretch well outside his or her area of expertise; connect with the local communities and develop opportunities for STEP collaborations; design, organize, and mentor sophisticated student projects; and oversee the adaptation of the course to meet student interests. In spring 2007 we brought together an interdisciplinary team of faculty and staff with the expertise and interest related to the program and renewable energy from LUC's College of Arts and Sciences, School of Communication, School of Education, School of Business Administration, CEL, and CUERP to further define the STEP model.

Two learning goals were established during these planning sessions that applied to STEP: Biodiesel and all future STEP courses:

1. Inform students about current and relevant environmental problems that are particularly meaningful to them.
2. Foster environmental leadership values, skills, and abilities by providing students with service-learning opportunities to address the environmental problem the course examines.

We involve our students in solving the STEP course environmental problem through a diverse array of service-learning experiences. Some STEP students conduct community-based research related to the course topic. Others form partnerships with campus or community organizations to provide direct services, such as workshops, after-school programs, or marketing materials. All STEP students deliver interactive presentations of the results of their service-learning projects at the STEP Public Forum, an event attended by members of the university and local communities featuring keynote speakers from inside and outside the university. These activities are a required part of the STEP curriculum, included in a total of about 40 service hours per student per semester.

Instructors accomplish the goals of the STEP program through lectures, discussions, and laboratories, in addition to the service-learning projects. All course components are interdisciplinary. For instance, in the last four semesters, STEP courses have involved over 35 members of LUC faculty (representing the College of Arts and Sciences, School of Communication, School of Nursing, School of Education, School of Business Administration, and

School of Social Work), LUC staff, and members of the local community. These academics and local professionals have given guest lectures, led discussions, and mentored STEP student service-learning projects. Additionally, our students, ranging from freshmen to graduate students, come from diverse majors, including sociology, accounting, secondary education, marketing, political science, philosophy, chemistry, English, communication, biology, and environmental studies. The most common STEP student major is environmental studies (22% of all students), followed by biology (20%), chemistry (8%), communications (7%), and sociology (7%). Student service-learning project groups, which typically contain multiple majors, reflect the diversity of ideas and people involved in the course.

The STEP courses also use student-directed learning to accomplish course goals. Student-directed learning experiences are focused on topics students have identified as meaningful. This pedagogy accepts that much of the motivation to learn and power for growth and development comes from the learner (Wilcox, 1996). Although we chose the initial STEP course topic, our students chose and will choose all future course topics based on their perceptions of campus and community sustainability needs. The changing topic model allows for exceptionally engaged students to take more than one STEP course in their undergraduate career. Each STEP course topic will repeat for several semesters before students choose a new topic. Furthermore, STEP students have a great deal of freedom in determining how they will address the course topic through their service-learning projects. After they become familiar with the resources available to them on campus and in the community, students take responsibility for selecting, planning, initiating, and evaluating the outcomes of their projects.

STEP: Biodiesel

Through two meetings in the spring of 2007, the faculty planning group defined the initial course topic, discussed relevant course content, and determined which service projects the campus and community could support. Over the summer, the course coordinator finalized the lecture topics and schedule, readings, assignments, and assessments and developed the syllabus (see the appendix). The coordinator's role was to finalize the course content to create a cohesive learning experience for the students.

Goals and Objectives

The goal of all the courses in the STEP program is to generate informed, capable, and active environmental leaders. In STEP: Biodiesel we sought to give students an interdisciplinary understanding of problems associated with the use of fossil fuels. Students not only learned about the environmental impacts of burning fossil fuels such as climate change, acid rain, and other forms of pollution, they also learned how these pollutants affect human and ecosystem health. Furthermore, they explored how professionals from diverse disciplines, including philosophy, political science, and economics, would approach these problems. Through this content, we hoped to demonstrate the principles of sustainability and the importance of taking an interdisciplinary approach to solving environmental problems. We also wanted STEP: Biodiesel students to understand the potential of renewable forms of energy (especially biofuels) to moderate these problems on national and global scales while providing an opportunity for students to participate in biodiesel and renewable energy–related service projects addressing these problems on the local scale. Specific objectives of student service projects in STEP: Biodiesel included building and staffing an economically sustainable biodiesel laboratory that would convert LUC cafeteria waste vegetable oil into biodiesel and educating various community groups about biodiesel and other forms of renewable energy.

Methods of Instruction

Students learned about sustainability and issues related to fossil fuel use through weekly lectures by LUC faculty and staff and community members. A wide variety of perspectives about the topic including lectures about the history of human energy use, politics of energy, energy and the economy, impacts of fossil fuel use on the atmosphere, biosphere, and human health, as well as ethical issues associated with the extraction and use of fossil fuels were provided.

Through discussions of popular and primary literature from across disciplines, students examined the efficacy of biofuels to reduce the use of fossil fuels and mitigate their harmful effects. The course coordinator facilitated the discussions, which were particularly exciting because of current controversies and conflicting opinions about biofuels. Issues discussed included the relationship between biofuels production and food prices, land clearing for biofuels production and the associated displacement of people and ecosystems, and economic subsidization of biofuels. It was interesting to hear students from diverse disciplines discuss these issues and develop an opinion about the sustainability of biofuels production. According to one former student, "The discussions were excellent. Because of our wide range of backgrounds, we all learned from the material as well as each other. It is critical to have these conversations."

In the laboratory section of the course, students learned the chemistry involved in making biodiesel from virgin and waste vegetable oil and procedures used to test the quality of biodiesel. In later labs students became proficient in making large batches (100 gallons) of biodiesel and built, modified, and staffed the LUC biodiesel production facility. In later semesters, after the biodiesel lab was fully functioning, students improved the efficacy of the reaction and manufacture of biodiesel and developed a recipe for producing soap from the waste glycerin.

Before each semester began, the course coordinator met with potential project mentors from the university and the community to discuss group project ideas. University mentors were identified based upon previous interest in the STEP program or sought out when STEP projects overlapped with their expertise. Community mentors were identified with assistance from the CEL, which maintains relationships with a diverse network of community organizations throughout Chicago. Community mentors were individuals with the appropriate expertise who needed help implementing a local sustainability project. We generated project ideas that were suitable for groups of three or four students to accomplish during the semester. All potential project ideas and mentors were then listed in the syllabus. The students had the opportunity to review these ideas and meet with potential group project mentors. They then identified the projects they wanted to complete based on their academic interests and their understanding of the resources available. Sometimes they selected projects and identified mentors who were not listed in the syllabus. Consequently, the course instructional method allowed for service projects to be largely student directed. We did not mandate that teams should be made up of students from diverse disciplines, but in three semesters all groups had students representing more than one major.

After selecting their projects and receiving basic training in proposal writing, STEP: Biodiesel students wrote project proposals. Because the student projects often required modest amounts of money (typically under

$100), we structured the proposals like a grant proposal. Students first met with potential stakeholders, conducted research, and discussed project ideas with their mentors. Next, they outlined the problem their project would address, their project goals and objectives, a detailed plan and timeline for meeting their objectives, a project evaluation plan, and a budget. The proposal assignment helped the groups organize their projects and gain important project development skills. Proposals also gave the group mentors and course coordinator many opportunities to advise the groups and help them refine the details of the projects.

Student Projects

In the three semesters the course was offered, STEP: Biodiesel students initiated and completed over 20 renewable energy service-learning projects. Ten of the projects focused on helping to develop and refine the biodiesel production process in the LUC Biodiesel Laboratory. These internal projects included writing a business plan for the laboratory; examining the possibility of growing algae to generate oil for biodiesel production; developing uses for the glycerin by-product of biodiesel production; as well as investigating the effectiveness of different catalysts, washing techniques, and varying quantities of methanol (the most expensive reagent) on biodiesel production. As a result of their scientific research, six STEP: Biodiesel students have presented their work at state and national conferences including the Illinois Academy of Sciences meeting; the National Sustainable Design Expo in Washington, D.C.; and the Inter-Collegiate Biodiesel Conference in Pennsylvania. Three additional outreach projects involved publicizing and promoting the STEP program and the biodiesel laboratory in the university and surrounding community. The following is a sample of the service-learning projects with local community involvement:

Fall 2007
- Two STEP: Biodiesel graduate students from LUC's School of Education worked with Highland Park High School's (HPHS) Green School Initiative club. Specifically, the STEP students developed and led three after-school sessions about biodiesel, developed a renewable energy curriculum for HPHS teachers, and helped HPHS build a biodiesel reactor it continues to operate successfully.

- Three STEP students developed a tailpipe exhaust collection apparatus they used to compare the quality of emissions of a vehicle burning different blends of diesel and biodiesel. The apparatus has become a community education tool and has since been used in high school education projects. Examining the particulate matter collected on a filter in the apparatus sends a powerful visual message to students about tailpipe emissions. Additionally, the filters provide clear visual evidence to students that biodiesel burns significantly cleaner than diesel fuel.
- Two students worked with LUC's vice president for public affairs to conduct a biofuels policy analysis for Illinois, draft a bill favoring the use of biodiesel in state vehicles, and identify a state representative to introduce the bill.
- STEP student and communication major T. J. Berdon submitted a documentary film about the course in a *National Geographic* Preserve Our Planet student film contest and was selected as a finalist.

Spring 2008

- Two STEP: Biodiesel students formed partnerships with the local nonprofit organization Friends of Parks to implement biodiesel after-school workshops. STEP students worked with the Earth Team Program, whose goal is to empower teens who otherwise do not have access to environmental programming through environmental education and involvement in environmental action. The STEP students developed and led a two-day workshop for 30 students from the Earth Team Program. Earth Team students were given a tour of the biodiesel laboratory and learned about biofuels and renewable energy.
- Three STEP students evaluated the feasibility of distributing LUC biodiesel as home heating oil. They analyzed census data and determined the density of local homes and businesses with heating oil furnaces (biodiesel is miscible with No. 2 heating oil). They worked with LUC's geographic information systems specialist to display the information as maps of the community. The students presented their maps and findings at a city of Chicago neighborhood greening meeting to generate community interest in the project. The students also made recommendations to the LUC Biodiesel Laboratory to begin distributing fuel to needy members of the community.
- One STEP student developed and wrote a $75,000 grant proposal submitted to the EPA People, Prosperity and the Planet (P3) program. The student met with mentors and stakeholders to determine how to best support

local high schools in integrating biodiesel and renewable energy lessons and activities into their curricula and cocurricular activities. This proposal was funded in April 2008 and currently supports our biodiesel and renewable energy outreach work.

Fall 2008
- Two STEP students became partners with the Field Museum to conduct emissions testing. Specifically, the students collected emissions from the museum's renewable energy vehicle (REV) that travels to local schools to teach students about renewable energy and is capable of running on biodiesel, waste vegetable oil, or diesel. The STEP: Biodiesel students conducted an analysis of particulate emissions the REV produced when burning each of the three fuels and gave their analysis to the Field Museum for use in its educational programming.

Evaluation

We assessed student understanding of course lecture material through a written examination. All faculty and community member lecturers developed four short-answer questions about their lecture, and the course coordinator chose a subset of questions for the exam. In addition, we tested student understanding of laboratory material in a lab practicum exam. The laboratory exam was administered at midsemester, and the goal was to identify any problems in student understanding of biodiesel production before the class began making large-scale batches of fuel.

Each semester the lecture and laboratory exam scores demonstrated good overall student understanding of the material and procedures. Instructors found it interesting that when preparing for the exams, students from the social sciences, humanities, and professional schools expressed how they felt intimidated by the chemistry and environmental science material in the lectures and in the laboratory. However, these students often achieved the highest exam grades, perhaps driven by a fear of failure.

We assessed student understanding of discussion materials by administering group quizzes at the beginning of most discussion class meetings. When quizzes were not administered, we asked students to write reaction papers about the material before coming to class.

Evaluation of student service-learning projects in the STEP: Biodiesel course was ongoing. During the project development phase, students met with and discussed content with mentors and the course coordinator and went through several iterations of their proposals before they were formally evaluated. (Mentors' contributions to this process varied, but this was a primary responsibility of the course coordinator.) Students later presented their revised project plans to the class for further feedback and assessment. Progress was monitored via project updates once every two weeks at the beginning of class. The course coordinator and mentors evaluated whether students had met their objectives by assessing their public forum presentations (which included a professional-meeting-quality poster summarizing their initial goals and objectives, project activities, and accomplishments) and student project self-evaluations. Student project self-evaluations involved students' assessing their original proposed work plan to determine whether their initial goals and objectives were met.

The self-directed learning process was new to many of our students, and it received mixed reviews. Some students appeared to thrive in this learning environment. On course evaluations, many noted they believed the self-directed aspect of their experience in STEP: Biodiesel greatly helped prepare them for graduate school or the professional world. Others said they would have liked more structure and guidance.

STEP: Biodiesel Outcomes

Through the service-learning projects completed over the three semesters that STEP: Biodiesel was offered, students created a successful biodiesel operation. They dramatically increased production efficiency and reduced the quantity of waste generated during biodiesel production. For example, after two semesters of soap-making research, STEP: Biodiesel students developed a recipe for a soap that uses the biodiesel laboratory's waste glycerin (a by-product of biodiesel production). The soap now serves as a valuable marketing tool for our program; it is distributed as a free sample at LUC's new student orientation and sold at the LUC Museum of Art and bookstore. The bus company that shuttles students between LUC's Lakeshore and Water Tower campuses now purchases the lab's fuel. LUC biodiesel is also being used internally. For example, LUC's Department of Facilities uses it to power its snow removal equipment, and students, staff, and faculty have used it to drive to local events such as conferences and meetings. As a result of all these efforts, three semesters after students wrote an initial business plan, the LUC Biodiesel Laboratory is nearly financially sustainable. Thus, we are confident the biodiesel laboratory will remain part of the LUC curriculum, the University Sustainability Initiative, and the community.

In our estimation, STEP: Biodiesel students have had an impact on thousands of people through biodiesel and renewable energy education and service learning. Over 500 people attended the STEP: Biodiesel course public forums, and hundreds more have been educated through student service-learning projects and programs supported by the student-initiated EPA biodiesel and renewable energy outreach program. Student-designed outreach materials such as the STEP website (http://www.luc.edu/cuerp/STEP_ Courses.shtml) and documentary films about the course have spread the message about the program to other audiences.

Impacts on Students

We believe the course has had positive impacts on student professional development. For example:

- Strong and lasting relationships developed between students and faculty, resulting from a high instructor-to-student ratio and the collaborative effort of students and faculty mentors working together to solve problems. Numerous students have benefited from these relationships by gaining access to research and work-study opportunities in subsequent semesters.
- Community organizations, such as the Uncommon Ground Rooftop Farm, have offered STEP students opportunities, such as internships, fellowships, and jobs. A variety of measures, numeric and anecdotal, indicate that the course has also positively affected student civic engagement. For example:
  - Over 40% of the students who took the STEP: Biodiesel course have remained active in the STEP program. Most of these students did so by taking another STEP course, volunteering for the program, or participating in academic internships that would allow them to continue the work they started on their service-learning projects.
  - Former STEP: Biodiesel students organized a group of 30 LUC students who traveled to Washington, D.C., for Power Shift 2009, a national student mobilization movement whose goal is to persuade

elected officials to take comprehensive and immediate action to combat climate change. Half of the participants traveled to the event in CUERP's Dodge Sprinter, which was powered by student-made biodiesel.

o The STEP: Biodiesel student who helped conduct a biofuels policy analysis and wrote a biofuels bill for the state of Illinois was, at the time of writing, a staff assistant to a congressman who sits on an agricultural subcommittee that defines our national biofuels policies.

The interdisciplinary nature of the course has provided powerful learning experiences for STEP: Biodiesel students. For example, communication students typically do not enroll in natural science courses. Although many students expressed intimidation at first, they quickly learned the chemistry, biology, and physics involved in biodiesel production. According to their mentor, Elizabeth Coffman, a documentary filmmaker and associate professor of communication, students experienced why an intimate knowledge of a subject is essential to appropriately communicate their work to the public. Because of their scientific knowledge, communication students were able to contribute to the success of the course by creating persuasive films, press releases, newsletters, and newspaper articles. Additionally, students from other disciplines witnessed the value of communication strategies for achieving class goals.

We saw dramatic transformations of many students involved in the STEP: Biodiesel course. On course evaluations, 22% of STEP: Biodiesel students indicated that the course had changed their career path. (This is likely an underestimation since these comments were voluntary; we did not ask a specific question about the impacts of the course on their career goals.) Two students changed their degree programs from bachelor of arts to bachelor of science as a result of their semester projects, which involved scientific research. A communication student became so involved with the course that after graduating he remained in Chicago to manage the biodiesel laboratory and has rethought his career options to include environmental goals.

Impacts on LUC Faculty and Staff

The LUC faculty members and staff involved in the course have been affected as well. Elizabeth Coffman reports that the interdisciplinary experience has exposed her to new ideas and encouraged her to reflect on environmental issues in her writings and in a current filmmaking project. LUC's director of university marketing, Maeve Kiley, said she has been inspired by the motivation of the STEP: Biodiesel students whom she helped in advertising the public forums and other class events. Furthermore, Kiley insisted that her marketing work benefited from these interactions with LUC students.

Other faculty members report that STEP has changed the way they teach. Most point to a new focus on designing courses with more emphasis on relevant problems and engaging students in authentic and community-based projects. Michael Welch, STEP instructor from LUC's School of Business Administration, had more specific and disciplinary reflections on his participation in the class:

> I believe that my participation in the course has focused my teaching more on sustainability in the business context. Business courses traditionally taught that corporations were in business for one purpose: to maximize the return to the shareholders. That concept has changed so that most businesses now recognize that they must consider the interests of many stakeholders (employees, vendors, customers, the government, and the community in which the company exists) when making strategic decisions. Moreover, decisions must be made not only in the context of short-term gain, but also in light of the long-term consequences those decisions have on their stakeholders. This has allowed me to emphasize concepts that might not have been adequately considered in previous decision making, particularly the impact of these decisions on the environment. As such, these concepts must be incorporated into the strategic planning process.

Impacts on the University

The STEP: Biodiesel course was acknowledged as fulfilling an important curricular need for LUC students in spring 2008 when STEP was accepted into the university's core curriculum. All LUC undergraduates are required to select 15 courses from specific knowledge and value areas. The STEP course model currently fills the civic engagement and leadership value area core curriculum requirement.

The STEP courses have spurred other interdisciplinary efforts at LUC. For example, STEP faculty member Coffman was inspired to initiate another interdisciplinary course about prison issues in which students worked with Illinois prisoners from Stateville Correctional Facility and produced a newsletter written by prisoners, prisoner advocates, and LUC students majoring in criminal justice, communication, fine and performing arts, and sociology. STEP is also being used as a model in the development of a capstone course for LUC women's studies majors and for another interdisciplinary course responding to public health issues that have an impact on the LUC community and its neighbors. The latter course is a collaboration between several departments in the College of Arts and Sciences, the School of Social Work, and the School of Nursing. These examples have compelled LUC administrators to begin addressing institutional barriers that thwart interdisciplinary courses, including difficulties listing courses offered by multiple departments and schools, registering students, and crediting faculty for their participation. LUC has developed a new committee through the College of Arts and Sciences dean's office that is working to address these problems.

The STEP: Biodiesel courses have also had an effect on LUC by generating institutional partnerships. For example, what started as a student project with the Field Museum has turned into much more. The museum, in partnership with CUERP, implemented the student-initiated EPA renewable energy education grant in which we are collaborating to provide professional development opportunities about renewable energy for local teachers. STEP: Biodiesel has also forged strong partnerships between LUC and Uncommon Ground, a local restaurant that donates its waste vegetable oil to the biodiesel laboratory, and in return has placed many LUC students in its green business and rooftop gardening internship programs.

We have also developed an exciting partnership with the city of Chicago. Two Department of Parks and Recreation employees enrolled in an LUC biodiesel continuing education course titled Small-Scale Biodiesel Production through CUERP and LUC's continuum program. The continuum course was developed in response to community demand; many community members who attended the STEP: Biodiesel public forums or were otherwise involved with the course were interested in learning more about small-scale biodiesel production. The continuum course helped city of Chicago administrators understand the steps necessary to begin producing biodiesel. They are currently in the process of building a biodiesel production facility that will produce enough fuel (about 100,000 gallons) to power all parks and recreation vehicles with B20 (a blend of 20% biodiesel and 80% diesel).

Impacts on the Community

Our education efforts in high schools have also been fruitful. HPHS is currently capable of converting 25 gallons of waste vegetable oil into biodiesel per week. The fuel is used to run campus maintenance equipment, including lawn mowers and snow blowers, and to power a concession stand at football games. According to HPHS assistant principal Tom Koulentes, "When the high school began this project, I had no idea how powerful the learning experience would be. It is not an overstatement to say that this project, and the experience of producing an alternative form of energy, has inspired our students and transformed many of their lives." According to Laura Berthold, the Earth Team Program leader from Friends of Parks, the student-led STEP: Biodiesel workshop was a positive experience for her students in many ways, including increasing her students' awareness about biofuels and their understanding of how their choices can make an impact on the environment. She also said that "[her] students enjoyed seeing a college and meeting with university students. College seems so intimidating to these high-school students. On this field trip they were able to ask questions to the Loyola students and learn about their experiences applying and finding the right major." We continue to expand our work with local high schools. Our former students' Environmental Protection Agency (EPA)–funded project has provided us with support to educate over 200 teachers about biodiesel and renewable energy and will allow us to facilitate biodiesel production at four more local high schools during the 2009–2010 academic year.

Impacts on the Environment

STEP: Biodiesel students' efforts have and continue to make quantifiable impacts on the local environment. Our students have produced over 3,700 gallons of biodiesel, and the LUC Biodiesel Laboratory is now capable of producing more than 100 gallons of biodiesel per week. Many of the community groups that STEP: Biodiesel students have worked with are also currently making and using biodiesel. Burning one gallon of diesel fuel emits 22.2 pounds of CO_2 (U.S. EPA, 2005). Thus, by producing a renewable fuel that replaces diesel fuel, STEP: Biodiesel students have helped reduce the emissions of CO_2 by more than 82,000 pounds. (When the city of Chicago's biodiesel production facility comes online, this number will increase to over 2 million pounds per year.) Because biodiesel also significantly reduces emissions of air pollutants such as carbon monoxide, polycyclic aromatic hydrocarbons, particulate matter, and unburned hydrocarbons (U.S. EPA, 2002), STEP: Biodiesel participants have improved local air quality. Thus, LUC students have made a small but measurable positive environmental impact in their local community.

Challenges

Along the way we encountered many obstacles, some of them related to the nature of biodiesel production. For example, the Chicago Fire Department temporarily shut down our lab during the first semester of the course, requiring us to improve our ventilation system. During the third semester of the course, LUC's general council advised us to stop distributing our biodiesel because of legal complications. (After months of dealing with the Internal Revenue Service, EPA, state of Illinois, and National Biodiesel Board, this issue has been addressed.) Many of these challenges offered great learning experiences for all parties involved. Students, in particular, were happy to be involved in navigating these challenges and appeared to learn a great deal from their involvement.

Other challenges were related to the current disciplinary structure of our institution. Because LUC had never conducted an interdisciplinary course like STEP: Biodiesel, we spent hours dealing with the registrar's office and nine department chairs to cross-list the course for three semesters. This situation improved when we received permission from our provost to list the course as a university (UNIV) course, a designation that does not lie within any particular academic department. Unfortunately, having the UNIV designation made the course somewhat obscure in the course-offering guide. Students typically look for courses in a given discipline and overlook the few courses that are offered under UNIV. To compensate for this, we had to do a great deal of advertising and recruiting. Finally, when the course was approved to fulfill a core requirement it became much easier for students to fit the course into their schedules, but the course does not count toward any major or minor except for the environmental studies/sciences program major. Thus, registration still presents a problem for some students who want to take the course but do not have room in their schedules for open electives.

The STEP courses are also very resource intensive. Interdisciplinary and service-learning courses demand extra time to coordinate. STEP also requires funds to support the course coordinator, student projects, and LUC faculty, staff, and community member instructor honoraria. As mentioned earlier, the course was initially funded by an EPA grant. We later received a generous gift from a private donor. In the short term, the financial benefits for the STEP program have exceeded the initial up-front costs. However, sustaining funding into the future will continue to be a challenge. Thus, while the STEP model has been extremely successful, it may be too resource intensive to serve as a model for more than a few keystone service-learning courses at any college or university.

Future Directions

During class discussions at the end of each semester, our former students indicated a strong desire to make the campus and local food systems more sustainable. In our current class, STEP: Food Systems, LUC students are learning about the historical, political, environmental, and ethical intricacies of our global food system. Meanwhile, they are working to bring a farmers market to our community, examining local food access issues for immigrant populations, starting a composting operation on campus, growing food for local food pantries, writing a business plan for producing honey on campus, and working with our dining hall staff to make the dining options at LUC more sustainable. We can only imagine what they will accomplish and what they, in addition to everyone else involved, will learn.

References

Astin, A. W., & Sax, L. J. (1998). How undergraduates are affected by service participation. *Journal of College Student Development, 39*(3), 251–263.

Brown, L. R. (2008). *Plan B 3.0: Mobilizing to save civilization.* New York, NY: Earth
Policy Institute.

Cortese, A. D. (2003). The critical role of higher education in creating a sustainable
future. *Planning for Higher Education, 31*(3), 15–22.

Eyler, J., Giles, D. E., & Braxton, J. (1997). The impact of service-learning on college students. *Michigan Journal of Community Service-Learning, 4*(1), 5–15.

Orr, D. W. (1994). *Earth in mind: On education, environment, and the human pros-
pect.* Washington, DC: Island Press.

Orr, D. W. (2003). Planning to learn. *Planning for Higher Education, 31*(3), 77–81.

Rockström, J., Steffen, S., Noone, K., Persson, A., Chapin, F. S., Lambin, E. F., et al. (2009). A safe operating space for humanity. *Nature, 461*, 472–475.

Senge, P. (2000). The academy as a learning community. In A. Lucas & Associates (Eds.), *Leading academic change* (pp. 275–300). San Francisco, CA: Jossey-Bass.

U.S. Environmental Protection Agency. (2002). *A comprehensive analysis of biodiesel impacts on exhaust emissions* (Report No. EPA 420-P02-001). Washington, DC: U.S. Government Printing Office.

U.S. Environmental Protection Agency. (2005). *Average carbon dioxide emissions resulting from gasoline and diesel fuel* (Report No. EPA 420-F-05-001). Washington, DC: U.S. Government Printing Office.

Wilcox, S. (1996). Fostering self-directed learning in the university setting. *Studies in Higher Education, 21*(2), 165–176.

Appendix

Solutions to Environmental Problems (STEP) Biodiesel Course Syllabus Spring 2008

Credit hours: 3.0

Meeting times: Tuesdays 2:30–3:45 pm; Thursdays 2:30–5:00 pm

Lecture and discussion location: 733 Damen Hall

Biodiesel lab and Lab Manager office location: 948 Damen Hall

Course Coordinator office hours and location: 422 Quinlan LSB, Tuesdays and Thursdays 9 am–10 am

Instructors

Elizabeth Coffman, Communication
David Crumrine, Chemistry
Marshall Eames, Natural Science
Marc Hayford, School of Business Administration
Rola Khishfe, School of Education
Maeve Kiley, University Marketing
Marilyn Krogh, Sociology
Daniel Larkin, Biology
Gina Lettiere, CUERP
Shane Lishawa, Lab Manager, CUERP
Philip Nyden, CURL
Christopher Peterson, Natural Science, ESP
Martina Schmeling, Chemistry
John Shea, S.J., Social Philosophy
Nancy Tuchman, Provost's Office, CUERP, Biology
Alison Varty, Course Coordinator, CUERP
Michael Welch, School of Business Administration

Course Description

STEP is an interdisciplinary service-learning course designed to develop practical solutions to pressing and complex environmental problems. This class will explore the potential for biodiesel to assuage global energy problems. While learning about the environmental, social, political, and economic aspects of energy production and consumption, we will maintain and staff the Loyola biodiesel lab that converts waste vegetable oil from Loyola food services into biodiesel for use at the university and within the community. We will also engage in other campus and community-based service-learning projects.

Course Format

This is a highly interdisciplinary team-taught course. Lectures and discussions will take place Tuesdays in room 733 Damen Hall. The goal of the lectures and discussions is to provide students with background information on issues of petroleum dependency, alternative fuels, greenhouse gasses, and sustainability.

In the beginning of the term Thursday lab sessions will take place in the biodiesel lab. Lab sessions will focus on teaching everyone the basic biodiesel reaction on small and large scales. After the production exam, every other week, students will work under the guidance of Shane Lishawa, the Lab Manager, and Zachary Waickman, Biodiesel Lab Intern, to improve the biodiesel laboratory, convert WVO [waste vegetable oil] into biodiesel, and test the quality of the biodiesel. During the alternate weeks, students will discuss current pressing biofuel-related issues in the lecture hall.

A significant portion of the course will be focused on small-group projects. Faculty will serve as mentors for the group projects (see last page for potential projects topics), and each project will provide a real-world interdisciplinary experience that will contribute to and/or complement the overall goals of producing a clean, renewable, petroleum-alternative fuel from a waste product. Substantial out-of-class time will be necessary to complete group projects, all of which will be outlined in a proposal that acts as a contract between faculty mentors and students.

On April 24th students will present their final projects in an interactive public forum.

Point Distribution

Production Exam (15%)

Content Exam (20%)

Discussion quizzes (5%)—Each discussion session will begin with a brief quiz on the readings.

Participation (10%)—Based on class attendance and participation in lecture and laboratory/discussion section.

Group project (50%)—proposal presentation (5%), proposal (10%), final product (20%),* and public presentation (15%)

* Not all students in the group will receive the same grade; effort will be assessed via self- and group evaluations.

Grading Scale

A = 93%–100%, A− = 90%–92%, B+ = 87%–89%, B = 83%–86%, B− = 80%–82%, C+ = 77%–79%, C = 73%–76%, C− = 70%–72%, D+ = 67%–69%, D = 60%–66%, F < 60%

Academic Integrity: You will be held to the university's standard of academic integrity, which is described at: http://www.luc.edu/academics/catalog/un dergrad/reg_academicintegrity.shtml

Cell Phone Use: As a courtesy to your instructors and your classmates, your cell phone should be off during all class meetings.

Schedule

T, January 15	Introduction: Discussion of syllabus, slide show of last semester (Tuchman and Varty) **research assignment given**
Th, January 17	Making biodiesel from virgin oil and lab intro and safety (Lishawa)
T, January 22	Strategic planning of successful business ventures (Welch) **students select group projects**
Th, January 24	Make biodiesel from waste vegetable oil (Lishawa)
T, January 29	Reflect on business plan; discuss STEP vision and goals (Varty and Lishawa)
Th, January 31	Biodiesel ASTM standards QA/QC (Varty and Lishawa)
T, February 5	Energy in natural systems: The carbon cycle and life-cycle analyses (Tuchman and Varty)
Th, February 7	Scaling up workshop (Lishawa) **group contract drafts due**
T, February 12	Production Exam
Th, February 14	Group Project Presentations (STEP community)
T, February 19	Historical role of energy in human societies (Peterson)
Th, February 21	Discussion topic 1: Biofuels compared **group contracts due**

T, February 26	Philosophy of technology and conservation values (Shea)
Th, February 28	Discussion topic 1: Biofuels compared
T, March 4	Spring break
Th, March 6	Spring break
T, March 11	Benefits and constraints of petroleum alternatives (Eames)
Th, March 13	Discussion topic 2: Biofuels: Social and environmental issues
T, March 18	Energy and environmental economics (Hayford)
Th, March 20	Discussion topic 2: Biofuels: Social and environmental issues
T, March 25	Greenhouse gases: Environmental impacts of fossil fuel use (Schmeling)
Th, March 27	Discussion topic 3: Beyond biofuels: Other alternatives
T, April 1	Petroleum and alternative fuel politics (Advanced Biodiesel student: Blake Anderson)
Th, April 3	Discussion topic 3: Beyond biofuels: Other alternatives
T, April 8	Why get the word out? Why go green? Reporting and promoting our projects (Coffman and Kiley)
Th, April 10	Exam review
T, April 15	Lecture exam
Th, April 17	Rehearsal for public forum
T, April 22	Discuss future of biodiesel and sustainability initiatives at Loyola (Varty)
Th, April 24	Public forum: Final presentations
Th, May 1	9:00–11:00 am—group projects due, course, self- and group evaluations conducted

Student Group Projects

1) **Community outreach and marketing** (*Coffman, Kiley, and Lettiere*)—This group of students will help promote STEP class efforts. Projects can include publicizing the public forum, maintaining the biodiesel website, writing articles to publish in local newspapers, producing a radio show, running biodiesel community workshops, or giving lab tours.

2) **Biodiesel quality assurance** (*Crumrine*)—This group of students will research the ASTM standards for biodiesel and improve the lab's QA/QC program.

3) **Algae for oil** (*Eames and Peterson*)—This group of students will assist in ongoing research focused on growing algae for oil to supplement our biodiesel feedstock.

4) **Loyola Fuels the Community** (*Krogh and Nyden*)—This group of students will research the benefits and constraints of using biodiesel to replace No. 2 heating oil in oil furnaces. This group will propose a plan for distributing Loyola biodiesel to families and/or charitable organizations in the Rogers Park community.

5) **Production research** (*Schmeling and Lishawa*)—This group of students will conduct scientific research on biodiesel production. They may choose to vary certain aspects of production, i.e., heat, or the amount of reagents used, and measuring the amount of product formed and product quality, to inform our production process and that of others. They may also research and make recommendations to increase the energy efficiency of our production process.

6) **Education and outreach to high schools** (*Khishfe, Tuchman, and Varty*)—The Highland Park High School (HPHS) and the Young Women's Leadership Charter School (YWLCS) are partnering with LUC in biodiesel production. This group of students will teach the HPHS and YWLCS students how to set up a biodiesel lab (including safety measures), build the reactor, and make biodiesel out of their cafeteria waste vegetable oil. LUC student mentors will provide short informative talks to the high school students, as well as oversight and training in the laboratory operations.

SECTION TWO

INCREASING CIVIC ENGAGEMENT

4

WHAT'S THE MATTER WITH AMERICAN DEMOCRACY?

Responding by Embracing Civic Engagement and Sustainability

Scott G. McNall

What's the matter with American democracy? Is it the fact that we have elected leaders who do not represent the majority of eligible voters, or is it the fact that less than half of those eligible to vote actually do so? Is it that national policy is crafted on the basis of ideology or party membership rather than informed social policies? Why does a government that professes to be pro-family favor legislation that makes it extremely difficult for families to survive as whole units? Why are there people who adamantly deny that the globe is warming or that human activity plays a central role in this dynamic? Why, compared to other democratic nations, do we fail to deliver appropriate health care to all our citizens? Why are so many of our citizens frozen in their cynicism, unable to act to create a healthy, humane, and durable society?

Whatever your answer to these questions might be (it's the media, it's money driving political decisions, it's a deeply class-divided society), let's place some of the blame squarely where it deserves to be: on the shoulders of America's colleges and universities. Simply put, we have not helped students develop the skills and confidence they need to become actively engaged citizens. We have failed. We have failed to create an educated citizenry. How else can we explain the lack of faith and participation in democratic elections?

Service, Service Learning, and Civic Engagement

Voluntary programs of service, supposedly, can create a social conscience. Service is seen as inherently good, and administrators of colleges and universities have been quick to compare their institutions with each other, enumerating the hours of community service provided by their students, faculty, and staff to local nonprofits, neighborhoods, and soup kitchens.[1] Faculty have come to understand that while service is important, students can better learn disciplinary content when the service is integrated into a course. For example, a student taking a course in introductory sociology or political science is going to be introduced to the topics of class, gender, and ethnicity. But how class, race, and gender are historically constructed and the difference they make in shaping opportunity can be hard to understand in the abstract. They are easier to understand if a student experiences helping someone without health insurance, or finding a place to live for someone who is homeless or who does not have a job. Concepts like the poverty line could become more than a textbook abstraction. Strong evidence (Battistoni, Gelman, Saltmarsh, Wergin, & Zlotkowski, 2003) shows the benefits of this feedback loop: Read the material, find a community context where it would apply, and then report back on it. Service learning, as opposed to just service, deepens disciplinary knowledge. That might be the end of the story if the mission of the university were solely to serve and increase disciplinary knowledge. But it isn't. Students need to have a broad understanding of the political, economic, historical, and social conditions that cause the problems they are studying (American Political Science Association Task Force on Civic Engagement in the 21st Century, 1998). There is no single reason emergency rooms are crowded, and in some hospitals, closed. But if our goal is to remedy the situation and to provide more citizens with better access to medical care, informed citizens must be willing to act. Civic engagement, unlike service learning, focuses on the problem and its solution, and any solution in a democratic society requires compromises. (The move to civic engagement is also about embracing these ideals in all aspects of higher education institutions.[2])

Embracing Civic Engagement

California State University, Chico has a long and proud tradition of service to the local community. In 1966 the Associated Students, an independent corporation of the student body at Chico State, created the Community Action Volunteers in Education (CAVE), whose goal is to make classroom learning relevant while also reaching out to the community. Over several years this volunteer effort evolved into a sophisticated structure of student-led projects designed to meet clearly articulated community needs.

CAVE members surveyed government and nongovernmental agencies to determine where student help should be directed. The group created a directorship position and developed protocols (interviews, references, résumés) to ensure that the service provided by the students was high quality, and that the agencies had an opportunity to provide not only oversight of the students but feedback on how the agencies' needs were being met and how well the students performed.

CAVE has worked well for the campus and the community. When faculty wanted their students to have a service experience, they sent them to CAVE. While a few members of the faculty had embraced models of service learning, the service-learning curriculum overall was underdeveloped. But a set of conjunctures spurred the growth of service-learning courses on campus and in the California State University (CSU) system. In 1998 the California State Legislature proposed that all students graduating from the CSU system complete a service requirement. The legislation was not enacted, but it did cause the Office of the CSU Chancellor to take a close look at service requirements, to hire staff with skills in service learning, and to support funding to create an infrastructure to support service-learning courses so that all CSU students would have at least one high-quality service-learning experience prior to graduation. As Chico State already had a well-developed structure, funds from the Office of the Chancellor were used to develop additional service-learning courses. Faculty mentors, with skills in service learning, worked with faculty, chosen on a competitive basis, to develop new courses. Then, in 2002 Chico State hired a new director of CAVE, who had been a CAVE volunteer when she attended Chico State. She replicated the engaged department model (Battistoni et al., 2003) and began to train staff of entire departments in the methods of service learning and civic engagement. The logic was that no single person in any department, and no single course, could create the kind of transformative environment necessary to help students serve and learn. This model is still being used and refined in 2011 at Chico, as faculty mentors work with an entire department to train everyone in the knowledge, skills, and attitudes necessary for student success.

In 2004 several things happened to alter our course of direction and to shift our focus from service learning to civic engagement. The university hired a new president, Paul J. Zingg, and the entire campus had a chance to participate in a special program of the American Democracy Project (ADP), which was cosponsored by the American Association of State Colleges and Universities, the Carnegie Foundation (under the direction of Tom Erlich), and the *New York Times*. We agreed to participate in the ADP because we believe that democracy is not a given, that it is endangered, that it needs to be created actively, and that universities need to do a better job of creating democratic citizens as part of their public mission. We saw that one way to do this would be to introduce students to issues of consequence and show them, through specific case studies, how contentious democracy is and how differing ideas must be considered if we are to find common ground. Participants were encouraged to choose issues and topics relevant to their campus, community, or region; there was no one-size-fits-all model. Chico State chose to participate in ADP's Stewardship of Public Lands project, which focused on management of public lands, for several reasons. First, Chico State had acquired a system of reserve that totaled more than 4,000 acres immediately adjacent to the city's more than 3,000-acre Bidwell Park, and use of the land stirred some controversy within the community. Some members of the public wanted open access, but the university wanted to regulate and minimize human impact on the reserves. Second, general environmental issues are of strong concern, not only to our local community but to the entire region. Concerns about land use, development, water rights, open space, and quality of life animate political discussions. Third, faculty and administrators believed the combined approach of civic engagement and a focus on the environment would allow us to build on our academic strengths and our existing resource base and achieve national recognition.

Building on Our Strengths

In early summer 2004, I went to Yellowstone National Park to participate in the Stewardship of Public Lands project, to watch wolves in the wild, and to learn about the controversies surrounding the reintroduction of wolves into the park in 1995.

Wolves were a keystone species in the park, but the last one had been shot in 1926 (Wolf reintroduction, 2011), part of America's notorious effort to eradicate wildness in the landscape and civilize more of the American West by fencing, farming, and ranching it. It's important to remember that Yellowstone is public land, and much of the land surrounding Yellowstone (though not all) is also public land, leased for grazing.

The story of the wolves' reintroduction is positive. The wolves have thinned the herds of elk overgrazing the land, chased the coyotes away that had been feeding on young pronghorn, increased the survival rate of grizzly cubs (because the mothers feed on the carrion left by the wolves), and increased the number of moose that needed the young willow shoots the elks had been eating. It's a great story until you talk to the guides who make a living hunting elks or the ranchers surrounding Yellowstone who believe the wolves are threatening their economic survival. The point from the perspective of the ADP is that democracy is messy, and studying the reintroduction of wolves will help students better understand how democracy depends on acknowledging controversy and working to resolve it.

However, when I returned to Chico and discussed the project with others who were involved, we concluded that as interesting as this story might be, it wasn't going to be as relevant to our students as the environmental issues in our own region. With those issues, we could forge a simultaneous commitment to civic engagement and sustainability.

Focusing on Sustainability

The concept of *sustainable development* was chosen by the students, faculty, and administration to guide our campus efforts after several campus discussions. We drew on the United Nations' (2002) definition of sustainable development and David Orr's (1991a, 1991b) definition, because we felt it essential to focus on the triad of economic justice, social justice, and environmental justice (see also Edwards, 2005). We did not want to separate these concepts and felt the unity would allow us to deepen student commitment to civic engagement (understanding the social, economic, historical, and political roots of current issues). Sustainability was thus a means as well as an end. What was and what was not sustainable? What would and would not create economic viability and a decent future? How can democratic citizens accomplish these goals?

We also deliberately chose the twin concepts of a sustainable future and sustainable development because we saw this as the best way to convene all units on campus: academic affairs, student affairs, business and finance, advancement and development, and the Associated Students (which is a separate corporation). Often, campuses that embrace the idea of sustainability do so primarily for business reasons, as a way to save money, and develop metrics related to the use of water and energy, reduction of the waste stream, dining facilities, and so on. Our goal was and is a bit more ambitious; we wanted to find opportunities for students to put their learning to work on campus and to develop campus-based projects focused on sustainability as a means of developing students' lifelong skills. We wanted them to know they could make a difference.[3] With the involvement of staff from the Office of Business and Finance, students involved in Green Campus (an offshoot of the Alliance to Save Energy), chose specific projects in consultation with other units on campus to reduce energy use and then worked to implement them. Green Campus also worked with housing to create green residence halls and sponsored competitions among residence halls and floors to reduce energy use.

To focus our campuswide efforts we adopted a new sixth strategic priority, which states:

> Believing that each generation owes something to those which follow, we will create environmentally literate citizens, who will embrace sustainability as a way of living. We will be wise stewards of scarce resources and, in seeking to develop the whole person, be aware that our individual and collective actions have economic, social, and environmental consequences locally, regionally, and globally.

Chico's Strategic Plan for the Future had guided the campus for a decade (1994–2004). Our new president, Paul J. Zingg, in 2004 offered the campus an opportunity to update that plan. A series of Environmental Summits drew faculty, staff, and students, resulting in the sixth strategic priority that was grounded in the following values and assumptions:

- A democratic society is a sustainable society, and a sustainable society is a democratic society.
- A few individuals working together can change the world.
- Students, faculty, and staff can make an immediate difference in shaping the future.

- Whatever our discipline or political perspective, we must address questions about what one generation owes to another, and we must address how we are going to sustain life on the planet.
- It is the mission of the university to connect to our region and community to help solve real problems.
- We have an obligation to provide our students with opportunities for meaningful engagement.

These are big ideas, and I do not want to give the impression that we have accomplished all we set out to do, but they did and do frame our actions. The business of creating a democratic society and helping our students become good citizens is a journey.

Value-Based Organizations

A journey toward a democratic society is complicated, and we need a map if we are to reach our destination. In his well-known work *Good to Great: Why Some Companies Make the Leap . . . and Others Don't,* Jim Collins (2001) provides some useful directions. Collins and his associates reviewed a list of over 1,435 companies to determine the difference between companies that were merely good and those that became great. He narrowed his list to 18 companies and concluded, among other things, that great companies had a well-articulated set of core values and strong but flexible leaders, gave people freedom about how to meet goals, put forth extraordinary and *consistent* efforts to achieve corporate goals, used facts to improve, and honored the commitments they made. There are always dangers in drawing parallels between what a great company does and what characterizes a great university. But if you were to make up your own quick list of comparisons, the list would probably include commitment, focus, flexibility, and a core set of beliefs. A core belief for universities (at least the great ones) is in the transformative power of education. We believe we can help students learn and that learning is an inherently good thing. As I argued earlier, it is the duty of universities to help create democratic citizens; to train students to be good citizens; and to reflect on how best to balance their economic, social, and environmental needs.

Frankly, our goal is to become a great university building *consistently* on our core values. We developed our first Strategic Plan for the Future in 1994, and that served as a strong guide for the allocation and reallocation of resources for more than a decade. Whether budgets expanded or contracted, we used the plan to craft a course of action. When Zingg arrived in 2004, he asked us to amplify the core values that were already informing our work. Briefly, we wanted to build learning communities within the university, and we were committed to diversity and academic freedom. Our core values reaffirmed our commitment to our students and our belief in them. We recognized that the hopes and aspirations students bring with them were the ones we should do best to honor. We needed to provide real service to our community and to accept our responsibility as a member of the community, to encourage, participate in, and develop a common ground for addressing meaningful social issues.

Building on Our Values and Creating an Infrastructure for Civic Engagement and Sustainability

The major addition to our Strategic Plan for the Future, the sixth strategic priority, embraced the concepts of sustainable development and citizenship. I have already partially explained how we were able to bring together and build on deep institutional values related to stewardship of natural resources and on student service to the community. The infrastructures we created may serve as a road map for other organizations wishing to follow a similar course.

As a sociologist, I know the importance of strong social organizations in implementing complicated goals or missions over time. Max Weber (Eisenstadt, 1968) noted that the charisma of an organization's leaders needed to be built into the routine of the organization if dynamic movements were to succeed. The problem in any organization is that good ideas may belong to just one person or to a small group of people, and if the person or group disappears, dissolves, or loses interest, the movement falters. Faculty and students must always confront this problem if they are to be successful. Ideas must have a structural or organizational framework to ensure they continue to drive the organization toward a new future.

A first step in encouraging and strengthening civic engagement and sustainability in an institution is to include the goals in a strategic plan and, of course, make sure the plan is followed. Since sustainability was our focus, we already had preexisting structures we could build on:

- The Associated Students Recycling Program, which has been in place since 1996, was created to address state mandates to reduce the waste stream. It was funded by the Associated Students to educate students about the need to recycle, which is often an easy entry point for training students to be wise stewards of scarce resources. The program has expanded to include community outreach, helping other organizations recycle, deal with e-waste, compost, and so on. A full-time student-funded director manages its work.

- In 1996 the Associated Students created the position of environmental affairs commissioner (elected by the student body) to ensure that student concerns about the environment were kept before the entire student body. The group also created an Environmental Affairs Resource Library with holdings about environmental and stewardship issues.

- The Department of Political Science supervised (with Associated Student funds supporting the organization) the Community Legal Information Center (CLIC), founded in 1970. In addition to providing legal services to students and community members, the center staff also addressed problems of environmental justice.

- Starting in 1994, and with the agreement of several key deans (agriculture, behavioral and social sciences, engineering and computer science, and natural sciences), it was decided that the university would begin to build up interdisciplinary research strength in areas relating to its bioregion and watershed. When a faculty opening occurred in, say, geology, the first question asked was whether the position would support a program in environmental studies or sciences. For about a decade, we developed substantial capacity in environmental studies and environmental sciences. The acquisition of the 4,000-acre reserve helped spur ecological research. Now, the university has close to 150 green courses that deal with some aspect of sustainability, that is, the interrelated nature of environmental, social, and economic justice. Our revised general education curriculum now has a sustainability track students can follow to complete all their general education requirements.

- The emergence of sustainable development as a national topic has meant an opportunity to expand existing programs and create new ones. The Department of Health and Community Services has added an option in environmental health, a welcome addition to the curriculum. Because of student interest in the College of Business, a new minor in managing for sustainability is growing rapidly.[4] (For a discussion of sustainability in business see Esty & Winston, 2006.)

- In 2002 Jack Rawlins, a former student, big-game hunter, and entrepreneur, funded the Rawlins Endowed Professorship of Environmental Literacy. Rawlins believed it is essential that all students be exposed to ideas about biodiversity, climate change, and how to address such matters. A new course was created and a professor of natural sciences was selected and charged with two tasks: teach environmental literacy and begin the process of embedding concepts of environmental literacy (sustainability) across the entire curriculum. The current holder of this chair, Jim Pushnik, has hosted campus workshops to discuss how sustainability can be addressed in virtually every academic discipline and began outreach to community college faculty to do the same thing (see Barlett & Chase, 2004). Many of us hope to make environmental literacy a required course for all students.

- Earth Day, founded as part of a nationwide effort in the 1970s, is now Earth Month (April) on the Chico State campus. In 2006 more than two events took place every day of the month to celebrate the environment and to identify environmental problems and issues. Needless to say, this depth of focus provides many opportunities for student involvement and engagement as the students organize presentations, identify speakers, and develop poster sessions.

As this brief list makes clear, Chico State targeted issues related to the environment that were of central importance to the campus and its surrounding community. The year 2004 marked something of a tipping point for the university: It welcomed a new president; updated its strategic plan; became part of the national ADP; and hired a director for CAVE, who initiated the engaged department program. But more was to come:

- In 2005 a sustainability director was hired to link student ideas and initiatives with the appropriate division or department in the university. The rationale was that students often have great ideas but don't always have the wherewithal or time (because they graduate) to carry good ideas forward. The director's job was to take a question such as,

"Why can't we grow our own organic food on the farm and sell it to the cafeteria?" and try to make it a reality. This particular and real example required working with the university farm, developing a business plan, seeking funding, and working with the Associated Students Food Services to ensure there would be a market. Students in chemistry and engineering, with the help of the sustainability director, developed a biodiesel machine to recycle the cooking oil from the cafeteria and turn it into fuel for tractors on the university farm.

- In the fall of 2005 our new Associated Student environmental affairs commissioner (EAC) decided that the Associated Students would create and host a conference titled "This Way to Sustainability," put together by the students and drawing on members from the local community to give presentations on sustainability, land-use planning, green buildings, composting, earthworm farms, and so forth. The conference attracted over 300 people. In the spring of 2006 the university also hosted a similar conference, which was broader in scope and brought in nationally recognized speakers on the environment, green building, and sustainability. An event called Sustainability Day preceded the conference and grew out of the interests of the Associated Students and key faculty in geography. Each year since then, students build a mountain of trash from throwaway materials and packaging from the student union, form an elephant from discarded materials, and make posters on sustainability issues and—especially—offer solutions.

- Courtney Voss, the EAC for the Associated Students, proposed an initiative in 2006–2007 that will have long-lasting consequences. She asked all students to tax themselves $5 per semester to do two things: hire a sustainability director for the Associated Student businesses and create a fund for student-initiated sustainability projects. The fund provides about $165,000 a year for student-generated projects, such as urban gardens, expanded recycling, and development of solar-powered bike shelters.

- Voss also was elected student body president, running on an environmental ticket. Once elected, she and I agreed that for the 2006–2007 academic year, we would have one conference, pooling our energies and resources. "This Way to Sustainability II" was held in November of 2006 and drew over 800 students, faculty, and staff from across

California, as well as members of the local community. What distinguished, and distinguishes, the conference is that it represents a combined community effort wherein community members serve as presenters and discussants. It also represents a deepening partnership with the local community college, Butte Community College (BCC). The Associated Students of BCC, as well as their administration, were sponsors of the conference and helped with planning and organization.

- Anthony Cortese served as keynote speaker for the 2006 conference and asked Zingg to endorse the national effort to reduce the carbon footprints of university campuses to 0%. Chico State's president was one of the original signatories of the American College & University Presidents' Climate Commitment. The full effect of this on the campus has yet to be realized, but it has heightened awareness that not only must we work to save energy and reduce our carbon footprint, but we have to change behaviors. A campuswide committee is developing a Climate Action Plan with specific targets and measures, which include energy (and its sources), water, management of the waste stream, and recycling—in effect, all those variables that affect our carbon footprint.

- Chico had one of the first chapters of Green Campus in California. Operating under the supervision of the campus sustainability coordinator, Green Campus identified easy ways to save money in residence halls—substituting compact fluorescent lightbulbs for regular bulbs, installing energy-saving appliances, and so on. Green Campus members also developed real-time metering in the residence halls, using equipment developed by students in engineering, and instituted competitions among the halls to reduce energy use. These projects and others resulted in rebates to the campus and Green Campus in 2007 of close to $150,000, which will be used for new energy-saving projects. Students are able to gain valuable practical experience and act as good stewards of the environment through such projects.

- As planning commenced for the 2007–2008 "This Way to Sustainability III" conference, it became clear that our community college partner, BCC, could carve out a part of the larger conference as its own. One of the community college's missions is to train students for the building trades. In the late summer of 2007, BCC hosted a conference that focused on the built environment, using contractors, architects, planners, builders, and others to focus on the details and costs of green building design and construction.

- "This Way to Sustainability III" was held November 1–4 on the campus of Chico State, cosponsored by BCC. More than 1,100 students, faculty, staff, and members of the local community registered, and 250 of the students who attended were from campuses other than Chico. The conference featured 5 keynote speakers, 80 sessions, and more than 110 presenters and discussants. The topics covered the wide spectrum of sustainable development, including population and the environment, agriculture, religion, art and the natural world, poetry, the built environment, and actions individuals could take locally and globally to create a sustainable future. Awards were also given to a local individual, nonprofit organization and a business that did the most for sustainability in 2007. This conference celebrates work on campus and connects us to our local community and region. It also provides an annual opportunity to reenergize members of the student body, and it provides new students with an opportunity to become engaged in conversations about how they can create their own future.[5] One day of the conference is devoted to helping students from other campuses learn how to take action on their own campuses, and all students discuss how to become involved in the political process. Finally, the 2007 conference included a student face by asking 80 students from BCC and Chico State to introduce the speakers in all sessions and manage the registration process, meals, and entertainment. Before the conference, the students corresponded with the people they were to introduce to learn more about them and sustainability. This practice continues.
- In the spring of 2007 the university created a new position of executive director of the Institute for Sustainable Development to give voice and direction to campus sustainability efforts; to continue to connect those efforts to the larger community; and to identify new resources to deepen the university's commitment to civic engagement, democracy, and a sustainable future. I was appointed by the president as executive director. The organizational structure draws together those responsible for campuswide sustainability efforts—such as the

university nature reserve's managers and staff, the university director of sustainability, the Associated Students director of sustainability, as well as others interested in and responsible for sustainability on campus.

The number of sustainability projects under way on campus is considerable, and the previous list could be expanded. The breadth of our activity has achieved national acclaim. For example, in 2007 the university received the National Wildlife Federation's grand prize for being the campus that had done the most to reduce global warming. The university has been able to respond to national initiatives such as Focus the Nation in February of 2008 to ensure that all political candidates address such issues as a national energy policy, global warming, and the relationship among social, economic, and environmental justice. The commitment to sustainable development also provides an opportunity to rethink how we engage students in our general education classes. The director of the Freshman Year experience coordinates a university-wide effort to help students succeed academically. This is done in consultation with the director of civic engagement and the dean of undergraduate education, who have instituted town hall meetings as a capstone experience for all students in beginning composition courses or other large general education courses. The students have chosen issues that concern them as citizens and as current and future voters. One of the major themes they have identified is sustainability. A strong infrastructure, communications across divisional lines, and open forums such as the annual sustainability conference allow us to continue pursuing the goal of creating democratic citizens and distinguishing the university as a leader in sustainable development.

Our commitment to sustainable development and to meeting community needs provides unexpected opportunities for our students. A partnership between the Institute for Sustainable Development (ISD) and the local chamber of commerce, which commenced in February 2008, sought to answer such questions as: What does it mean to be a green business? What are the risks and opportunities presented by a changing climate? How can one manage toward goals of sustainability? Having answered these questions, the ISD then presented to the business community a catalog of fee-based services. Two groups of business students, supervised by faculty from the College of Business (Net Impact and SCORE/SEED) will provide sustainability audits to local businesses as a way of helping them save energy and better understand sustainability. Our students conducted an energy audit for our local municipal government. The city of Chico, which signed the Mayors' Climate Change Resolution (a national effort to get cities to lower their carbon emissions), hired a former student and interns from Chico State to provide an assessment of the city's carbon footprint. One of the university's foci, as it relates to sustainability, is to seek out more paid and unpaid internships for our students in sustainable businesses, communities, and nonprofit organizations.

Developing a System of Metrics

A reasonable question, and not just from accrediting bodies and legislators demanding accountability, is, How do you know whether this integrated effort will work? To answer this question, the following are the measures to be used:

- *Voter turnout in local and national elections.* This will serve as one benchmark, as well as the number of our students who register to vote. We have historical data on participation rates, which have been high.
- *An increase in the number of paid and unpaid environmental internships.* We anticipate that our partnership with the local business community will yield a greater number of opportunities for engagement here and elsewhere.
- *Civic engagement.* This will be measured by the NSSE, as well as our own internal number of hours of service, number of service-learning courses, and number of civic-learning activities. We are still involved in developing good measures of civic engagement, as opposed to service and CAVE. Additionally, the director of civic engagement has been asked to develop more civic engagement opportunities, as opposed to service, and to focus them on the environment.
- *External funding.* We anticipate funding from private individuals and foundations for our efforts to blend civic engagement and sustainability.
- *National recognition.* This would include honors such as the 2007 award from the National Wildlife Federation.

- *Success of our annual conference.* In 2007 the conference had a maximum attendance of 1,100 people.

Making a Difference

Civic engagement is now seen as an important goal for American universities. We've been good at delivering hours of student service, but, as I've said, creating engaged citizens is not a simple task. My intention has been to provide an example of one organization's continuing effort to connect to its community and region and to provide real and meaningful opportunities for student engagement. Given our core values, our location, our commitment to the community, and a previously developed set of structures to address environmental concerns, it made sense for us to choose the dual focus of civic engagement and sustainability. We also needed to ensure that whatever we did could be sustained, and we have done that by creating positions, organization, and a strategic priority that can serve as a road map to the future. Sustainability will capture the attention of many universities, just as other educational movements have. Whether that is the best focus for helping develop a democratic society will depend a lot on an organization's existing structure and history. There must be some mechanism for engaging students each year, there must be some mechanism for continually connecting to the community, and there must be people who focus on helping develop projects that will engage students. This is no small mandate. Institution administrators cannot make such efforts meaningful unless they are willing to set these mechanisms in motion.

Notes

1. The National Survey of Student Engagement (NSSE) measures community engagement primarily in terms of number of hours served.
2. For some background on defining the engaged campus, see http://www.compact.org/advancedtoolkit/.
3. This is an intentional way to create opportunities for civic engagement (and service learning) on campus where activities can be closely monitored and students can be provided with frequent and positive feedback.
4. As we develop new courses and programs, it is with the understanding that sustainable development is a multidisciplinary effort and that all disciplines have something meaningful to say about what one generation owes to another.

5. The sustainability movement is characterized by hope and optimism on the part of the students and not as oppositional. It differs substantially from the environmental and political movements of the 1960s in that students seem to be more interested in focusing on solutions and what they can do as individuals that is practical and will serve the common good.

References

American Association of State Colleges and Universities. (2007). *Presidents' Climate Commitment.* Retrieved from http://www.presidentsclimatecommitment.org

American Political Science Association Task Force on Civic Engagement in the 21st Century. (1998). Expanded articulation statement: A call for reactions and contributions. *Political Science and Politics, 31*(3), 636–637.

Barlett, P. F., & Chase, G. (Eds.). (2004). *Sustainability on campus: Stories and strategies for change.* Cambridge, MA: MIT Press.

Battistoni, R., Gelman, S., Saltmarsh, J., Wergin, J., and Zlotkowski, E. (2003). *Engaged department toolkit.* Boston, MA: Campus Compact.

Collins, J. (2001). *Good to great: Why some companies make the leap . . . and others don't.* New York, NY: HarperCollins.

Dale, T., Elliot, J. M., & Scourfield McLauchlan, J. (2011). *Civic engagement II.* Retrieved from the American Political Science Association website: http://www.apsa net.org/content_41303.cfm

Edwards, A. R. (2005). *The sustainability revolution: Portrait of a paradigm shift.* Philadelphia, PA: New Society.

Eisenstadt, S. N. (1968). *Max Weber on charisma and institution building.* Chicago, IL: University of Chicago Press.

Esty, D. C., & Winston, A. S. (2006). *From green to gold: How smart companies use environmental strategy to innovate, create value, and build competitive advantage.* New Haven, CT: Yale University Press.

Orr, D. (1991a). *Ecological literacy: Education and transition to a postmodern world.* Albany, NY: SUNY Press.

Orr, D. (Winter, 1991b). What is education for? Six myths about the foundations of modern education, and six new principles to replace them. *In Context, 27,* 52. Retrieved from http://www.context.org/ICLIB/IC27/Orr.htm

United Nations. (2002). Resolution 57/254. United Nations Decade of Education for Sustainable Development. Retrieved from http://www.un-documents.net/a57r254.htm

Wolf reintroduction. (2011). Retrieved from http://en.wikipedia.org/wiki/Wolf_reintroduction

5

SUSTAINABILITY STARTS AT HOME

A Hybrid Service-Learning Model for Teaching Environmental Sustainability

J. Marshall Eames and Jeremy Brooks

T he imperative for environmental sustainability has grown strongly in the nearly 25 years since the Brundtland Commission issued the first definition of the term, which is "meeting the needs of the present without compromising the ability of future generations to meet their own needs" (United Nations World Commission on Environment and Development, 1987, p. 43). Barbier (1987) elegantly refined this concept, describing sustainability as the intersection of successful economic, social, and environmental systems.

At Loyola University Chicago, an important part of our mission directs the university to be a steward of the environment. This goal manifests itself in an increasing number of courses and community outreach events that emphasize the multidimensional nature of environmental sustainability. One such course at Loyola is Natural Science 180, Environmental Sustainability.

One of the challenges instructors face in the area of environmental sustainability is its interdisciplinary nature. At the United Nations World Civic Forum 2009 in Seoul, Korea (United Nations Department of Economic and Social Affairs, 2009), leaders from government, higher education, nongovernmental organizations, and business stressed the need for interdisciplinary teams of scholars and planning and development practitioners and engineers to work together on humanity's most pressing global problems: climate change, renewable energy, and sustainable agriculture. Tackling these subjects requires instructors to reeducate themselves and stretch their own knowledge and understanding of the world. We have intentionally designed our Environmental Sustainability course, and particularly its service-learning component, to allow students and instructors to understand the interdependency of the social, economic, and environmental aspects of sustainability.

In 2005 Loyola revised the undergraduate core curriculum to reflect the university's mission emphasizing leadership and environmental stewardship. Environmental Sustainability satisfies the scientific literacy requirement and is one of a small number of courses that satisfy Loyola's civic engagement core value. The faculty has been challenged to adapt or develop courses that simultaneously provide academic rigor and a meaningful civic contribution. Previous approaches to integrating civic engagement into science courses were doing outreach at local schools or involving students in community cleanup or greening projects. Feedback from course evaluations showed that students often considered the projects as busywork that lacked a deeper connection to the fundamentals covered in class. We have found that students are most engaged by projects they feel make a significant and lasting contribution to improving the environment.

One impetus for our work appeared when Loyola's administration prevailed upon Marshall Eames to conduct a campuswide environmental sustainability assessment of energy, water, waste, food, transportation, and other major systems so that a sustainability action plan could be developed. Time was short, the budget was tight, and the work was in addition to a full teaching load. Students in the Environmental Sustainability course were asked to conduct the studies on campus to complete the assessment. Through the assessment, we learned that the functions and actions of urban universities like Loyola are intimately interwoven with the surrounding communities and that the next step in developing a sustainability action plan required a different way of thinking about the relationship between town and gown.

In early spring 2007 Loyola's Center for Environmental Research and Policy (CUERP) was approached by community council members from an adjacent neighborhood, Edgewater, to help them develop a sustainability action plan to make Edgewater Chicago's greenest community. The community sought the participation of Loyola faculty and students in conducting studies, gathering data, and analyzing the results to help the Edgewater Community Council (ECC) make more informed decisions regarding the creation and implementation of its sustainability plan. We recognized this partnership's potential to contribute to the university's mission. The partnership has since allowed Loyola faculty to engage undergraduates in meaningful service to the community and the university in ways that involve true academic learning. At the same time, Loyola has enjoyed an unprecedented opportunity to reconcile the sustainability goals of the university with those of the community. The experience we describe and the course that emerged are the results of those events.

Loyola and the Community

Throughout this chapter, we use the term *community* in a broad sense to represent the faculty, staff, and students of Loyola University and the nearby Edgewater neighborhood. Loyola University Chicago, founded in 1870, had outgrown its original campus by the end of the 19th century and needed to find a new location. The university purchased 20 acres of lakefront to build what is now Loyola's Lakeshore campus. In 1955 the first dormitory opened, an event that triggered a fundamental change in the relationship between the university and the community of Edgewater. Today the 50-acre Lakeshore campus has a resident population of 3,850 students, an additional 450 students living nearby in off-campus apartments, and a daily population of nearly 10,500 people. Students are significant stakeholders in the community and represent a considerable economic force. Loyola itself is the largest landholder and employer in the community.

With a population of 62,198, Edgewater is the second most densely populated community in Chicago and, consequently, has little open space (Fischer & Schwieterman, 2008). Edgewater has an active community council, development corporations, and a chamber of commerce. These entities helped us forge a strong alliance with the community and allowed for student involvement.

Edgewater's mission to become the greenest community in Chicago focuses on making transportation, energy, water use, and schools more sustainable. Also important is increasing parks and open spaces and building a stronger overall sense of community. After discussions with the ECC, we saw a great opportunity for service learning. Built upon what we learned in an earlier sustainability assessment of Loyola's operations and our discussions with the ECC, the idea for a new course emerged. The course is a hybrid that emphasizes service learning within the context of a traditional lecture/lab-based science course. This hybrid approach ensures the academic rigor of lecture/lab-based science courses and simultaneously engages students in applied problem solving in the local community. Providing the academic foundation remains the responsibility of the instructor, while providing service and civic engagement opportunities is the responsibility of our primary contacts in the community. Before each semester, we contact the participating community organizations to develop a list of projects that would benefit from student involvement. During this time, we roughly define the scope of the students' involvement, agree upon deliverables, and identify the primary contact people in the community organizations. By the second week of the semester, students list their top three project preferences, and assignments are made based on that and estimated workloads. Student teams are responsible for contacting the organization and coordinating their involvement with the primary contact. In many cases, the primary contacts mentor the students by discussing research ideas that would most benefit the community, assist students in contacting other relevant community members, facilitate data collection through community contacts, and provide insight into community affairs and functions in relation to environmental sustainability.

Overview of the Course

Course goals and structure. Our intention is that the course demonstrates to students the inextricable relationships among politics, business, social organizations, and ecosystems, and allows students to recognize the ramifications of the decisions they make. Our own backgrounds are interdisciplinary, a strength we feel adds value to the learning experience. Marshall Eames is trained in engineering, ecology, and public administration and brings to the classroom 25 years of experience working in the government sector and as a consultant. Jeremy Brooks is trained in human ecology, a field that blends anthropology, economics, political science, sociology, psychology, and ecology.

We designed the course to accomplish three things: educate students about global environmental problems, their causes, and potential solutions; fulfill the university's civic engagement core requirement; and design a course that would fulfill Loyola's core curriculum science requirement for nonscience majors. Thus, we use community-based research projects that allow students to interact with community members and gain insights into the community's role in making the urban and campus environments more sustainable. Our learning objectives reinforce the belief that true academic learning takes place through service-learning projects (Howard, 2001; Jones, 2003). The course objectives and the various forms of assessment we used are listed in Table 5.1.

The course is not team taught, although we share course objectives and organize our sections similarly. Each of us independently teaches multiple sections of the course during the same semester, and we coordinate our sections to avoid redundancy in student projects. Some service-learning projects focus directly on Loyola's effects on community sustainability, while others are targeted at the roles business and residents play in affecting sustainability. Although we have crafted our individual lectures, discussions, and assignments according to our personal strengths and disciplines, and some of the reading materials differ in each of our courses depending upon the types of project the students will be conducting, we cover the same fundamental content in all our sections.

Since the course fulfills dual undergraduate core curriculum requirements for civic engagement as well as scientific literacy, it is a very attractive option for students. The course is open to students from all majors and academic levels. We use a variety of teaching approaches to satisfy different learning styles, combining traditional lectures, in-class discussions, short discussions (think-pair-share), films and short video clips, and student presentations. A strong experiential learning approach is common to both of our courses.

Course topics. Eames adapted the course for a section dedicated solely to students in the green living/learning community portion of Loyola's First-Year Experience, which aims to ease the transition to campus life for incoming students. The syllabus for that section is in Appendix A, and a sample of Jeremy Brooks's syllabus, which describes areas of coverage, is in Appendix B.

While the first part of the course focuses on teaching content areas, early in the semester we introduce the service-learning component. Students are provided with the suggested thematic areas that have been developed by the instructors in consultation with community organizations. We also solicit ideas for thematic areas from the class during the first week. Students are encouraged to identify the thematic areas and projects that build upon their

TABLE 5.1
Learning Objectives for the Course

Objective	Form of Assessment
Describe how ecological systems function, how biological diversity relates to ecological dynamics, and why biodiversity conservation is important.	Exam
Discuss the origins of environmental problems and potential solutions from scientific, ethical, and philosophical perspectives.	Exam, personal reflection essays, book review
Demonstrate the ways in which human activities differ from natural ecological processes and analyze how human actions alter ecosystem functioning and ecological dynamics.	Exam, book review
Describe social, political, and economic inequities and social justice, and explain the implications these factors have on resource use and access to healthy environments.	Personal reflection essays, project report/presentation
Explain the concept of *trade-offs* and how they are relevant to a sustainable society, and identify the potential conflicts that arise between different stakeholders (e.g., corporate interests vs. citizen interests, rich vs. poor, rural vs. urban)	Exam, project report/presentation
Compare different approaches to solving environmental problems (new technologies, policies, approaches, etc.) and explain the science behind existing or emerging environmental problems.	Short presentation, research project
Explain the theory of evolution by natural selection and how this theory can help us understand human behaviors and the roots of our environmental problems.	Exam, project report
Use and apply scientific methods (identify problem of interest, state hypothesis, design study, analyze data and draw conclusion, communicate results) to analyze an environmental problem or test a potential solution through a semester-long, community-based research project.	Research project
Differentiate among various theoretical perspectives on human behavior and decision making from the fields of political science, economics, anthropology, and other social science disciplines, and relate them to patterns of resource use and conservation efforts.	Exam, book review
Employ the concepts and practices addressed throughout the semester in the different stages of the research project.	Research project

interests because we consistently see more engagement and better quality in student-driven projects than in instructor-generated projects. Our goals at the beginning of the course are to provide the students with background information about the campus and the Edgewater community; discuss the university's rationale for civic engagement projects and their benefits to students, the university, and the community; provide an overview of environmental sustainability in an urban context; reinforce fundamentals of the scientific method, with an emphasis on experimental design and hypothesis testing; and discuss the nature of scientific knowledge and the inherent uncertainty of scientific investigation.

After the introductory part of the course, we cover a number of topics from basic ecology, conservation biology, environmental science, and engineering and introduce social science topics that are crucial for understanding the current and potential future of environmental problems and their solutions. A discussion on the impacts of transportation illustrates our different approaches to the topics. Eames focuses on improved technologies that lead to greater efficiencies and reduced energy consumption, and Brooks looks at changes in behaviors that lead to modal shifts, fewer or reduced trips, and lower energy consumption. We devote the remainder of the semester, usually about three weeks, to assisting the project teams in applying the concepts presented throughout the semester to their service-learning projects. We focus on individual consultation with the teams since the projects vary greatly in nature. The semester culminates when teams present their projects during the final week of classes. A final research paper is submitted in lieu of a final exam.

Description of the Service-Learning Projects

The centerpiece of the course is the semester-long group research project that begins in the first week of class and culminates with a comprehensive report and presentation during the last week of the semester. The service-learning projects are intended to provide an exercise for the students to become familiar with the processes of experimental design and hypothesis testing; encourage students to explore the multidisciplinary facets (e.g., social, economic, environmental, and political) of a particular environmental issue; provide useful data, insights, and suggestions that will assist the university and the ECC in refining and implementing their long-range sustainability plan; provide an opportunity for the students to explore the neighborhood adjacent to their campus (and homes), interact with their neighbors, and view their surrounding community through the lens of environmental sustainability; and allow students to serve as ambassadors for Loyola University to increase the interaction between the campus and the community.

Figure 5.1 shows the relationships among classroom actions, outside research and reading, and milestone assignments. This general outline for the service-learning project portion of the course can be tailored to different teaching styles, course objectives, and instructor preferences. The success of the student projects and the quality of the learning experience are related directly to the level of advanced preparation and interaction with community members and mentors in identifying useful and feasible projects. The bulleted points at the top of Figure 5.1 signify this aspect of planning.

Student teams were composed of three to six people, based on student preference, project complexity, and anticipated workload. Once group assignments were made, students were asked to focus on a specific research question that falls within the thematic area. Projects focused on important sustainability issues in the community.

The lead organization in Edgewater is the ECC, but several other community organizations were involved in the service-learning projects in a variety of ways. Students worked with diverse entities, such as environmental consultants, development corporations, the parks district, the ward's aldermanic office, and local schools and businesses. Businesses included a local restaurant with Chicago's first certified organic rooftop garden. With rare exceptions, individuals graciously gave of their time to meet with and mentor students, provide data and information, and include students in public forums.

These organizations played three main roles, but not all individuals or organizations were intended to fulfill each of these roles. The first role was to provide opportunity through contact and mentorship. Each student group was assigned a primary contact/mentor whose task was to provide suggestions about research questions that were interesting and relevant to the community. The primary contacts were from organizations like those listed previously.

The second role was as a partner. In this case, the student groups identified an organization whose interests aligned with the group's research interests and questions. For instance, one group studying green businesses paired with the Andersonville Development Corporation and its Eco-Andersonville

FIGURE 5.1
Service-Learning Flowchart

Before the Semester

- Meet with community leaders to discuss potential topic areas
- Identify key community contacts/mentors for each topic area

In Class	Outside of Class	Assignments
	Weeks 1–4	
Introduce students to the project goals and expectations	Students read reports from previous classes to help with research ideas	Draft of research proposal is due
Community leaders introduce students to community background and their goals	Students contact community mentors to discuss research ideas	Professor makes comments and returns them to students
Students introduced to Leadership in Energy and Environmental Design (LEED) for Neighborhood Design and urban sustainability	Students explore the community to help generate research ideas	
Discuss topic areas with students and brainstorm research ideas as a class		
Students pick top three topic areas and are assigned to groups		
	Weeks 4–6	
Class time devoted to group meetings to refine hypotheses and study design; each group meets with professor	Students continue to meet, communicate with mentors, and design their project	Final draft of research proposal is due
Other class time devoted to group meetings for students to organize the project	Once hypotheses, study design, and survey questions are OK'd by professor and community, students begin data collection	Students are to begin crafting survey questions (where applicable)
		Survey questions and research proposals sent to community leaders for comment

Weeks 7–10

Some class time is allotted for student group meetings	Student groups continue with data collection	First personal reflection essay is due (week 7)
	Professor and TA compile survey instruments from each group, create surveys online, and send links to surveys to community block leaders for distribution to community members via e-mail	Group project update is due (week 8 or 9)
	Links to surveys sent to students so they can incorporate data	

Weeks 11–14

Some class time is allotted for student group meetings	Student groups continue with data collection	Second personal reflection essay due (week 11)
Some lecture time devoted to basic statistical analyses and data management and presentation		
Some lecture time devoted to discussion of writing scientific reports		

Week 16

Class time is devoted to student presentations. Each group has approximately 25 minutes for presentation and questions	Students prepare presentations and final group reports	Final reports are due
		Personal portfolios are due (final reflection essay, detailed outline of contribution to the project, peer review)

Semester End

- During finals week, a group of student volunteers will compile group reports from their section of the class into one document and submit an electronic version.

initiative to develop green business practice guidelines for local small businesses. Another group examining religion and sustainability paired with Faith in Place, a local ecumenical organization promoting stewardship of the earth's resources. Students worked hard with their partners to design research questions that maximized the usefulness of the information for the organization.

The third role was as research subjects. Some organizations/businesses were the focus of the students' projects. These organizations were selected because they shed light on community sustainability or because their practices could be valuable examples to others. Individuals in these organizations provided the information/data for the projects and helped the students understand how their organization interfaced with the community.

Because this class is part of the core curriculum and is open to all majors at all levels, we encourage the students to draw on their own disciplinary background knowledge and skills as they select and design their projects, analyze and interpret results, and write their reports. When we select the teams, we also attempt to match talents and skills to the project. This is a big attraction for students who are normally insecure in science courses. One can relate almost any major to environmental sustainability, and having the opportunity to pursue a research topic that has personal interest and incorporates one's existing knowledge base allows the students to connect their own knowledge base with those of students pursuing different majors. The students are encouraged to emphasize the connections between their majors and the service-learning projects in personal reflection essays submitted throughout the semester. One particularly anxious senior commented, "This wasn't too bad, I actually got to use stuff I learned in my education classes." She worked with a team that developed a sustainability awareness video for new faculty and staff orientation.

Some other specific examples of projects include

- frequency of community reuse/recycling;
- analysis of demand for parks/open space in Edgewater;
- levels of adult environmental education and awareness;
- motivations for using alternative transportation (bicycling, public transportation, car sharing);
- water usage—consumption patterns and student behaviors in residence halls;

- analysis of social capital, community cohesion, and trust in the community;
- feasibility of local/urban/community agriculture;
- noise exposure—indoor and outdoor noise levels in the community;
- Dumpster Diving in the Dining Halls—an analysis of Loyola's food waste stream;
- contributions of religious organizations to sustainability efforts;
- trends in green business/consumerism;
- paperless campus—an analysis of Loyola's copier/printer paper consumption; and
- transportation demand management—an analysis of community parking demands.

Such projects would not be possible without the active participation and support from the local community government, nongovernmental organizations, and university administrators and staff. Students worked throughout the community and interacted with vice presidents, directors, and managers from all divisions of the university, including finance, facilities, campus safety, transportation, student life, and food services. Their work included coordination with neighborhood organizations to ensure that campus-planning efforts were compatible with those of the Edgewater community.

Evaluation of Student Learning

In-class assignments. We use a variety of approaches to evaluate student progress in the course. Although we differ somewhat in our preferred approaches, philosophically we agree on giving students the opportunity to succeed through assignments that are geared toward a variety of learning styles. One approach we both rely on is assigning multiple three- to four-page book synopses. This assignment is particularly effective with students who have weak quantitative skills or who are science phobic. Students could draw upon lectures, discussions, and other educational and personal experiences in summarizing and evaluating the book. Further, by giving students a wide choice of books, they are able to select ones that match their interests, talents, and level of scientific sophistication. Examples of reading lists and assignments are contained in Appendix A.

Another approach we successfully employ is structuring the midterm exam as a sustainable design problem (see Appendix C). This is an effective way of assessing students' true grasp of the concepts presented in lectures and readings, and it compels them to apply their learning through analysis and synthesis. The midterm is a take-home exam, which the students have one week to complete. They are expected to synthesize their own solutions, but they have the option (encouraged) of discussing ideas with fellow students, mentors, faculty, or other professionals. The advantage to this approach is that the exam itself becomes a learning tool.

An alternative to such midterms is a more traditional exam. In the past, we used exam questions that required students to construct a well-stated hypothesis, design a simple scientific study, identify key variables, and point out the shortcomings of a hypothetical research design. Other questions require students to apply their knowledge of theories of human behavior to explain different scenarios depicting environmental problems, including a case study that appeared in *National Geographic* about the water crisis in Australia.

In addition to the exams, we require student pairs to do a short (7- to 10-minute) presentation on any topic related to environmental sustainability. This assignment allows the students to be creative and to draw on their own disciplinary backgrounds. Students majoring in physics did a presentation on the potential benefits (and drawbacks) of nuclear power, biology majors discussed advancements in using bacteria to clean up waste, and economics majors informed students of tax incentives for using solar power. The topic areas were entirely open and included creative presentations, such as how to have a green Halloween, the environmental consequences of the drug trade, and environmentally friendly alternatives to traditional burials and cremation.

Evaluation of the service-learning project. The service-learning project is the centerpiece of the course and represents about half of the total grade. Throughout the semester, we required milestone submissions, such as project proposals, updates, and personal reflection essays to keep the teams on schedule and to give the instructor a preview of the final product. Evaluating the individual student's contribution to the team service-learning project was challenging. Students complained about being saddled with unproductive teammates, conflicting schedules, and last-minute defections. Giving students the opportunity to work on the project during class time eliminated or reduced the problems with schedule conflicts and coordination. We required our students to use peer review as part of the evaluation process. Teammates anonymously rated each other's work in four categories: timeliness, cooperation, contribution, and participation. At the end of the semester, each student submitted a portfolio documenting his or her personal contribution to the project. After using this procedure for 10 sections of the course, we observed a remarkable correlation between portfolio scores and the peer evaluations.

At the end of the semester, all students submit a personal portfolio containing their final personal reflection essay (the last of three such essays submitted throughout the semester), an outline of their contribution to the project including the approximate amount of time devoted to each task they performed, notes, drafts and analyses, and an evaluation of their peers. The portfolios are graded, first using a checklist to ensure that all the required components are included, and then, more holistically, using the instructor's evaluation. The reflection essays are graded based on the students' ability to address particular points in their essays. Students who convincingly demonstrated progression in comprehending and analyzing the complex nature of environmental sustainability throughout their three essays received the highest grades, while those who provided only an update of their contribution to the project received the lowest grades. These grades were combined with scores for the other components of students' final portfolios.

Each group writes a final report on its project. The first five or six students who express interest in an extra-credit project are selected to compile and edit the final reports from their class section into one document. Essentially, each final report represents a chapter in the overall document. These student editors write an introduction and conclusion, provide a table of contents, and write brief introductory paragraphs for each of the final reports. The full class report is then published electronically and made available to all members of the class and provided to the ECC and the university. It is too early to provide many concrete examples of how the results from the students' projects have been incorporated into the planning and implementation of the ECC's long-term sustainability efforts. However, results from transportation studies in Edgewater showed that the Chicago Transit Authority did not facilitate movement within and around the community, which resulted in the creation of a circulator route in which buses travel around the community on a set schedule to serve students, residents, and local businesses. In another example, based upon a suggestion from the initial food waste study, Loyola adopted trayless buffet dining. A follow-up student study two years later demonstrated a 29% reduction in plate waste in Loyola dining halls. An added benefit for the students was the sense that through service learning and civic engagement, they could have a positive impact on sustainability. A study on transportation patterns led to a student-operated, university-supported free bike-loan program. Program participants take abandoned bikes found on campus and donate them to other students. During the first semester of operation, the demand exceeded availability by 100%. Waste stream analyses for local restaurants and campus dining halls helped optimize the production of waste-derived biodiesel fuel by providing a consistent supply of waste vegetable oil.

Value of the Service-Learning Project

The Loyola/Edgewater community benefits in numerous ways because of student work. For example, the ECC wanted to become a showcase community for sustainable urban redevelopment. Student projects helped the ECC decide which actions were most appropriate and which areas needed emphasizing. The projects provided information about how environmentally aware Edgewater's residents were, the number of and reasons why people used public transportation, and whether consumers expressed shopping preferences for businesses that operated sustainably. This type of information provided insight into why particular environmental problems exist and what the best approach may be for addressing them. For instance, one group found there was a great demand for more open space, even from residents who did not frequently use existing parks. Another group found that the main reason many Edgewater residents do not bicycle throughout the city is not because the streets are busy and there are few bike lanes but because they do not own bicycles, a result that points to the utility of a bike-sharing program. Yet another group found that while the demand for local and organic produce is high, awareness of the few existing farmers markets is low, as is access to organically grown food in local grocery stores. This information is useful not only to local leaders, who might be willing to donate funds to a bike-sharing program, but also to local business owners, who now know more about the growing demand for healthier, locally produced food options.

A second benefit to the community is that the projects require students to make specific recommendations that can be incorporated into Edgewater's sustainability plan. For instance, one group studied pedestrian traffic in two separate Edgewater locations thought to be conducive to walking (Farr, 2007). One location had wider, tree-lined sidewalks along narrower streets, while the other had sparse greenery, more automobile traffic, and busier, more dangerous intersections. Contrary to its hypothesis, this group found that aesthetic characteristics did not necessarily provide a greater incentive for people to walk. The group suggested that Edgewater should initially focus more on providing attractive destinations for pedestrians (grocery stores, coffee shops, restaurants, etc.) and less on streetscape beautification. They also suggested that given the relatively high levels of pedestrian traffic, Edgewater could devote its limited manpower and funds to other arenas of sustainability, such as identifying land to be purchased for green space or building a bike-sharing program. Another group identified state grants that Edgewater schools could seek to bolster their environmental education programs and reduce their ecological footprint. Programs like the Illinois Environmental Protection Agency's Clean School Bus Program, Lake Education Assistance Program (LEAP), and Green Youth Award provide funding to replace older existing buses with cleaner models; funds for field trips that focus on watershed and lake education; and money for student projects that reduce waste and pollution, restore land and waterways, increase energy efficiency, and preserve or restore natural areas. The students also informed the community about the state of Illinois's Zero Waste School Grant Program, which funds school efforts to become zero waste environments. These recommendations not only provide a starting place for the community to begin to move forward with long-term sustainability plans but also specific information about programs that can be implemented in the short term.

A third benefit of the service-learning component is a greater sense of connection between students and the community that results from conducting the projects. One group of students who recognized that older residents without automobiles had difficulty shopping proposed a bicycle delivery service operated by students under the auspices of the university and the community council. Another group of students developed a how-to guide for creating a community garden, based in part on the successful gardens that exist in the south side of Chicago. These students also professed an interest in getting the garden started even after the class had finished. Following the completion of the semester, another student went on to work for the local alderman as an environmental affairs assistant.

Additionally, some students extended their community work to environmental projects in other courses. A student who majored in fine arts designed advertisements for an environmental awareness campaign for her course, and other students interviewed business owners and the director of the Andersonville Development Corporation as part of a business class. As testimony to the success of the course, members of the nearby Rogers Park neighborhood asked to involve students in their community-planning project in future semesters.

There were tangible benefits of the service learning for the university as well. Students worked and interacted with staff from areas across the university including the libraries, human resources, food service, resident life, facilities, and strategic planning. As a result of the initial sustainability assessment, the university created an office of environmental sustainability, and four students who completed the course went on to work as interns to develop an overall sustainability plan. In addition, student volunteers support our libraries and help develop sustainability guidelines for Loyola's campus in Rome, Italy. Comprehensive transportation and parking studies have been used to support the recently updated planned urban development documentation for the campus. Several members of student government and the Student Environmental Alliance have taken the course and are increasingly active in university committees such as the Reduce, Reuse, Recycle Committee and the Transportation Demand Management Steering Committee. Furthermore, student analyses of paper consumption led to an initiative by Loyola's information technology department to go paperless.

Finally, the service-learning projects are a benefit to students by complementing the in-class components of the course and by providing a forum grounded in practice for student learning. In all the projects, students are asked to do some level of experimentation and hypothesis testing and to apply what they learned to community environmental issues using concepts that were discussed in lectures. The students have shown they are able to link the responses from community members to the concepts covered in class, thereby providing a direct, tangible connection between the classroom and the real world. This component of the project is especially beneficial for students who are concrete thinkers. Perhaps the most dramatic lesson for students is demonstrating the real-world complexity belied by Barbier's

(1987) simple Venn diagram for sustainability. Many students comment about this in their reflections, reports, and presentations. Students often see only the proximal effect of an action. For example, taking a long shower results in more water consumption, but students often fail to look at the causal web, which includes additional energy to treat, pump, heat, and sanitize the extra water. Even more broadly, they do not see the connections among water consumption, Great Lakes water elevation, shipping, and even power generation at Niagara Falls. The Barbier diagram can compel students to engage in deeper systems thinking about the environment.

Suggestions for Faculty at Other Universities

The story of the genesis of this course provides what we believe to be an important message: Instructors must be flexible and open to opportunities that present themselves. Although we are generally pleased with the design of the course and the student outcomes, improvements are needed with regard to the instructor workload. The service-learning project makes the course demanding of the instructor's time, and we suggest that faculty not teach more than two sections per semester. At Loyola the course has an enrollment cap of 32 students per section and historically has a very low attrition rate. We recommend keeping class size at this limit and perhaps reducing it should the instructor incorporate the more writing-intensive assignments described previously. Teaching assistants can sometimes ease the burden. We also suggest limiting some sections of the course to juniors and seniors who bring the requisite academic skills for conducting meaningful research projects. We have found the disparity in intellectual maturity in a mixed class, its effect upon group cohesion, and the quality of the research projects to be a problem.

A 15-week-semester setting allows students to be involved in complex projects without being overwhelmed at the end of the term. A 10-week quarter may be too short to accomplish course goals. However, it may be useful where possible to turn this into a two-quarter or two-semester course. The additional time would allow the students to do more background research on their topics, strengthen their study design capabilities, and increase the quantity and quality of the data they collect, all of which could provide more useful information for the community and create stronger bonds between the students and community members. With this two-term arrangement, outstanding students would have the opportunity to conduct research at a level that may be suitable for publication in a peer-reviewed journal. We recognize there are obstacles to such a configuration, such as constraints imposed by graduation times and difficulties scheduling faculty; however, such obstacles have been overcome as illustrated by the Freshman Inquiry program in sustainability at Portland State University (see http://www.pdx.edu/unst/freshman-inquiry-sustainability).

Throughout the two years of teaching this course, we have also identified changes we would make to the service-learning project to increase benefits for students and the community:

- Have each group include in its proposal a short summary of the specific research in the thematic area conducted by the students in previous semesters. This assignment will ensure that the groups are aware of and can build upon the previous research results and recommendations without repeating earlier work.

- Have the groups critique each other's research proposals. This assignment will give the students more experience with hypothesis testing and study design and strengthen each group's study.

- Provide a forum for students to post their personal reflections anonymously. As instructors, we enjoyed reading the reflection essays and think the students would benefit from seeing the transformations their classmates have undergone.

- Actively encourage creativity in presentations and reports. Encourage students to explore multimedia presentations or tools that can benefit the community. Student groups often present their work in a standard PowerPoint format that sometimes turns an interesting project into a dry presentation that generates little excitement among the other students. By encouraging groups to harness new media such as YouTube and social networking sites, and present their projects through videos, narratives, games, or other formats, there is a greater likelihood the other students will learn from their projects. For instance, one group included a game in its PowerPoint presentation and another group modeled its presentation on a newscast. Both approaches piqued the interest of the class more than other approaches. The instructors can encourage such approaches by incorporating these techniques into class lectures throughout the semester and emphasizing that the students can use such techniques in their own presentations.

- Have the students explicitly state a revised hypothesis, or hypotheses, based on the outcomes of their study to gain experience with the next step of the scientific process and to give future students a starting point for the next study.

The Course's Future at Loyola

We tested a new variation of this course during fall 2009, with a First-Year Experience, green living learning for 30 freshmen in a living-learning community. Our experience in 2008 showed that the students in the community are highly motivated and very enthusiastic about sustainability. What these freshmen lack in academic training, we hope they make up in enthusiasm. The course was taught in a dedicated section in a three-hour block and revolved around guest speakers from the community who introduced issues related to sustainability. Students took on the challenge of doing a research project. Each group of four to six freshmen was assigned an upperclassman mentor who helped guide the team project.

In addition, because the Rogers Park neighborhood, in which the majority of Loyola's academic campus resides, had already requested student participation in its own sustainability planning project, its community leaders were kept abreast of the collaboration in Edgewater and were excited to be a partner with the students in the Environmental Sustainability course in 2009.

Conclusion

We were fortunate to be presented with a unique and timely opportunity to take advantage of the confluence of ideal circumstances at the university and in the community. While successful implementation of the course depends in large part on the interest and cooperation of the community, environmental issues are at the forefront worldwide, and we imagine many communities want to promote sustainability. Although this course requires time and effort from the instructors, students, and community partners, they all say that the sense of accomplishment and the information obtained from the class are well worth the effort.

References

Barbier, E. B. (1987). The concept of sustainable development. *Environmental Conservation, 14*(2), 101–110.

Farr, D. (2007). *Sustainable urbanism: Urban designing with nature.* New York, NY: Wiley.

Fischer, L., & Schwieterman, J. P. (2008). *A kaleidoscope of culture: Measuring the diversity of Chicago's neighborhoods.* Chicago, IL: School of Public Service Policy Study, DePaul University.

Howard, J. (2001). *Service-learning course design workbook.* Ann Arbor, MI: MPublishing.

Jones, S. (2003). *Introduction to service-learning toolkit: Readings and resources for faculty.* Providence, RI: Campus Compact.

United Nations Department of Economic and Social Affairs. (2009, May). World Civic Forum 2009, Seoul, Korea.

United Nations World Commission on Environment and Development. (1987). *Report of the World Commission on Environment and Development: Our common future.* Oslo, Norway: Author.

Appendix A

Sample Syllabus—J. Marshall Eames

NATURAL SCIENCE 180
ENVIRONMENTAL SUSTAINABILITY
COURSE INFORMATION

Course Description: As we enter the 21st century, the higher education community is becoming increasingly concerned about campus sustainability. Loyola is no exception. Through the Center for Urban Environmental Research and Policy (CUERP), the university is looking at issues that reflect the need for low-impact, sustainable, urban environments. For example, the Division of Facilities Management is currently evaluating the effectiveness of recycling on campus.

This course must support a core curriculum value area by promoting civic engagement and leadership. To accomplish this, we will take a hands-on approach to learning about and contributing to the understanding of sustainability at Loyola University Chicago and our surrounding community.

We will explore relationships between modern higher education, the Earth's resources, and our environment. We will examine issues such as climate change, the energy crisis, water shortages, air pollution, urban noise, deforestation, biodiversity, and land use from global and local perspectives. Through our explorations, we will learn some physics, chemistry, earth science, biology, and (hopefully) some ecology. We will learn about the interconnectedness of nature and how society impacts the environment.

You are all members of the Green Living Learning Community that affords you a unique educational experience and simultaneously creates a laboratory to observe and reflect upon the impacts of student behaviors on the environment. We also have chosen an unusual format for this class, "A Dinner Meeting," during which a wide array of guest speakers will join us for dinner and talk about aspects of sustainability ranging from water consumption to climate action plans to community greening initiatives. During the first weeks we will get to know each other, learn how science works, and I'll share with you things we have learned about the infrastructure and operations of our campus. Then, the fun begins as we bring in our guests. Be active learners: Engage our guests in discussions and ask lots of questions. The most discouraging experience for a speaker is to conclude a talk and then have no one ask questions.

Here's how a typical class should work:

5:00–5:15	Reception for speaker, buffet line open
5:15–6:15	I'll introduce next week's topic with an informal lecture
6:15–6:30	Intermission
6:30–7:30	Guest speaker
7:30–8:00	Questions and discussion

The centerpieces to this course are the civic engagement projects. In the past, students in this course conducted a preliminary sustainability assessment for Loyola's Lakeshore campus, and the results shed much light on the issues facing the campus community as we strive to meet our mission and create a sustainable campus. We will again focus our energies on the campus community by working with various departments to bring about a positive environmental change in the campus culture and our relationship with Edgewater and Rogers Park. Our overarching theme will be "Environmental Awareness."

We will talk more about the projects and process in class. You will work in small teams (2–3 students) and also will discover the panoply of talents needed to effect change. Think about the 3–4 projects that interest you the most. I will try to assign students to their first choices, but you should have alternates in mind.

Tests and Grading: Education should be both challenging and fun! To that end, this course offers several types of activities to earn points. The course grade is based upon 1,000 total points and the following schedule:

A:	920–1000	A−:	900–919		
B+:	870–899	B:	820–869	B−:	790–819
C+:	760–789	C:	710–759	C−:	680–709
D+:	650–679	D:	600–649		
F:	< 600				

Your grade is determined by the total number of points you accrue. Some of you may think I'm math challenged since the total possible points sums to 1,050 not 1,000. You may accrue 600 pts before submitting the final project. Consider this a safety net if you feel that colleagues on your team are not pulling their weight. You are only limited by your own initiative and the quality of the work you submit. You must submit one book synopsis from each category. (No substitutions allowed!) Each book synopsis is worth 150 points. The take-home midterm is worth 150 points. There is no final exam but there is a class project that is worth 450 points. There will be more information on that class project in a separate handout. See the course schedule for the due dates for the synopses and midterm. The final projects are due on the last scheduled class meeting.

Midterm (150): A take-home exam that will be fun and challenging.

Book Synopsis: Read and summarize the book in a well written 3- to 4-page paper. You must read one book from each category (that's a total of 3 synopses), but you may read them in any order you wish. Incorporate the principles we discuss in this class when writing your paper. Relate the authors' ideas to the environment, sustainability, and your class project. Be especially mindful of the authors' thesis.

CATEGORY 1 (150 PTS)

Collapse: How Societies Choose to Fail or Succeed. 2005. By Jared Diamond.

Changes in the Land: Indians, Colonists, and the Ecology of New England. 1983. By William Cronon.

Guns, Germs, and Steel: The Fates of Human Societies. 1997. By Jared Diamond.

Nature's Metropolis: Chicago and the Great West. 1992. By William Cronon.

1491: New Revelations of the Americas before Columbus. 2006. By Charles C. Mann.

The Worst Hard Time. 2006. By Timothy Egan

The Revolt of the Elites and the Betrayal of Democracy. 1995. By Christopher Lasch

CATEGORY 2 (150 PTS)

Tapped Out: The Coming World Crisis in Water and What We Can Do About It. 1998. By Paul Simon.

Food Politics: How the Food Industry Influences Nutrition and Health. 2007. By Marion Nestle

Sanitary City: Urban Infrastructure in America from Colonial Times to the Present. 2000. By Martin Melosi.

Road Ecology: Science and Solutions. 2003. By R.T. Forman et al.

Miracle Under the Oaks: The Revival of Nature in America. 1995. By William K. Stevens.

Cradle to Cradle/Remaking the Way We Make Things. 2002. By W. McDonough & M. Braumgart.

Down to Earth: Nature's Role in American History. 2002. By Ted Steinberg.

Race, Place, and Environmental Justice after Hurricane Katrina. 2009. By Robert D. Bullard & Beverly Wright.

CATEGORY 3 (150 PTS)

Ecological Design. 1996. By Sim Van der Ryn & Stuart Cowan

Natural Capitalism. 1999. By Paul Hawken, Amory Lovins, & L. Hunter Lovins

Transportation & Sustainable Campus Communities: Issues, Examples, Solutions. 2004. By W. Toors & S. W. Havlick

Sustainability on Campus: Stories and Strategies for Change. 2004. By P. F. Barlett & G. W. Chase.

Environmental Urban Noise. 2001. By A. Garcia (I recommend this for science majors—it gets a bit technical.)

Biodiversity Recovery Plan. 1999. By Chicago Wilderness

The Tallgrass Restoration Handbook: For Prairies, Savannas, and Woodlands. 1997. By Stephen Packard & Cornelia F. Mutel

Energy in Nature and Society: General Energetics of Complex Systems. 2008. By Vaclav Smil

CLASS PROJECT (450 PTS):

This course must satisfy a core value for civic engagement and leadership, and the class project is the mechanism for doing that. You will work in small groups on a specific element of a larger class initiative. Our focus this semester will be on environmental awareness. As residential students, you have a special interest in greening the campus, its operations, and those of the surrounding communities. Here is an example of what we have in mind.

Several years ago, undergraduate and graduate students at the University of California, Berkeley prepared a sustainability study for their campus. A copy of the assessment may be found on the Blackboard site for this course. The Berkeley assessment looked at 9 major campus systems. During spring and fall semesters 2007, and spring semester 2008, Loyola students developed assessments for our campus (copies also are available on Blackboard) that represent an extraordinary effort by undergraduate students. The culminations of their projects were written reports and presentations to the CUERP at the end of each semester. This semester we will pick up where the students left off. The current project will be focused on, and intended to augment, the preliminary assessment, and we will begin educating the campus and surrounding communities about sustainability. The outputs from this project will be written reports and educational/training materials and a presentation to CUERP and your peers. I will provide more details on the projects in a separate document.

I hear the groans and "feel your pain." Group projects always seem "unfair." "What if I get a bad group?" "I end up doing all the work because I don't want a bad grade!" "John went missing and at the last minute expected us all to get together to finish up." The list of complaints is endless and if I haven't heard them all, I have heard most of them. Sadly, throughout your life you will be working with other people (ascetics, hermits, and trolls excepted). To alleviate some of the "unfairness," you will be graded on your contribution to the overall effort. I will survey your teammates and evaluate your personal portfolio. Your portfolio must contain all your research notes, data analyses, draft submittals and any other materials relevant to your contribution to the effort. Your personal portfolio and class project are due on Tuesday, 1 December 2009, at 5:00 p.m. Submit the portfolio materials in a large manila envelope labeled with your name, class section, and date.

Grading scheme:	weight	category
	0.3	output quality
	0.3	portfolio
	0.3	peer evaluation
	0.1	instructor observation

REQUIRED TEXTBOOKS:

Loyola University Chicago—Campus Sustainability Assessment 2007. (available free on course Blackboard site)

Loyola University Chicago—Campus Sustainability Assessment Fall 2007. (available free on course Blackboard site)

Loyola University Chicago—Campus Sustainability Plan Spring 2008. (available free on course Blackboard site)

UC Berkeley Campus Sustainability Assessment 2005. (available free on course Blackboard site)

Course Strategies: Study! Just showing up for class is not enough. I am old-fashioned and expect students to commit to about 2 hours' outside preparation for each hour in class. Keep current with the reading and assignments. I believe in the "Preview and Review" approach, so read the material before you come to class. I expect students to be engaged in the learning process and actively participate in class. I *will* call on students to explain or critique reading assignments. Be prepared! Since you are college students, I expect you are equipped with an arsenal of scholarly weapons (The good kind!) and you will use them in this class.

My handouts are targeted for a general audience. Understanding units, conversions, scientific notation, and some simple ecological principles will be important to understanding the lectures later in the course. If your quantitative skills are rusty, you should put in some extra time with these topics. Still having difficulty—stop by my office.

Before you begin writing that first assignment, go to the Blackboard site and download the instructions on writing papers for this class. Yes, there are rules governing margins, font size, and other format issues. A couple of cautionary notes are in order. First, a 2-page paper means just that: 2 full pages of text (I don't round the page count). If you give me 1½ pages, you have given me 75 percent of what was required so I will start grading at 75 percent. Don't tell me "that's not fair"—you wouldn't expect to pay for 2 full gallons of gasoline if you only received 1½ gallons, would you? Second, lengthy direct quotes from sources will be deducted from your page count. Most probably the author(s) already graduated from college, so I'm not interested in grading their work. Finally, a picture may be worth a thousand words, but not in my class. Use charts, graphs, tables, pictures, and other illustrative material, but make sure they are relevant and advance the clarity of your writing. If they are just "padding," I'll deduct them from the page count.

Class Conduct: I prefer to conduct class as a forum with a free but orderly exchange of ideas. To accomplish this, you must be prepared. Read the material, do the homework, and bring questions and ideas. You may interrupt my lecture with questions, but be polite. Remember, if you're lost, most of your classmates are too. Besides, the little side-trips make learning fun. Class discussions are a fun way to learn, but in large classes, they require courtesy and some patience. You may use your laptop to take notes but no texting, web surfing, etc., during the class and especially during the guest speaker's presentation.

Since we will have guest speakers, a different level of courtesy is due them. Unless they instruct you otherwise, please hold questions until the end of their presentation. Ask questions, engage the speaker in conversation, and when the opportunity presents, thank them for their time. All our speakers have volunteered their time and some have traveled as well.

I have high expectations for students. My role, as a teacher, is to be your guide and help you to learn. If you have difficulty with the material, make arrangements to see me as soon as possible. Anyone with special needs should see me immediately. I will be happy to provide a list of supplemental resources that may clarify and enhance your understanding of the material, so do not hesitate to use those texts.

Please, read and understand the university's policies on academic conduct. Since you will be working on research papers, be especially careful of plagiarism. Know what constitutes plagiarism. Be clear in your understanding of the penalties and sanctions you face if you plagiarize. I do take academic misconduct seriously and I will seek sanctions against students violating university policy.

Attendance: I take attendance and I expect students to attend class. Studies have shown that there is a very high correlation between attendance and success in a course. Things happen! In each person's life there are unexpected events that require attention. I allow one (1) unexcused absence without penalty. Subsequent unexcused absences will result in a loss of 10 points/absence. If you must miss class, make arrangements with me beforehand to avoid a penalty. If your project team has scheduled an interview or some activity that takes you away from the classroom, check with me first so you are not marked absent.

Information, handouts, assignments, etc: Check the course's Blackboard site frequently. You are responsible for checking and I will not accept the "I didn't know excuse." I will post homework assignments, work sheets, the syllabus and schedule, short reading assignments, and other valuable information there. Also, I am not your accountant. So keep track of your own grades and assignments. Do not destroy or throw away assignments until your final grade is posted. If there are discrepancies between your records and mine, you will need the assignments to support your claim.

FINALLY! If you have any questions, concerns, difficulties, or just need to talk about the course, see me.

Appendix B

Sample Syllabus—Jeremy Brooks
NATURAL SCIENCE 180
ENVIRONMENTAL SUSTAINABILITY
COURSE DESCRIPTION

This course explores interdisciplinary thinking about how to address the contemporary environmental crisis and work toward a more sustainable society. You will be introduced to the fundamental principles, concepts, and knowledge from ecology, environmental science, and various social science disciplines that are essential to understanding how we can minimize human impacts on the environment. A scientific perspective on how the natural world works is critical to helping us understand not only how we impact the functioning of the environment, but also what steps we need to take to reduce those impacts. In addition, a scientific understanding of human behavior will help us understand why humans have had such a drastic impact on the planet and what the obstacles are to implementing solutions for our environmental problems.

This course must support a core curriculum value area by promoting civic engagement and leadership. To accomplish this, we will take a hands-on approach to learning and contribute to the understanding of sustainability in the surrounding community of Edgewater. In recent years, students in this course conducted sustainability assessments for Loyola's Lakeshore campus and the results shed much light on the issues facing the campus community as we strive to meet our mission and create a sustainable campus. This semester we will focus outward from Loyola's campus to assist the neighborhood of Edgewater in its efforts to become the greenest neighborhood in Chicago. The centerpieces of this course are the group projects that we will undertake as we identify ways to make Edgewater a more sustainable community. You will learn more about the topics we will focus on and how the group projects will work in the first two weeks of the course.

COURSE OBJECTIVES

- To introduce the complex issues entailed in the efforts to achieve a sustainable lifestyle from a scientific, ethical, and philosophical perspective

- To explore key conceptual principles within ecology, environmental science, political science, economics, anthropology, and other social science disciplines related to patterns of resource conservation and use
- To focus on the potential conflicts that arise between different stakeholders with respect to sustainability (e.g., corporate interests vs. citizen interests), to determine how these conflicts can be resolved
- To engage in critical analysis of contemporary issues relating to the conservation of natural resources, progress toward sustainable development, and the effects of globalization
- To discuss social, political, and economic inequity, social justice, and the implications for resource use and access to healthy environments
- To review a book that will provide more depth into a particular topic or pressing issue related to sustainability and gain experience with peer review
- To participate in a group project that is part of a larger class project to help the people of Edgewater create a more sustainable society. Through this project you will learn and gain experience with experimental design and the scientific method, as well as get real-life experience with the complexities of understanding the links between human-environment interactions and the difficulties of implementing initiatives for sustainability.

Please, read and understand the university's policies on academic conduct. Since you will be working on research papers, be especially careful not to plagiarize. Know what constitutes plagiarism. Be clear in your understanding of the penalties and sanctions you face if you plagiarize. I do take academic misconduct seriously and I will seek sanctions against students violating University policy.

INFORMATION, HANDOUTS, ASSIGNMENTS, ETC.

Check the course's Blackboard site frequently. The following syllabus is only a rough approximation. I reserve the right to change readings or the order of classes based on how the class evolves. I will inform you about such changes well in advance. You are responsible for checking and I will not accept the "I didn't know excuse." I will post homework assignments, worksheets, the syllabus and schedule, short reading assignments, and other valuable information on Blackboard. Keep track of your own grades and assignments. Do not destroy or throw away assignments until your final grade is posted. If there are discrepancies between your records and mine, you will need the assignments to support your claim.

READINGS

There is no textbook for this class. There are, however, required readings that will be posted on the course website. The content of these readings will be included in the exams to help you follow the topic in class that day.

In addition, I ask that you read over the following reports over the duration of the course this semester. These are reports that students have produced from the last two semesters of this class. These reports, particularly the one from fall 2008, can help you develop your civic engagement projects and will give you an idea of what is expected for the project.

1. Loyola University Chicago—Campus Sustainability Assessment 2007

2. Final Reports from NTSC—180 Fall 2008

ASSIGNMENTS AND GRADING

Grades will be based on your performance on two exams, two book reviews, one short presentation, the portfolio you create detailing your involvement in the civic engagement project, and participation in class.

1. 2 Exams (100 points each): These exams will include multiple-choice and short answer questions. I will provide a skeleton study guide that you can all fill in as a class.

2. Paper (200 points): First Draft (50 pts), Peer review (50 pts), Final Draft (100 pts)

Read and summarize one book in a well-written, 12-point font, 3-to 4-page, single-spaced paper. You may read the two books in any order you wish. It is important that you incorporate the principles we discuss in this class when writing your paper and to relate the authors' ideas on sustainability and our class project. I will provide a more detailed rubric for how I will grade the papers and post it on the course website.

Choose *one* book from the following:

Natural Capitalism. 1999. By Paul Hawken, Amory Lovins, and L. Hunter Lovins

Bowling Alone: The Collapse and Revival of American Community. 2001. By Robert Putnam

The Omnivore's Dilemma: A Natural History of Four Meals. 2007. By Michael Pollan

The Nature of Design. 2002. By David Orr

The paper assignment will also include a peer review. Each student will hand in a draft of his or her paper. I will not see this draft other than to pair you with another student who has read another book. You will then (anonymously) correct and comment on the paper, providing the author (who is also anonymous) with feedback about how to make the paper better. You will each get comments back from the anonymous reviewer and will submit both the first draft and the final draft to me to be graded. I will provide detailed instructions for this assignment.

3. Informational Session (50 points)

You will have to pair up with another student for this assignment. Each pair has 7–10 minutes maximum to present an issue related to environmental sustainability. You must find a website, blog, database, YouTube clip, or other movie clip, piece of artwork, newspaper article, etc.—anything that addresses a pertinent issue or some way that people are trying to address environmental problems. You will have 5 minutes to present to the class why the piece you found is important, how it addressed your topic, what you learned from it and how it could be of use to the rest of the class. This is your chance to be creative!! I would encourage you to not Google the topic title and look at the first web page that pops up. You all come from diverse academic backgrounds and have diverse interests; this is your chance to use your skills and interests to introduce something new to the class. This is your chance to add something to a science course in a way that scientists might not be suited to doing. Remember almost everything can be linked in *some* way to sustainability. These will be graded on 3 criteria: relevance, the quality of information presented, and creativity.

4. Civic Engagement Project: Sustainability in Edgewater (500 points)

Throughout your life you will often need to work with others on group projects regardless of what career path you choose. To alleviate some of the perceived "unfairness," you will be graded on your contribution to the overall effort. I will survey your teammates and evaluate your personal portfolio. Your portfolio must contain all your research notes, data analyses, draft submittals, personal reflection essays and any other materials relevant to *your* contribution to the effort. Please be diligent about maintaining your portfolio throughout the semester. Get a folder now and collect everything as you go. I will allow you to work in your groups one day a week during class as the semester progresses. Submit the materials in a large manila envelope labeled with your name, class section, and date.

5. Components of the Civic Engagement Project

   1. Research Proposal
   2. One group update/progress report
   3. Three personal reflection essays (the last one turned in at the end of the semester)
   4. Final Group Report
   5. Final Group Presentation
   6. Final personal portfolio (consists of your 3 reflection essays, a peer review, description and evidence of your contribution to the project, and a detailed outline of your work on the project including estimates of the time devoted to each task)

Grading scheme:	weight	category
50	pts.	midterm progress report
150	pts.	*your portfolio*
150	pts.	final presentation in class
150	pts.	group final report
50	pts.	instructor observation—general quality of *your* work

Total 550 points

6. Class Participation (50 points)

A large portion of this class will be based on case studies, discussion, debates, and other activities that require a lot of engagement and participation.

Total Points that can be earned for the course:

Exams	200
Paper	200
Information session	50
Civic engagement	550
Participation	100
Total	1,100

If you are having any problems throughout the semester, have any questions, or are just interested in talking about environmental issues and sustainability, please don't hesitate to stop by my office.

	Date	Lecture	Reading (see course website for material)	Assignments
		PART 1—EDGEWATER SUSTAINABILITY PROJECT		
Week 1	Mon 1/12	Intro—background—overview		
	Wed 1/14	Guest Speaker—Allen Stryczek—Edgewater Community Council	Chapter 1 Farr	
	Fri 1/16	Topics graffiti—brainstorming about research topics	Chapter 2 Farr	
Week 2	MLK DAY	NO CLASS		
	Wed 1/21	Group Formation: Scientific Method—Experimental Design		
	Fri 1/23	Guest Speaker—Peter Locke—LEED Neighborhood design		
Week 3	Mon 1/26	Scientific Metho—Experimental Design—Presentation 1	ES (47–50)	Experimental Design assignment—due next day
	Wed 1/28	What is sustainability? classroom graffiti		
	Fri 1/30	Groups Meet—Presentation 2		

PART 2—ECOLOGICAL SYSTEMS				
Week 4	Mon 2/2	Energy flow in ecosystems—Presentation 3	Ehrlich (23–24) (30–38) ES (61–63) Golley (37–43)	PROPOSAL DUE
	Wed 2/4	Nutrient Cycles	ES (68–72)	
	Fri 2/6	Community assemblage and disturbance—Presentation 4	Ehrlich reading (268–279)	
Week 5	Mon 2/9	Ecosystem ecology and the Serengeti	Ehrlich (240–254, 256–264)	
	Wed 2/11	Biodiversity and Conservation	Earth on Edge Discussion Guide	
	Fri 2/13	Groups meet		Paper 1—Draft Due
Week 6	Mon 2/16	Biological populations Presentation 5	ES (126–129, 133–134)	
	Wed 2/18	Human Populations and environmental sustainability—Presentation 6	ES (139–144, 149–153, 155–156)	
	Fri 2/20	Demographic transition and population control		
Week 7	Mon 2/23	EXAM I		
PART 3—HUMAN SYSTEMS & THE ENVIRONMENT				
	Wed 2/25	Social science I—disciplinary perspectives—evolution and human behavior		
	Fri 2/27	Tragedy of the commons game	Hardin (1969)	Paper 1—comments due
Week 8	Mon 3/2	SPRING		
	Wed 3/4	BREAK		
	Fri 3/6	NO CLASSES		
Week 9	Mon 3/9	FILM 11th Hour		
	Wed 3/11	FILM 11th Hour		
	Fri 3/13	11th hour discussion—comparison of human and natural systems—Presentation 7		Paper 1—final draft due

Week 10	Mon 3/16	Climate Change I	IPCC FAQs	
	Wed 3/18	Climate Change II—Presentation 8	IPCC FAQs	
	Fri 3/20	Groups meet—Presentation 9		
Week 11	Mon 3/23	Urbanization/Suburbanization		
	Wed 3/25	Food Systems I—soil & industrial agriculture—Presentation 10	Scientific American article	
	Fri 3/27	Groups Meet—Presentation 11		
Week 12	Mon 3/30	Food Systems II—food miles—Presentation 12	Conservation Magazine paper/Nat Geo article	
	Wed 4/1	Groups meet		
	Fri 4/3	EXAM 2		
Week 13	Mon 4/6	Consumption I—Story of Stuff		
	Wed 4/8	Groups meet		
	Fri 4/10	EASTER		
Week 14	Mon 4/13	NO CLASS		
	Wed 4/15	Consumption II—Ecological footprint and Happiness Index—Presentation 13	Ecological footprint case study readings	
	Fri 4/17	Groups meet		
Week 15	Mon 4/20	Student presentations		
	Wed 4/22	Student presentations		
	Fri 4/24	Class Wrap-up	Personal Portfolio due	

Appendix C

Take-Home Midterm Exam—Sampling Design Problem

Instructions: You will need a 22-inch-x-28-inch poster board, scale (ruler), straight edge, and colored pencils. Use both sides of the poster board. On the front side, create a plan view of your sustainable campus. Your plan will be implemented over 20 years. The plan must be drawn to scale and have a north arrow and legend. You need not be artistic but neatness does count. The plan may be schematic (sometimes called a bubble plan) showing the general locations of facilities and their orientations. You must account for all the normal functions of a college or university, including but not limited to instructional facilities, residential facilities (dorms, dining halls, etc.), transportation (parking, streets, sidewalks, and paths, commuter stations, etc.), administrative offices, maintenance, recreation, open space, and sports facilities. Also show access points to campus and indicate the general relationship between campus and off-campus commercial and service locations.

The back of the board must contain a justification for your design (economic, social, and environmental). Explain how your design integrates function with the natural and built environment. Highlight and justify the key sustainability elements in your design. Remember to consider quality-of-life factors, such as noise and light pollution, in developing your design. This should be accomplished in 3 pages of 12-point font, Times New Roman, double-spaced text, with half-inch margins.

You must do your own unique design, but you may discuss the project with classmates and others to get ideas and feedback on your design. Stop by and discuss your ideas with me if you wish.

Scenario 3:

Enrollment:	1,200 Full Time Equivalents (FTE)
Location:	Rural, Midwestern, 240 ac
Funding:	Private (church affiliated), residential
Type:	Bachelor, liberal arts
Age:	165 yrs
Endowment:	$475,000,000

The college is located at the southern outskirts of a midwestern village (5,400 people). The academic buildings are clustered on a 10-ac academic

campus. Most of the academic buildings, including the library and administration buildings, are small, constructed of local limestone, and predate
WWII. The cozy residence halls (= 60 students/hall) are located around the
periphery of the academic campus, as are the support facilities. The architec-
ture is coherent throughout the campus. The school has a large thriving
Greek system and many students live in on-campus fraternity and sorority
houses owned by the college. Most students live on campus and very limited
opportunities exist for off-campus housing. The campus is hilly and parklike
with many large mature trees and winding lanes and walkways connecting
the buildings. In addition to the academic campus and surrounding residence halls (40 ac), the developed campus is surrounded by a 200-ac nature
preserve. Intramural sports and several club sports are popular on campus.
There are many opportunities for outdoor recreation nearby, including
whitewater canoeing, backpacking, rock climbing, cycling, skiing, and water
sports. The college sponsors movies, concerts, and cultural and recreational
activities on weekends, but many students still leave for weekends. Most students bring cars to campus. At its peak in the 1970s, enrollment reached
1,600 FTE but more recently the college has seen declining enrollments and
difficulty recruiting students. The trustees capped enrollment at 1,250 in
order to maintain the character of the institution.

There is no public transportation. Restaurants, taverns, and limited
shopping (groceries, hardware, auto services, and general merchandise) are
located in the village about 0.5 miles from campus. The village is served by
a major interstate highway and is 1.5 hrs from three large cities. The local
economy is service based, but there is one small manufacturing company in
town. The surrounding area is dominated by dairies, vegetable farms, and
orchards. Unemployment is at the state average and good-paying jobs are
available for blue-collar workers. Town/gown relationships are good and the
college serves as the cultural center for the village and surrounding area. Population in the town has declined slowly from a peak of 5,900 in the 1950s
and the average age of residents has increased.

LEARNING BY DOING ACROSS DISCIPLINES

Activism, Environmental Awareness, and Civic Engagement

Cheryl Swift and sal johnston

O ur interdisciplinary approach to learning and civic engagement is deeply rooted in the history and mission of our institution, Whittier College, which integrates interdisciplinarity into its curriculum through its liberal education program and has long emphasized and valued praxis. Whittier is unusual in that it is a small, private residential liberal arts college and a Hispanic-serving institution in a major metropolitan center (greater Los Angeles). As such, it serves a diverse student body; in 2009, 51% of the students were of color and many were first-generation college students. In an effort to support and improve retention and learning in its diverse, nontraditional student body, the college developed a First-Year Experience program involving each student in overlapping learning communities. All first-year students enroll in a small freshman writing seminar (FWS; see appendix), which is also an advising group for academic mentoring and a living learning residential community. They are also required to coenroll as a group in a course in one of the academic disciplines. This structure, called the *first-year link*, thus generates several learning communities embracing different spaces, classes, and academic disciplines (Cross, 1998). We used these communities and their rich potential for interdisciplinary thinking as the basis for our investigation of the impact of interdisciplinary pedagogies and service experiences on achieving learning outcomes and promoting environmental civic awareness among our students.

We linked an introductory science course, Environmental Science 100 (ENVS 100; see appendix), to an FWS taught by a sociologist because we wanted specifically to explore the efficacy of interdisciplinary approaches in demystifying science for students to improve student engagement with sustainability. There is ample evidence that interdisciplinary learning communities are a successful strategy for connecting students to other students and faculty (Goldey, 2004) and for facilitating learning for individuals from underrepresented groups (Cross, 1998; Farrell, 2002). This is particularly important in the sciences. Students from underrepresented groups often find science unengaging; they feel isolated because content is presented in the abstract rather than as knowledge that affects them personally, and role models or peers are lacking. Learning communities facilitate the formation of peer groups; interdisciplinary communities, where connections can be made between science and other disciplines, make science less abstract and more relevant (Committee on the Guide to Recruiting and Advancing Women Scientists and Engineers in Academia, Committee on Women in Science and Engineering, & National Research Council, 2006; Farrell; Seymour, 1992).

Service, Engagement, and Environmental Awareness

Our goal was not only to enhance students' learning about issues of environmentalism or sustainability in the abstract or in isolation from their own activities but also to encourage their self-aware participation in those issues as engaged agents in their environments rather than as simply students of them. Thus, our course content was fully coordinated with service learning or praxis. Proponents of service learning generally value learning strategies that emphasize self-discovery or guided learning (in contrast to learn first, do later learning) and thus value praxis as a particularly effective pedagogical strategy (Kirschner, Sweller, & Clark, 2006; Rocheleau, 2004). We agree but assert further that it is praxis *in conversation with content* that animates the value of service learning (Cross, 1998; Exley, 2004). In our project, service-learning activities were clearly connected to course materials and to scientific research on human impacts on resource availability. In this regard, our contribution to debates concerning the utility of service learning takes the form of rejecting the question of whether service learning is valuable in the abstract: Its value depends on how you do it (Astin, Vogelgesang, Ikeda, & Yee, 2000; Covitt, 2002; Exley).

Our courses used traditional service-learning models in which students performed service in the community, but we also defined and used a more expansive model of service learning nested between the models outlined by Morton (1993) as participatory democracy (students build capacity as participants in self-governance) and social justice (students gain a personal understanding of their role in the social fabric). We hybridized problem-based learning and service learning to promote activism through an on-campus investigation of food waste and through assignments that asked students to measure and reflect on their resource consumption. These opportunities involved students with a real local community (food waste in the campus dining facility) or with global problems (personal impacts on global resource availability; see Hovland, 2005). Rather than serving the community as in the philanthropist model of service learning (Battistoni, 1997), such course activities used the community as a source of environmental problems needing solutions. They were also essential to two of the most important learning outcomes in ENVS 100: that learners will be able to identify the ways their own actions contribute to altering material cycles and resource availability, and the lifestyle changes they can make to reduce their resource consumption (see appendix).

Achieving these outcomes involved effectively communicating the principle of sustainability, which environmental writers generally treat as an ethical imperative that actions in the present must not result in a reduced quality of life for future generations (Rosenbaum, 1993; United Nations, 1987). Like many other observers of the processes of social and cultural change, we assume that individuals must be able to grasp the relationship among their individual choices, actions, and changes in biogeochemical cycles resulting from consumption habits that lead to ecological degradation. We assert that activism prompted by service learning, or learning by doing, helps students make this connection and thus serves as a resource for ecological consciousness-raising (Schnick & Petrequin, 2007; Waterman & Stanley, 2000).

The Project

Our project involved a total of 31 students enrolled in the fall of 2008 in ENVS 100, 15 of whom were first-year students coenrolled in an FWS titled

The World Without Us (see appendix). The remaining 16 students in ENVS 100 were mainly seniors from several different majors taking the course to satisfy Whittier's general education requirement in science and society (see Table 6.1). These two learning communities—mixed-major seniors and co-enrolled first-year students—were useful groups for comparative assessment of the project's outcomes.

The two courses were coordinated in methods, content, and structure. ENVS 100 focused on acquainting students with the dynamics of biogeo-chemical cycles—water, carbon, and nitrogen—tracking the movement of these critical resources through living and nonliving compartments. It examined the ways human consumption practices have altered theses cycles, either by depleting resource reservoirs or by increasing their size, and in either case causing other environmental problems. Human impacts on the environment were studied in the context of place, history, economics, social structures, religious practice, and so on, from different disciplinary perspectives (see appendix). Similarly, the FWS explored the ways environmental thinking is expressed, examining discursive/intellectual communities and how they shape inquiry and the transmission of information. This meant paying attention to how those in different disciplines write, who their assumed audiences are, and what types of writing might be needed to effectively communicate issues of ecological sustainability to the general public (see appendix).

The two courses interacted across the semester in specific structural ways. ENVS 100 was divided into three units devoted to the study of water,

TABLE 6.1
Breakdown of ENVS 100 Class Participants by Class Standing, Major, and Motivation ($N = 32$)

	Senior (%)	Junior (%)	First Year (%)
Enrollment	42	6	52
Majors represented			
Social science	58		22
Natural science	8	100	33
Humanities	33		44
Reason for taking class			
General education requirement	100		33
elective			33
Major requirement		100	33

carbon, and the basic principles of ecology (see Table 6.2). The FWS employed a similar three-part structure as students were introduced to various forms of writing (see Table 6.3). Its first section, focusing on Alan Weisman's (2008) *The World Without Us*, examined critically our cultural pretension that the world exists for our use as resources whose primary value can be expressed in commodity form, and sought to decenter human beings in the concrete biogeochemical processes that constitute our habitat. Its second part was a focused intensive study of climate change and the challenges of writing clearly about complex scientific phenomena, culminating in a research paper. The final section was more abstract, questioning the meaning and significance of human life and our place in the world through two novels: Jim Crace's (2001) *Being Dead* and Kazuo Ishiguro's (2006) *Never Let Me Go*. Although the three sections of each course did not mirror each other perfectly, we designed them with the idea that they would generate a dynamic

TABLE 6.2
Summary of Syllabus for ENVS 100

Unit	Topics Covered	Evaluation	Service-Learning Components
Introduction			
Water	• Energy flow on Earth • Global climate • Water cycle • Global water availability • Local water availability • Famine, water and climate change • Fire, water, and climate change	• Water footprint project • Pre-/post-survey • Exam questions	• River/beach cleanup • Water use journal • Water footprint calculation
Carbon	• Carbon cycle • Rock cycle (integrating ocean sequestration of carbon) • Carbon and climate change • Carbon and food production • Linking carbon and water cycles: industrial farming • Linking carbon and nitrogen cycles: industrial farming	• Carbon footprint project • Exam questions	• Measuring food waste • Action to reduce carbon footprint • Carbon footprint calculator
Ecology	• Population growth, global sanitation, and water • Endangered species and water in the West • Ecosystems and habitats and water in the West • History of water and Los Angeles	• Ecological footprint project • Exam questions	• Measuring ecological footprints

TABLE 6.3
Summary of Syllabus for FWS

Unit	Topics Covered	Evaluation
Weisman: Describing a World Without Us	• Effective descriptive writing • Field observation • Human impact on the environment • Human location within ecosystems	• Observation paper and the process of draft and revision
Kolbert: The Science of Climate Change	• Analysis and argumentation • Audience and effective communication • Literature review • Research • Carbon cycles • Ecosystems, specifically ocean systems • The politics of environmental change and regulation	• Research-based analysis paper • Peer review • Revision process
Crace and Ishiguro: Science and Love	• Writing compare/contrast papers • Synthesis • Science as a practice • Science as culture • Social change • Relationships • Love	• Compare/contrast paper • Peer review • Revision process • Portfolio and reflection on the development of their writing over the semester

interaction of course content; environmental awareness; and community-oriented, experiential, and service activities. In ENVS 100 such activities included participation in a local river cleanup and the calculation of students' water, carbon, and general ecological footprints; in the FWS they included trash observations in local parks and a major project monitoring wasted food in Whittier College's dining facility.

We drew upon three pedagogical strategies to structure our collaboration. First, we asked students to examine the problem of excessive resource consumption in light of their own service or community-based experiences. We assumed that these activities would provide a personal context to learning about human impacts on the environment, and that they would motivate changes in behavior. We felt strongly that unless one directly confronts resource consumption practices by measuring them, it is too easy to see consumption as someone else's problem; in other words, we assumed that by confronting their own consumption, students would become more aware of resource depletion as a problem at the local and global levels (Hovland, 2005; Schnick & Petrequin, 2007). Based on previous studies assessing service learning, we also felt that conceptually and literally inserting oneself into biogeochemical cycles would make the cycles more meaningful and thus increase learning (Astin et al., 2000; Burns, 2005; Eisenhut & Flannery, 2005).

Second, as we have said, students in our classes were situated in complex layers of learning communities as defined by Cross (1998) so that their "doing" was always relational. They had to evaluate their own actions, but they did so in the context of multiple, layered communities: As members of a living learning community, the coenrolled first-year students constituted a residential community of shared academic experiences; the linked courses themselves were an interdisciplinary learning community mixing introductory and advanced students from a number of academic disciplines; the first-year students' collaboration with upper-division sociology students on food production as one of their service-learning activities produced yet another interdisciplinary learning community; students involved the diverse communities of Whittier, Compton, and Riverside in their service-learning projects; and students engaged the globe—the largest human and nonhuman community—as they calculated their water, carbon, and ecological footprints. All of these relations helped students understand that individual actions aren't actually individual; actions occur in and have an impact on communities.

Third, and finally, we relied on a fundamentally interdisciplinary approach to confront the problem of sustainability. In ENVS 100, biogeochemical cycles were framed in the context of human impacts, and human impacts were framed in the context of the global and local community. For example, the water cycle was presented in three different frameworks: through analysis of human uses of water for products we use every day, particularly agriculture, as food production accounts for the majority of water used in California and worldwide (Postel, 1998); through analysis of population growth, development, water delivery, and sanitation; and through analysis of the history of water projects and their impact on humans and other species in the southwest United States. At the same time, the FWS examined nonscientists (Kolbert, 2007; Weisman, 2008) communicating about the relationship of humans to the environment, used novels as a tool for understanding ecological concerns, and explored the role of feelings as well as analysis in problem solving. The FWS writing assignments complemented the footprint projects of ENVS 100, as learners were asked to first write down observational notes and use those notes as the basis for a research paper, an analytical process analogous to the precise examination of one's own consumption as a basis for addressing the problem of water in California.

Learning Goals

Our short-term goal was to improve learners' understanding and retention of knowledge, but our long-term goal was to challenge learners to reinterpret the ecological significance of their own and others' daily practices. For individuals to evaluate the effects they have on the availability of future resources, they must have knowledge about the physical and societal processes that control that availability. They must also understand personal implications in those processes. Thus, we wanted students to experience—literally to see—the collective impact of seemingly small individual actions by having them participate in the service and footprint activities at our pedagogy's core. An understanding of a sustainable lifestyle requires that learners confront their own actions and evaluate how changes in daily practices contribute to or work against sustainable use of resources.

Student Outcomes

Assessment: Principles and Process

We assumed that the effectiveness of our pedagogical strategies would need to be measured in two ways. The first was the degree to which our strategies prompt a change in behavior or greater awareness of the world; in other words, did our pedagogical strategies promote more sustainable resource use, thus demonstrating increased civic engagement? Certainly the service-learning literature is rich with examples demonstrating increased civic engagement of students after service-learning projects (Eisenhut & Flannery, 2005; Goldey, 2004; Schnick & Petrequin, 2007; but see Exley, 2004). The second measure of effectiveness would be the amount of learning, defined by us as internalization of information, about resource cycles and human impacts that students either identified or reported. Like our pedagogy, our assessment would have to focus on praxis and content, on enhanced engagement and increased knowledge.

Formal assessment data about learning outcomes after linking these courses were acquired from several sources. Students enrolled in ENVS 100 completed an online pre- and postsurvey of the course evaluating how well they understood the water cycle and human impacts on it; they also completed a more general online evaluation of the course at its conclusion. The coenrolled first-year students evaluated their experience of the FWS with a concluding questionnaire; their writing skills acquisition was assessed using portfolios assembled for Whittier College's Writing Program. Finally, and importantly, less formal data concerning learning outcomes emerged frequently in the seminar, whose size and format encouraged its students to reflect with their instructor on the effectiveness of the course's interdisciplinary and service elements.

Service Learning and Learning Outcomes

The impact of service learning and related experiences on learning outcomes was evaluated by the pre–/post–water project survey and the general course evaluation in ENVS 100. When students commented on course activities they found useful in learning the material, more students (77%) reported the footprint projects as being more helpful than the field trips (55%). When students commented on what they liked most about the course in an open-ended question on the general course evaluation, 60% of the students reported liking either the projects involving self-examination of resource consumption or the service-learning opportunities.

Narrative comments such as the following, made in course evaluations and in class meetings, suggest that paying attention to what gets thrown away helped students make their own connections between lifestyle choices and consumption.

> Scraping plates taught me things that books and my professor combined could not teach me. Books and my professor would be able to spill out numbers and percentages of food wasted per person, per day . . . but until you see it, it does not matter, it is not personal.

After reading a chapter in Weisman (2008) detailing how plastics pollute the ocean—particularly how they break down into tiny pieces and become part of the food chain—students were horrified. Several students rummaged through their health and beauty products, discovering hidden plastic pollutants. One student brought a bag of offending products to class; she held it in front of her asking, "What am I supposed to do with it? I can't throw it away because it will escape!" Students who measured waste in the campus dining facility made similar connections and shared the problem of waste as it contributes to consumption in class discussions of what contributes to ecological footprints. This project's participants reported they were amazed at the volume and type of waste they witnessed: untouched hamburgers, sandwiches, pizza slices, salads, and whole hot meals sent back to the dish-washing stations. They consistently said that seeing the amount of waste really opened their eyes. The concrete connection between the course materials on sustainability and the empirical experience of handling hundreds of pounds of wasted food proved to be a potent combination.

In all categories, 66% or more of students reported that they could outline and explain biogeochemical cycles, and more than 75% reported understanding human impacts on water and carbon cycles, and more than 80% reported understanding how their lifestyle changes could affect the carbon cycle (Table 6.4). The pre- and postsurvey of the water unit suggested that self-evaluation and analysis of water use in the context of reading and talking about which human activities consume the most water was helpful. The percentage of students who became aware of the fact that most of the world's

TABLE 6.4
Student Self-Reported Demonstration of Mastery of Course Outcomes

	First-Year Students (%)	Seniors (%)	Class (%)
Understand and outline			
Carbon cycle	67	75	68
Water cycle	56	91	77
Understand human impacts on			
Carbon cycle	78	100	86
Water cycle	78	99	91
Understand why water in developing countries is a problem	78	100	91
Understand how changes in lifestyle affect carbon cycle	88	100	85
Understand relationship between carbon and nitrogen cycles and agriculture	67	92	77
Know their ecological footprint	89	100	95

and California's water is used for food production increased by 30% (see Table 6.5). More students correctly identified the source of Los Angeles's water after the water unit was completed, and students seemed to be somewhat more aware of how landscaping might contribute to water conservation (Table 6.5).

Service Learning and Civic Engagement

Civic engagement often begins with self-awareness, and students demonstrated awareness of their personal use of resources, the college's use of resources, and the global problem of potable water and sanitation. For example, after completion of the water project, a student commented: "My attitude matured. Before I analyzed my water consumption I thought since

TABLE 6.5
Evaluation of Learning Outcomes Related to Water Consumption and Distribution

Learning Categories	*9/22 (%)**	*10/22 (%)***
General awareness of water consumption		
I know what a drought-tolerant plant is	74	100
I know what happens to water when it runs down the street	81	96
I notice when sprinklers are running		
All the time	68	72
Sometimes	29	28
Never	3	0
Most of our water is used for		
Bathing and drinking	16	4
Agriculture	65	96
Industry	19	0
Knowledge of California water delivery system		
Most of the water that Los Angeles uses comes from the		
Colorado River	52	32
San Gabriel River	32	24
Sacramento River	16	44
The California Aqueduct moves water from		
San Francisco to Los Angeles	20	16
Sacramento Delta to Los Angeles	30	52
Sierra Nevada to Los Angeles	50	32

I was only one person I wouldn't make a difference." Another student who participated in the dining facility project said, "Seeing the waste accumulate connected small individual actions to the 'big picture.'"

In an open-ended evaluation question, 45% of students commented that the class had made them more aware of their impact on Earth's resources, and 86% reported they knew what their ecological footprint was and understood their impact on the carbon cycle (see Table 6.4). Nearly 80% reported being willing to make lifestyle changes to reduce water consumption, including taking shorter showers (although fewer than 20% were willing to turn the water off in the shower when not rinsing; see Figure 6.1). Awareness of water use at Whittier College also increased as students reported noticing when sprinklers were running (see Table 6.5) and noticing how individuals used water (see Figure 6.1).

Students said that plate scraping, evaluating water consumption, and the ENVS 100 course in general were eye opening, suggesting increased awareness of resource consumption. In the case of examining campus food waste,

FIGURE 6.1
Postlearning Student-Reported Behavioral Changes

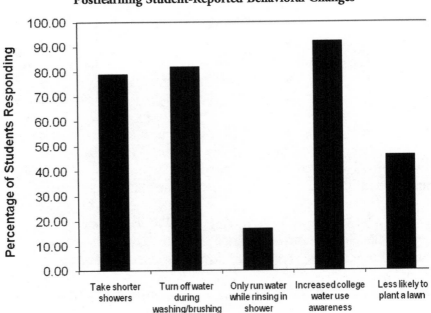

it is worth noting that students demonstrated the value of praxis, linking research and daily individual actions to social change. Whittier is a small institution—about 1,300 students—and an average lunch service handles 800 to 850 individuals. At the beginning of the fall 2008 semester, students measured an average of 10.4 ounces of food waste per person; after the removal of trays, students measured an average of 5.6 ounces of food waste per person. Thus, not only were students able to assess the impact of their actions, they were also able to effect measurable institutional change. This combination of outcomes created a level of engagement best seen in the sense of student agency that the project instilled: Three members of the FWS, for example, were still working on food waste projects with their instructor nearly a year later.

Learning Communities and Learning Outcomes

We compared learning outcomes between the ENVS 100 seniors, who were not coenrolled in the FWA, and first-year students enrolled in both courses. More than 80% of the former, but fewer than 50% of the latter, reported they had completed all the readings for the environmental science class. Despite the fact that the majority of the first-year students did complete the readings and, in fact, complained there was too much reading, their self-reported ability to understand and explain biogeochemical cycles and human impacts ranged from 67% to 78% (see Table 6.4). While other factors (attention to lectures, prior knowledge, self-reporting error) may explain why students who did not do the readings reported mastery of course materials and concepts, it seems likely that being part of a learning community in which the same information was presented in different contexts may have contributed to first-year student learning. In fact, 78% of first-year students reported that the readings they did complete were helpful in learning the material presented in ENVS 100, as compared to 67% of seniors and 73% of the class overall (data not presented); in other words, the contextualizing experience of the FWS may have made the readings in ENVS 100 more accessible, comprehensible, and useful to the first-year students. Anecdotal information from FWS further supports this contention: First-year students often commented in class that they preferred the readings in FWS to the "boring science" readings in ENVS 100. For example, students found Kolbert's (2007) discussion of climate change more accessible and engaging than academic scientific articles. The seminar instructor was able to use this sentiment to explore basic writing issues such as audience, voice, and discursive community. Seminar members discussed why scientific articles are constructed in a particular manner and whom they are written for, and contrasted this with the audience and goals of a text like Kolbert's *Field Notes From a Catastrophe*. The connections between the courses could also be seen in the topics that students in the seminar selected for their research papers. Many of them built on topics discussed in ENVS 100. In this way the linked courses provided students with additional resources and opportunities for learning.

Conclusion

Linking the FWS with ENVS 100 courses appears to have facilitated learning in the first-year student cohort. Clearly the layers of learning communities (the linkage itself, group field trips and activities, collaboration with another course in measuring food waste) were successful in promoting student learning. Placing students in biogeochemical cycles and asking them to self-evaluate or change behavior also seems to have been successful in helping new and more advanced student learning.

The courses' methods succeeded in demystifying science for all students. ENVS 100 can pose problems, since many nonscience majors take the class as a science requirement as seniors, having postponed the requirement for as long as possible. Yet the course also serves majors and potential majors. But an overwhelming majority of seniors found the class useful, expressed greater interest in the topic, and reported increased knowledge of the material, suggesting that learning by doing, whether picking up trash, evaluating personal consumption, or evaluating college consumption, involves learners with the topic and transforms the abstract into the material, as some evaluations of service learning predict (American Association of Colleges and Universities, 2008; Astin et al., 2000). Some sort of service-learning activity may be important in helping nonmajors learn to appreciate and not fear science. This not only has implications for teaching sustainability, but it may be an effective tool for any nonmajors science class (Burns, 2005; Weaver, 1962).

There was no baseline of knowledge needed before learners were able to engage in learning through doing (Kirschner et al., 2006), but service learning did not take place in isolation from reading, writing, reflection, and conversation. In our experience, simply having students go pick up trash, measure waste, or track personal resource use would not have been an effective tool in teaching sustainability. First, all the service-learning options or projects were embedded in course reading materials, discussion, and written reflection. Exley (2004) makes the point that simply picking up trash does not teach civic engagement, but when picking up trash is coupled with self-reflection and reading, it leads to an understanding of the real-world implications of a culture more concerned with convenience than with sustainability. In our project, in fact, service learning was connected to research questions and thus framed as investigation or data acquisition. Second, at least one professor was present and actively participated in all activities. Discourse between learners and instructors during the service learning provides an intellectual context for the activity. Finally, writing was an important component of both courses, and without the analysis and reflection in the papers, the self-evaluation activities and service-learning opportunities would not have been as important to learning.

Our project will continue to evolve in future versions. When we next offer the linked courses, we will allow more time in both courses for reflective discussion of the students' evaluation of their consumption habits and impact on resources (rather than confining this evaluation mainly to written products). We will involve the students more directly in our own ongoing exploratory discussion of the nature of service learning and civic engagement. At a more pragmatic level, we will fine-tune the internal structures of each course and their interface with one another. For example, students in ENVS 100 found the completion of three similar footprint projects repetitive, a complaint that seems reasonable enough, and we will seek to introduce more varied experiential ways students may directly explore their relationship to environmental sustainability.

The entire experience of linking ENVS 100 to the FWS, from casual observations to formal assessment results, suggests that it was an unusually effective teaching instrument whose core structures—interdisciplinarity, learning communities, and experiential and service learning—interacted synergistically to engage the students forcefully and directly as responsible, knowledgeable agents in the problems of sustainability.

References

American Association of Colleges and Universities. (2008). *Our students' best work: A framework for accountability worthy of our mission.* Washington, DC: Author.

Astin, A., Vogelgesang, L. J., Ikeda, E., & Yee, J. (2000). *How service learning affects students*. Los Angeles, CA: Higher Education Research Institute.

Battistoni, R. (1997). Service-learning and democratic citizenship. *Theory Into Practice, 36*(3), 150–156.

Burns, W. D. (2005). What does it mean to be liberally educated in the 21st century and other small questions: A reprint and reflections on a recent meeting. *PKAL, 4*, 1–4. Retrieved from http://www.pkal.org/documents/LiberallyEducatedInThe21stCentury.cfm

Committee on the Guide to Recruiting and Advancing Women Scientists and Engineers in Academia, Committee on Women in Science and Engineering, & National Research Council. (2006). *To recruit and advance: Women students and faculty in science and engineering*. Washington, DC: National Academies Press.

Covitt, B. A. (2002). *Motivating environmentally responsible behavior through service learning*. Retrieved from http://www.nationalserviceresources.org/files/legacy/filemanager/download/451/covittmot.pdf

Crace, J. (2001). *Being dead*. New York, NY: Picador.

Cross, K. P. (1998). Why learning communities? Why now? *About Campus, 3*(3), 4–11.

Eisenhut, A., & Flannery, D. (2005). Fostering an environmental ethic through service learning. *California Journal of Health Promotion, 3*(1), 92–102.

Exley, R. J. (2004). A critique of the civic engagement model. In B. Speck & S. Hoppe (Eds.), *Service learning: History, theory, and issues* (pp. 85–97). Westport, CT: Praeger.

Farrell, E. F. (2002). Engineering a warmer welcome for female students. *The Chronicle of Higher Education, 48*(24), A31.

Goldey, E. (2004). Disciplinary integration: The sciences and humanities in learning communities. In American Association for the Advancement of Science (Ed.), *Intervention and impact: Building excellence in undergraduate science, technology, engineering and mathematics (STEM) education* (pp. 209–216). Washington, DC: Author.

Hovland, K. (2005). Shared futures: Global learning and social responsibility. *Diversity Digest, 8*(3), 1, 16–17.

Ishiguro, K. (2006). *Never let me go*. New York, NY: Vintage.

Kirschner, P. A., Sweller, J., & Clark, R. E. (2006). Why minimal guidance during instruction does not work. *Educational Psychologist, 41*(2), 75–86.

Kolbert, E. (2007). *Field notes from a catastrophe*. New York, NY: Bloomsbury.

Morton, K. (1993). *Models of service and civic education*. Providence, RI: Campus Compact.

Postel, S. (1998). Water for food production: Will there be enough in 2025? *BioScience, 48*(8), 629–637.

Rocheleau, J. (2004). Theoretical roots of service-learning: Progressive education and the development of citizenship. In B. Speck & S. Hoppe (Eds.), *Service learning: History, theory, and issues* (pp. 3–42). Westport, CT: Praeger.

Rosenbaum, M. (1993). Sustainable design strategies. *Solar Today, 7,* 34–36.

Schnick, C., & Petrequin, P. (2007). Deconstructing the American dream through global learning. *Diversity & Democracy, 10*(3), 11.

Seymour, E. (1992). "The problem iceberg" in science, mathematics, and engineering education: Student explanations for high attrition rates. *Journal of College Science Teaching, 24*(4), 230–238.

United Nations. (1987). *Report of the world commission on environment and development: Our common future.* Retrieved from http://www.un-documents.net/wced-ocf.htm

Waterman, M., & Stanley, E. (2000). Lifelines Online: Curriculum and teaching strategies for adult learners. *Journal of College Science Teaching, 29*(5), 306–310.

Weaver, W. (1962). *Science for everybody.* Retrieved from http://www.pkal.org/docu ments/ScienceForEverybody.cfm

Weisman, A. (2008). *The world without us.* New York, NY: Picador.

Appendix: Syllabi for ENVS 100 and INTD 100, The World Without Us

Environmental Science 100, Fall 2008

Course Description

We live in a time of unprecedented challenges to the integrity of the life support system for the planet—the environment. The media warns us of climate change and drought, and our wallets feel the pinch of diminishing resource availability to fuel an economy based on fossil fuel. In this class, we will examine material cycles and the effect humans have had on those cycles with particular attention paid to water and water in the western United States. We all recognize the importance of water to sustain our bodies, but without water we have no food, no clothing, and no economy. Indeed, ready access to water keeps the economy in a dry western United States afloat. But is there going to be enough water to maintain the economy of California into the future given population growth and climate change? Will there be enough water to support ecosystems? What might our future look like with decreasing water supply? This class is focused on addressing these very questions.

Course Objectives

1. Learners will be able to outline carbon, water, and nitrogen cycles.
2. Learners will be able to link human actions to alterations of material cycles.
3. Learners will be able to identify the ways in which their own actions contribute to altering material cycles and resource availability.
4. Learners will be able to identify lifestyle changes they can make to reduce their resource consumption.
5. Learners will become better able to understand and evaluate media reports about environmental issues.

Course Structure and Attendance Policy

The course meets twice weekly for 80-minute lecture periods. In addition, there is a 50-minute colloquium that meets once a week. Learners are expected to attend all class meetings. Excused absences will be granted for athletic competitions or for illness with a note from a doctor. There are no makeup exams given. If you must be granted an excused absence on the day of an exam, those points are deducted from your total points in the class. On the fifth unexcused absence, learners will be penalized one letter grade on the final grade. If a learner is more than 15 minutes late to class, that is considered an unexcused absence.

INTD 100, Freshman Writing Seminar, The World Without Us Fall 2008

Prof. sal johnston   Peer Mentors: Jessica Hencier
115 Platner   Alex Maupin
907-4200 x4225
sjohnston@whittier.edu

While Copernicus successfully challenged the view that the earth was the center of the universe, human beings still often act as if the universe revolved around *us*. We view the planet and its other inhabitants as mere resources for our own desires. This writing seminar will evict humans from center stage and ponder *a world without us*. We will explore the question of what the world would be like without us—and the configuration of that *us* will vary— through a variety of different types of writing: scientific analyses, speculative journalism, fiction, and science fiction. What connects these different types of writing is the writer's ability to imagine alternatives to the world as we currently know it, alternatives to the way human beings presently live in their world, alternatives to the way that human beings presently relate to the natural world around them, and alternatives to human beings' presumed centrality to the world.

This writing course is linked with Introduction to Environmental Science (ENVS 101).

FROM WOLVES
TO WIND POWER

Fostering Student Understanding of Science, Stewardship, and Civic Engagement

Karen Whitehead and Mary Kay Helling

B uilding on their experiences of a weeklong institute sponsored by the American Association of State Colleges and Universities (AASCU) and the American Democracy Project (ADP) at Yellowstone National Park (YNP), faculty at the six public universities in South Dakota collaborated in teaching a common course for students from multiple disciplines from all six universities. This chapter describes the experiences of faculty, administrators, and student participants at the YNP institute; the course development process and content, service-learning, and civic engagement activities; the importance of partnerships; and the lessons we learned and future directions to take to improve the experience.

The YNP Experience

Activities in YNP were organized and delivered by the Yellowstone Association, an organization dedicated to fostering the public's understanding, appreciation, and enjoyment of YNP.[1] The association in partnership with the National Park Service offers educational products and services. The primary on-site instructor was a wildlife biologist with more than 10 years of teaching experience at the K–12 and college levels. The week consisted of the following components:

1. Lectures by and discussions with park officials and other experts on a wide variety of issues facing the park.
2. Guided discussions, wildlife viewing, and extensive touring of the park to observe firsthand practices (e.g., wolf reintroduction) that had become controversial issues among various park stakeholders.
3. Interviews with community members and other external stakeholders to learn about issues from disparate viewpoints. Interviews were set up to reflect opposing interests on specific policy issues such as bison management and the use of snowmobiles in YNP.
4. Small-group discussions on the development of curricular opportunities at the home campuses. In our case, the South Dakota contingent discussed the development of a statewide course or curriculum.
5. Informal discussions among participants and workshop staff.

The content of the workshop focused on a number of issues under active policy debate and public scrutiny associated with the park and the surrounding area. Specific topics of discussion included brucellosis (a bacterial disease) in bison, boating on Yellowstone Lake, snowmobiles and their winter use, grizzly bear management, and the reintroduction and management of wolves. Because the park is part of the Greater Yellowstone Ecosystem (GYE), and because there is no way to keep the park and its inhabitants isolated from the surrounding area, all the issues involved management of a resource in the park and the conflict arising when that resource moved beyond the bounds of the park.

During the course of exploring these issues, it became quite apparent that no topic could be understood in isolation. Every topic was a complex issue with connections to a large number of other areas, and each was the focus of numerous policy matters. For example, the decade-long wolf reintroduction and management project has been highly successful, with wolf populations exceeding projections. Interactions between wolves and other fauna in the park, conflicts with wolves in the surrounding region (two wolves were killed legally by a rancher outside the park while we were at the workshop), and possible indirect effects of wolves on vegetation in the park were discussed. Another example is grizzly bear management. The grizzly has thrived in YNP and is scheduled to be delisted as an endangered species. Major challenges face the grizzly, as its food supply of trout and pine nuts decreases because of stresses on those foods as well. Grizzlies also do not recognize the park boundaries and can venture beyond its borders, potentially threatening the safety of humans and domestic animals.

Course Development Process and Considerations

In preliminary discussions during the weeklong institute in the park, the South Dakota team developed the idea of offering a specific course for students who attend one of the state's public institutions of higher education. A collaborative interdisciplinary approach was used to develop the course titled Interdisciplinary Studies (IDL) 399, Issues of the Yellowstone Ecosystem. Individuals from the disciplines of biology, mathematics, human development, sociology, history, wildlife and fisheries, chemistry, and economics attended the summer 2006 AASCU institute in YNP. Every member of the South Dakota team was an enthusiastic participant and brought a unique perspective to the project, along with a commitment to fostering civic engagement.

The course development planning team was also committed to incorporating experiential, service-focused learning into the course, recognizing the contextual nature of knowledge (Liu, 1995) and the value of learning from experience (Giles & Eyler, 1994). Learning in context provides direct experience with what is being studied and promotes learning through group processes, which help foster communal problem solving. Content and pedagogical decisions were based on an inquiry-oriented perspective that employs the process of becoming informed student citizens (Giles & Eyler). Through such a process, students are required to study a problem in depth and propose solutions focused on the public good, while balancing multiple stakeholder views and actions.

The team met throughout the 2006–2007 school year to finalize the course and make all the necessary arrangements for a field trip and distance education needs. The course development team believed it was critical to include a field trip to YNP to provide an intensive, inquiry-based experience to kick off the course in August 2007.

Because of long distances between the universities, using the Dakota Digital Network (DDN), a statewide network that offers real-time audio and visual connectivity, reduced the need to travel to all group activities.

Information about the course was distributed in spring 2007 to faculty and students to allow time for student recruitment and registration. Posters about the course were displayed, and students were actively recruited via one-on-one discussions with involved faculty.

Overview of Course Structure

The course was piloted during the 2007 fall semester, beginning with a one-week session in YNP, which was similar to the summer 2006 AASCU institute for faculty members and administrators. All IDL 399 students and instructors participated in the YNP field trip, which lasted one week and was followed by a semester of small-group work. The students from all South Dakota higher education institutions who were involved had engaged in independent study and statewide interactions about a national resource issue of importance in South Dakota. The culminating event was a presentation on a topic selected by the students for policy makers in the state capital. The course had no specific prerequisites or corequisites. Enrollment was specifically limited to 24 students in the South Dakota System of Higher Education to enhance the small-group learning experience and to control costs. Thus, two to four students from each of the state universities participated. The course was taught by instructors who attended the YNP field trip and were part of the course development process.

Student Learning Outcomes

The goal of this course was to involve students in the examination of specific policy issues and to expose them to the process of civic engagement through advocacy for public policy recommendations. We hoped the course would allow students to demonstrate a working knowledge of key social, environmental, and political issues associated with the management of wildlife in the GYE; recognize and articulate through various modes of communication the complexity and interrelationships of political, social, and environmental controversies of the GYE; apply knowledge and skills from the GYE field trip to YNP to the management of similar natural resource issues in South Dakota; and experience civic engagement by contributing to the development of policy recommendations related to natural resources in South Dakota.

Course Requirements

Prior to arriving in YNP, students and instructors were encouraged to read the booklet *Yellowstone Resources & Issues* (YNP, 2007), which provided a good overview of YNP's history, geology, vegetation, the effects of fire, wildlife, cultural resources, park issues, and major areas of the park.

While at YNP, students were required to keep journals describing knowledge gained and their reactions to the types of advocacy they encountered. In addition to daily large group lecture and discussions, half the group spent one afternoon with ranchers while the other half visited with a businessman in West Yellowstone and an advocacy group called the Buffalo Field Campaign. The two student groups reported to each other the following day, generating considerable discussion on the relative impacts of appearance, passion, and knowledge of the efficacy of advocacy.

Yellowstone Association Institute instructors provided the students with multiple research papers on the three focus areas: reintroduction of wolves, bison and brucellosis, and snowmobiles and winter use. Students left Yellowstone with instructions to choose one of the topics, to study the research papers provided, to locate other research, and to write a paper on the topic. The final papers were to address the history of the issue, the various positions regarding the issue, the current status of resolution of the issue, and the students' own recommendations for a resolution. These papers constituted a warm-up exercise and a template for the work to be undertaken during the fall semester, namely, identifying a South Dakota issue the class wanted to dig deeply into and developing a recommendation for it.

Returning to South Dakota

Following the field trip to YNP, guest speakers, who were scheduled each Friday during September, were the South Dakota secretary of Game, Fish, & Parks; the South Dakota coordinator of Partners for Fish and Wildlife, a representative from U.S. Fish and Wildlife Service; a professor from a western regional university who gave the American Indian perspective; and a South Dakota state legislative representative. The first three speakers presented their views on what they believed were important and controversial issues in South Dakota. The final speaker described the political process in South Dakota and how public policy is developed and influenced.

During the last weekend in September, all class members and instructors met in a central location to brainstorm issues important to South Dakota and study them in depth with the goal of developing a policy recommendation, form working groups to identify how to approach the study of the identified issues (stakeholder groups, content specialists, etc.), and develop a work plan to accomplish assigned tasks.

After identifying several dozen potential topics, students cast votes for their top three choices and reduced the number of topics to five. In order of initial preference, the topics were loss of native prairies (sod busting), uranium mining and land restoration, Missouri River water usage, wind power, and snowmobile/ATV use in the Black Hills. Interestingly, none of the wildlife issues, such as mountain lions and prairie dogs, made it through the first cut. The students argued that significant progress had been made on these issues and they preferred to tackle an emerging problem. Also of note was how students cast their votes. They were told they could cast votes for three different topics, or if they felt passionately about a specific topic, they could cast all three of their votes for a single topic. One group of four students formed a coalition and cast 10 of their 12 votes for the uranium-mining topic, which none of the remaining 16 students voted for, thus providing an object lesson in how small organized groups can have a disproportionate influence. Ultimately, the students decided they would study wind power.

Following a broad-ranging exploration of the issues regarding wind power, during which one of the students stood up and took charge of the discussion (to the delight of the instructors), students decided to assign one of the components of the topic to each university. The components were the impact on wildlife and ecology; economics and private enterprise (providers, jobs, etc.); economics and government (tax, incentives, etc.); siting (geography, aesthetics, sound pollution, procedures); the power grid and infrastructure (conversion, transmission, storage, safety); and building costs, materials, operations, and repair (what types of materials are used and their effects on the environment).

In October students worked independently to gather information on these aspects of wind power, interviewed public officials, and contacted people in the industry. At the beginning of November the group reconvened in central South Dakota to present its findings. A significant outcome of this meeting was the realization by the students that each group had uncovered fundamental, difficult questions that would need to be answered before any informed recommendation could be developed. Examples of such questions were, What is the actual carbon footprint of a wind farm? and How would South Dakotans benefit when the massive investment required would mean that wind farm development would be financed and controlled by outside investors?

The choice of the topic presented a challenge to the instructors who had arranged for the class to make its final policy recommendation to the South Dakota Department of Game, Fish, & Parks, anticipating that the class would select a topic directly related to wildlife management. It was ultimately decided that meeting with members of the South Dakota Public Utilities Commission (PUC) for an informed discussion about these hard questions would be more appropriate than meeting with Game, Fish, & Parks staff, and that writing a letter to state representatives in the legislature would replace the development of a group recommendation. The student teams spent November developing their questions for the PUC, sharing their thoughts with each other via a WebCT-based chat room. Simultaneously, they wrote letters to legislators explaining what they had learned and made their recommendations regarding the wind power issue. In most cases, the recommendations centered around the need to proceed with caution and to obtain answers to open questions before the state committed to a particular course of action.

Assessment of Student Learning

Continuous assessment of student learning outcomes was accomplished through small- and large-group discussions, research assignments, oral presentations, and writing assignments. An end-of-course survey was also taken to establish baseline data with a focus on civic engagement. Plans are to track the student cohort over a four-year period or longer.

Service-Learning and Civic Engagement Activities

The course was designed to specifically include the following service-learning and civic engagement activities:

- *Public advocacy.* Faculty and students served as advocates for the sustainable and ethical use of public lands and natural resources.
- *Problem-based learning.* Specific problems in the areas of natural resources/public lands management faced by the GYE and the state of

South Dakota were addressed. The problems of the GYE included wildlife management and use of public lands for economic development and recreational activities (boating and snowmobiling, use of motorcycles). The focus in South Dakota on wind energy generation encompassed issues of renewable energy, land use, and protection of wildlife habitat and flyways.

- *Participant observation.* Students and faculty were immersed in the natural resource issues of the GYE. Participants observed wildlife and human behavior and confronted conflicting perspectives in public policy issues. One of the highlights of the Yellowstone field trip was observing the interplay between a pack of wolves with cubs and a grizzly bear with her cubs. The interaction ended in a stalemate. In discussions with one rancher, all students were moved by the sincerity of the individual and the obvious importance her cattle has to her. In contrast, there were a variety of reactions to the bison advocacy group: Some were impressed by the passion of the individuals they met and their willingness to sacrifice physical comfort for their cause, while others reacted negatively to the primitive living conditions—small space for numerous people, little heat, and a remote location with limited access to supplies.

- *Policy analysis.* Class participants interviewed representatives on multiple sides of identified issues while they were in YNP and in South Dakota. Snowmobile policy in YNP, in the process of being reviewed and revised, was examined from the perspective of the National Park Service and that of the businesses in West Yellowstone that made their living from snowmobile recreation. The choice of wind power as a topic lent itself well to this component, since students had to familiarize themselves with state and federal policies on power generation and transmission.

- *Self-directed learning.* Much of the course was deliberately designed to be student driven. The choice of a topic for in-depth study and organization of the group into study teams was left to the students themselves to determine.

Importance of Partnerships

Numerous partnerships were integral to the success of this course. The collaboration among the six public institutions of higher education in South

Dakota was refreshing and helped make this experience possible. The interdisciplinary approach was critical for broad appeal to students and faculty, as well as the need to consider policy issues from multiple perspectives. The collaborative approach to the course illustrated the realities of how change happens in communities. Additional partners included the Department of Game, Fish, & Parks; Partners for Fish and Wildlife; U.S. Fish and Wildlife Services; a South Dakota legislator; and a faculty member from Boise State University representing an American Indian perspective. Individuals from these agencies and organizations shared their time and expertise on selected topics. The Yellowstone Association Institute was also a critical partner, providing on-site teaching and organization for the YNP component of the course.

Lessons Learned

Numerous lessons resulted from the field experiences in YNP as well as the course development process and delivery.

Lesson one. Given a framework for investigating an issue, students can be effective in organizing themselves in a meaningful learning experience. The fact that a broad range of disciplinary interests was represented appeared to stimulate the exchange of ideas and build respect for the knowledge each team brought to the table. Faculty members were available to provide guidance, but students rose to the challenge when told it was their job to organize the work to be done as a class and in their individual teams.

Lesson two. In organizing a student-directed course, instructors need to beware of assuming they can predict the direction the course will take.

Lesson three. Careful delineation of the parameters for topic selection is needed to prevent students from tackling too broad a topic. We decided from the start that the choice of topic should be a student-driven effort. Thus, after the students brainstormed potential South Dakota topics to investigate and produce a related policy statement for, it became clear that the chosen topic of wind power was so complex and had so many unanswered questions that it was unrealistic to expect the class to develop a policy recommendation in the time remaining in the semester. Next time, we will at least discuss with the students the need to select a more specific topic or develop a list of potential topics in advance.

Lesson four. Much value is added to the educational experience when faculty, students, and administrators work across institutions and disciplines. The planning team approached the process of course development and delivery from a collaborative, community-building perspective. This orientation provided a positive and safe environment for sharing varying perspectives, different approaches to problem solving, and consensus building.

Lesson five. Complex issues are best addressed through an experientially based approach as opposed to a single-focus, traditional in-class approach. The focus of this class was on natural resource issues. To understand the multiple perspectives, one needs to consider the science as well as the social and political issues on a variety of levels (individual, family, community, regional, and national). The experientially based approach also fosters a greater sense of communal rather than individual learning. Students gain an appreciation for problem solving and engagement that value multiple (and many times varying) perspectives based on firsthand, direct experiences.

Future Directions

The IDL 399 course was offered again in summer and fall 2008. The team is attempting to identify possible funding sources to help offset the costs of the field trip to YNP and in-state travel expenses. Long-term goals include offering the course each summer and fall, increasing the number of field venues, and increasing the number of students enrolled. Another long-term goal is to investigate the possibility of developing a systemwide undergraduate certificate or minor focused on sustainability and civic engagement.

Some modifications to the course structure are under discussion. The field trip in YNP was critical in modeling the exploration of controversial issues and in forming a cohesive group with students whose institutions are 400 miles apart. In the next iteration of the course, more deliberate attention will be paid early in the week to the topic of civic engagement and how individuals can have an impact on policy development. The goal of having the class develop a policy recommendation was an ambitious one and is being reconsidered. If retained, more constraints will need to be placed to avoid choosing a topic that is too broad. Nonetheless, giving students free rein to influence the direction of the course in itself provided a valuable learning experience.

Given the importance of student learning and long-term change and impact, another long-term goal is to follow a subset of students after the completion of the course, and possibly postgraduation, to assess the degree of their continued interest and activity in natural resource issues and civic engagement.

Conclusion

A field-based, student-directed, multidisciplinary, and multi-institutional course can provide a direct experience in civic engagement. Faculty members and students alike learned valuable lessons about developing an advocacy position, using the strengths of individual team members, and working together over significant distances. All involved agreed that the course should be continued and expanded. An open question is the degree to which such an experience will increase civic engagement postgraduation, and further study is needed.

Note

1. The Yellowstone Association serves as the primary partner in education at Yellowstone National Park. For information, go to http://www.yellowstoneassociation.org.

References

Giles, D. E., & Eyler, J. (1994). Theoretical roots of service-learning in John Dewey: Toward a theory of service-learning. *Michigan Journal of Community Service Learning*, *1*, 77–85.

Liu, G. (1995). Knowledge, foundation, and discourse: Philosophical support for service-learning. *Michigan Journal of Community Service Learning*, 2, 5–18.

Yellowstone National Park. (2007). *Yellowstone resources & issues*. Mammoth Hot Springs, WY: Division of Interpretation.

MULTICULTURALISM AND SUSTAINABILITY EDUCATION

Engagement With Urban School Communities via Food and Learning Gardens

Dilafruz R. Williams

T he goal of this chapter is to tell the story of how I have connected my courses over almost a decade with themes of sustainability to involve students at Portland State University (PSU) with poor people and people of color in our communities most affected by ecological injustices. Often, urban areas are segregated by neighborhoods along racial and income levels, a trend that is de facto reflected in neighborhood public schools. Portland, Oregon, is no exception. Hence, for me, public schools and their communities in Portland have provided a critical forum to build partnerships for my students at PSU to engage in comprehending and addressing issues of multiculturalism and sustainability education.

Since food and health are emerging as significant issues, the establishment of and participation in school gardens, also known as learning gardens, at pre-K–12 school sites has enabled PSU students in my classes, most of whom are White, to not only develop skills that are highly prized but also to interact with poor and non-White children and youth in the Portland Public School (PPS) district. Involvement with these communities has encouraged a fair number of students to pursue ongoing community relationships beyond the particular courses. Plus, their involvement often results in centering their master's theses or culminating research projects on the sustainability themes they address in class. The convergence of food security, food access, hunger, and learning gardens enables students to ask questions about how sustainability affects disenfranchised communities in their own backyard— the city—where the poor and non-Whites, including Native Americans and refugee and immigrant families, have hitherto been invisible to them. I present samples of reflections of three graduate students who specifically focused their master's culminating projects to capture their research related to this issue.

PSU: Context

I have been using community-based learning as a form of pedagogy in my classes at PSU for almost two decades. In 1990 PSU president Judith Ramaley launched a comprehensive initiative to transform the institution by designing and aligning the curriculum to connect academia with the community in meaningful ways. With our newly defined urban mission, we designed courses to make engagement integral to learning. Since PSU is located in the heart of downtown, it is rather convenient to put into practice our motto, Let Knowledge Serve the City. We take seriously our charge to be of and in the community. With a student population of about 28,000, most of whom are commuters, the university is frequently recognized for its integration of student learning with service to the community through close ties with the metropolitan region.

At PSU we use the term *community-based learning* to broadly include service learning, practica, and also internships. As Williams and Bernstine (2002) explained,

> Through service-learning, [PSU] students are educated in an academic discipline while preparing to be contributing citizens. By becoming involved in community activities students provide benefits to others while learning about teamwork, civic responsibility, and the application of intellectual skills to community issues. Service-learning courses include in-depth theoretical and practical applications that allow for maximum integration of service and classroom work. (p. 259)

My graduate-level courses, thus, are part of a larger context of civic engagement at PSU that includes hundreds of undergraduate and graduate courses and senior capstones in practically all the disciplines.

Conceptual Framework for Courses With Sustainability Themes

In 2002 my colleague Pramod Parajuli and I founded a program—Leadership in Ecology, Culture, and Learning—and with a multiyear grant awarded by the Environmental Protection Agency, we started learning gardens (previously also known as FEED: Food-Based Ecological Education Design) at several schools in PPS in partnership with teachers, parents, administrators, PSU students, and community organizations using food as a unifying concept to integrate gardens in the school curriculum.

Parajuli served as my colleague at PSU until 2008, and together we designed several courses with themes of sustainability, such as Leadership for Sustainability, Global Political Ecology, Ecological and Cultural Foundations of Learning, Sustainability Education, Global Indigenous Cultures, Learning Gardens and Sustainability Education, Urban Education Farm and School Policy, and Nonviolence and Gandhi's Philosophy of Education for Sustainability, among others. The following concepts (Parajuli, 2006) guided our courses:

1. Intra- and intergenerational partnership: social class, gender, caste, race, ethnicity, and other human-created constructs, institutions, and practices of social inequities
2. Interspecies partnership: ecological, philosophical, and ethical aspects of humans' relationship with the more-than-human world, namely, the rest of the species
3. Intercultural partnership: an examination of the field of biological, cultural, and linguistic diversity; diversity of knowledge systems; and ways of knowing, teaching, and learning
4. Intereconomic partnership: social and economic institutions, arrangements of exchanges and surplus, fair trade and free trade between global north and global south, rural and urban relationships, agriculture and industry, producers and consumers

Across the courses, in covering issues of sustainability in the global context, I engage students in critical thinking about several themes: the triple-bottom-line discourse often connected with sustainability, the cultural underpinning of the discourse on development and poverty that primarily the north has shaped for the south, and the ways pursuit of ecojustice requires a revitalization of the commons that traditional societies took for granted. Moreover, the courses examine whether a sustainable society can also be socially just and bioculturally diverse. To address this, students critically examine what social class and ethnic/racial relations have to do with sustainability. The location of people within particular cultures of habitat and global structures of power informs the pedagogy and content of the courses.

What is important to me is to involve students in an understanding in our own communities of how culture and nature might thrive together and how a monoculture, for human societies and for biological species, causes problems. The students recognize that the discourse on sustainability requires a deep critique of Western paradigms. But we cannot stop with critique. While we look for subtle and overt ways that disenfranchise many of the communities in our own Portland backyard, we address ways to regenerate the communities through serving them. In several courses, themes of global ecological justice movements regarding soil, agriculture, biomass, food, water, and health are integrated. In engaging with the community, students develop a sense of agency to take responsibility for the earth. Food and the learning gardens have provided a means for mutual engagement.

The common thread that runs through my courses is a requirement of 30 hours each quarter (an 11-week period) for a student to serve in the community, which covers the mandatory community-based component of the course. The connections students must make with the academic content of the materials I cover in class are important, even as they serve in the community. Reflections are a significant part of the learning experience. I have used several sites and organizations over the years as partners for service learning in the area of sustainability, such as PPS, Oregon Tilth, Bureau of Environmental Services/City of Portland, Metro, Watershed Councils, Multnomah Food Policy Council, Native American Youth Association, African American Health Coalition, Immigrant and Refugee Community Organization, Slavic Coalition, Schools Uniting Neighborhoods, and the learning gardens, among others.

Food, Schools, and Learning Gardens

Food and learning gardens, seen as an important connection to embodied learning, have enabled PSU students to think not only about their own health but also that of the planet, resulting in a shift in the way they learn.

The learning gardens project is guided by several urgent issues: The percentage of hungry children in the state of Oregon and the nation is increasing, obesity and diabetes among children are on the rise in alarming numbers, there is a growing gap between the academic performance of White and ethnic minority students, and urban school students are particularly vulnerable given their loss of connection with and the less than desirable likelihood of exposure to nature (Williams & Brown, in press).

The courses I teach at PSU are integrated with the service-learning component for university students who work hand in hand with grades pre-K–8 in PPS. Interestingly, the learning gardens nurture students' love for nature, increase their understanding of the production and uses of edible plants, educate them about nutrition and the benefits of healthy eating habits, allow them to explore the cultural significance of foods including those from their native cultures, and demonstrate the healing properties of nature and gardening. The goals of the learning gardens are to

1. Promote multicultural learning representing multiple agricultural and culinary traditions of the parent community.
2. Foster multidisciplinary learning, connecting math, science, social sciences, languages, arts, and aesthetics.
3. Cultivate intergenerational learning between young adults and their parents, grandparents, and other relatives.
4. Nurture multisensory learning by involving not only our head but also our hands, heart, skin, tongue, intestines, and palate.
5. Promote a local food economy by valuing, respecting, and patronizing local farmers and suppliers who offer local, seasonal, and sustainably grown produce.

Using food systems as a unifying concept, PSU and PPS students learn how to grow, harvest, and prepare nutritious seasonal produce. Experiences in the kitchen and garden foster a better understanding of how the natural world sustains us and promote the environmental and social well-being of our school community. In the learning gardens program, curricular experiences between classroom learning and what is learned in the gardens are integrated. Seasonal learning is emphasized. As children and youth learn to grow food, build gardens, and see how the health of individuals, the land, and their communities are intertwined, they learn to rebuild healthy relationships with each component: Sustainability takes on tangible, pragmatic, and embodied meaning.

Urban Public Schools Context: Lane Middle School and Learning Gardens Laboratory

In addition to 10 learning gardens at school sites, including Title 1 high-poverty schools, PSU has also been involved in the initiation and design of the Learning Gardens Laboratory (LGLab) used by Lane Middle School as the key partner at this site. It is located opposite the school on a 10-acre property that includes several greenhouses and a community garden. Students and their teachers participate directly in the gardens for a one-hour block every week or for a two-hour block every other week. PSU students offer an integrated seasonally based curriculum coordinated with the topics taught in different subjects, especially science that incorporates Oregon state education standards. Focusing on principles of ecological systems, permaculture, multicultural contexts, and active learning, the curriculum is grounded in a sense of place and of stewardship for the land. The soil-to-supper curriculum focuses on gardening, eating, and community in each topic and each lesson, and progresses developmentally, for example, from water to watersheds and from food to foodsheds, as students move from lower to higher grades (Parajuli, 2006). Participation in LGLab not only engages low-income and culturally diverse youth in the challenging academic activities, but also provides a connection between their lives at school and at home.

Lane Middle School, with about 500 students ages 11 to 14 years in grades six to eight, is one of the most culturally and linguistically diverse schools in PPS: In 2005–2006, 54% of its students were minorities (12% African American, 25% Hispanic, 12% Asian, and 5% Native American), 41% spoke English as a second language, and 19 languages were spoken in their respective homes. Socioeconomically, students came from predominantly poor families with 75% of students qualifying for free or reduced-cost lunches. The school is located in Brentwood-Darlington, an outer-southeast Portland neighborhood, with the unfortunate nickname of "Felony Flats." The crime rate index (in all areas except murder) is 1.5 to 3 times higher than the national average. The community has historically lacked vitality, and the lives of students often include family instability because of underemployment, new immigrant or refugee status, violence, drugs, and incarceration. The school had a reputation for students' low academic achievement and high rates of truancy and dropout, and for their involvement in delinquency, drugs, and gangs. The school, which was under sanctions and threat of reconstitution/closure for not making adequate yearly progress under the No Child Left Behind Act of 2001, has turned around in the last two years, and the school community attributes the PSU-PPS partnership at the learning gardens as significant to this accomplishment.

The families at Lane, being culturally diverse, are drawn to food and gardens as a mechanism to be involved in the school community. Furthermore, the PSU-PPS partnership has resulted in a resident farmer program that involves Slavic, Somalian, Asian, and Hispanic parents in creating multicultural gardens and teaching the community about their traditions of growing and cooking food. LGLab provides PSU students in dozens of senior-level capstones and in undergraduate and graduate classes with opportunities for service learning under the broad umbrella of sustainability and, specifically, concerning food issues as they affect low-income and diverse communities.

Service-Learning Partnership Outcomes

PSU and PPS students work in partnership with community organizations at the learning gardens and feel they make a difference when there are tangible outcomes, such as

- establishing or supporting learning gardens at school sites, connecting with school personnel and nonprofit organizations, neighborhood associations, parent-teacher association, and government agencies;
- designing innovative learning gardens materials and multicultural curricula in the form of seasonal lesson plans, teacher guidebooks, and resource handbooks for pre-K–12 schools or community-based organizations on themes such as soil, food, crops, herbs, nutrition, health, farm economies, and so forth;
- conducting food waste audits and working with children and youth to address ways to cut down on waste;
- critically examining and addressing school food policy and food behavior during recess;

- serving on committees to develop a school wellness policy and food policy for the city and county;
- distributing food grown in the school gardens to the Oregon Food Bank and understanding issues related to food security and poverty;
- establishing multicultural family learning gardens to include immigrant families' knowledge and understanding of growing food; and
- supporting farm-to-school initiatives and designing logistics and protocols for low-income populations to be able to use food stamps at the farmers markets by starting and supporting markets in low-income neighborhoods.

Reflections

Course assignments include reflective and critical inquiry papers in which students are expected to integrate their service-learning experiences with the content of the texts they read in class. Reflections take various forms, as explained by Collier and Williams (2005), including such forms as journals, portfolios, integrative papers, discussions, and presentations in class. In their journals students are prompted to record their observations and analyze not only the activities but also their own thoughts, emotional reactions, and responses. This is not a one-time activity. The journals can be either free-form or structured with the overall direction for students to address specific issues and questions connected to course content. Students are also encouraged to develop a portfolio, which is a collection of exhibits related to the courses. This helps students when they are ready to undertake a master's thesis or project. I also encourage students to use formal and informal discussions with classmates, teammates, and community members to introduce them to different perspectives and challenge them to think critically. Furthermore, reflections support students during in-class presentations where they are required to discuss some aspect of their service-learning experience in terms of the concepts and theories covered in the course.

Although given other options for service sites, the majority of my students are drawn to examining issues of food, health, and obesity as they affect low-income and minority communities and schoolchildren via the learning gardens partnership. Using various types of reflection activities, I have encouraged students to think critically about representation and voice and culturally sensitive approaches to working with PPS students and their families. More than half my students continue to work at the gardens for service-learning assignments in other courses they take in the program. They often do their master's research or theses on food- and garden-based education, as demonstrated by the following project titles: *Tongue-tied No More: Garden-Based Education and Social Justice* (Anderson, 2009); *Green Paths to Health and Healing* (Bluehorse Skelton, 2008); *Sowing Seeds of Social Change Through Multicultural Gardens: A Guide to Practices and Resources in Portland, Oregon* (Nicola, 2007); *Building Community Food Systems Through Assessment, Projects, and Policy: A Study of the Lents Example in Southeast Portland, Oregon* (Fehrman, 2008); and *Youth Voices of Bounty and Opportunity: High School Students' Experiences With Food and Community* (Gilbert, 2010).

Sample Student Reflections: Food, Learning Gardens, and Multiculturalism

I present samples of three students' reflective writing as part of their master's culminating project.[1] Jennifer Anderson is now a teacher at the Southwest Charter School in Portland, where she is bringing the knowledge gained through her work with the learning gardens to her own classroom and school. Judy Bluehorse Skelton is an adjunct instructor at PSU teaching several senior capstones with themes of learning gardens. Jill Nicola, who had never considered teaching prior to her work in school gardens with multicultural communities, has now graduated in teacher education with an interest in teaching adolescents after she saw the power of their involvement in the learning gardens. Several other graduates are working in Portland and the state of Oregon promoting local food, school and community gardens, and food security policies. Through their organizations, they support a new generation of PSU students involved in service learning with multicultural communities.

Tongue-tied No More: Garden-Based Education and Social Justice
Jennifer Anderson (2009)
   In my graduate classes I was discussing White privilege, culturally responsive instruction, ESL teaching strategies, cross-cultural communication and sustainability education. As I acquired more knowledge about

these important concepts, my purpose at the Learning Gardens began to change. I was bothered by the fact that most of our staff and volunteers were White. Were we connecting to these culturally and linguistically diverse students? I wondered how, as a White woman, I could positively influence their experiences at the Learning Gardens. How could I teach children from Russia, Ukraine, Vietnam, Mexico, Honduras, Somalia, and Laos the joys and wonders of the garden?

From many of my graduate classes and from my current research on diversity pedagogy and multicultural education, I gained a deeper awareness of how my White culture influenced what happens in the garden. I realized the importance of understanding my own self-identity, which meant recognizing my race and ethnicity and the advantages and disadvantages associated with it. In order to be an effective, culturally competent educator, I needed to have a solid grasp on who I was, where I came from and how my culture affected my personal beliefs and practices. . . . Additionally, I acknowledged that the discovery and defining of my racial identity was a difficult, life-long process, and one that I must continually revisit and reevaluate through critical reflection.

I realized that every person brings to the table a unique set of values and beliefs that affects how she interprets and makes sense of the world. I acknowledged the connection between culture and learning and was reminded of how ethnicity plays a role in students' social and cognitive development (Sheets, 2005). Moreover, my PSU classes and experiences as an educator at the Learning Gardens further challenged me to see and understand through various cultural lenses.

With this deepening awareness of my White privilege I could no longer take my daily life experiences for granted. As McIntosh (1988) claims, "describing White privilege makes one newly accountable" (p. 1). Because I was cognizant of how the unearned advantages due to my skin color contributed to institutional racism, I needed to take complete responsibility for my White privilege. . . . As White educators, "we are accountable for how we respond to racism and dominance in our schools and communities" (Howard, 1999, p. 83). . . . In my work at the Learning Gardens with Lane middle schoolers, I knew I could be an "agent of change" (McIntosh, 1998).

Adolescence is a crucial time to address racial identity and combat negative stereotypes. During this time youth are trying to figure out who they are, where they come from, where they belong, and what it means to be a member of a particular group. While my students were actively engaged in exploring their racial identity and asking lots of questions, I could begin the conversation and confront racism head on through cross-racial dialogue in the garden. During their visits to the Learning Gardens, I could provide adolescents with identity-affirming experiences and information about their own cultural groups.

Karen Payne (1998) states, "there are significant social and cultural meanings attached to gardening and agriculture, which have an impact on people's responses to working the soil" (p. 40). Payne discusses the challenges and successes of working with adolescents from various cultures in the garden and suggests that we can value cultural differences by connecting history, earth knowledge, art, and creativity, "respecting each person's story, [and] taking an active role in helping people think about how issues of race and culture impact students' experiences in the garden" (p. 41). For culturally and linguistically diverse students, the garden has potential to empower and to encourage pride and respect in their cultural heritage. At the Learning Gardens, students could learn to value cultural differences by connecting history, ecological knowledge, and food experiences through sharing of personal stories.

During our year together at the Learning Gardens, my English language learners eagerly shared their stories. We spent a significant part of the year building trust and nourishing our relationships. . . . The food, the plants, the weather, the garden, and the place reminded students of moments, people, memories, places, and recipes, triggering the stories they told, often in their native language. In the Learning Gardens, they could speak Spanish, Russian, or Vietnamese. They could speak from their hearts. It was safe to be themselves. They were immigrants and refugees. English was not their native language. But at the Learning Gardens they could ask questions, laugh, enjoy and learn more than what science offered in the classroom. I discovered that through their stories they were discovering more about themselves, about each other, and about the land of their families. They were tongue-tied no more. Gardens helped them connect with their culture.

Green Paths to Healing
Judy Bluehorse Skelton (2008)

The 10-acre Learning Gardens Laboratory (LGL) provides students with hands-on experiences in growing food and learning about nutrition, soil, water, composting and more. Sixth and seventh graders from Lane [Middle School] visit LGL for two hours every two weeks to participate in curriculum that incorporates cultural components into its science focus and is designed to follow the seasons and cycles of life. Students design gardens, dig, sow seeds, journal, sing songs of thanks to the resident cedar tree, and study soil under the microscope. Lane families have attended the two harvest celebrations hosted at the LGL this past year and students have taken their seedlings home to create backyard gardens.

By participating in the community-based learning (CBL) process with the Learning Gardens program, our team focused on engaging children with the earth and her "natural capital." In his collection of essays, *The Nature of Design*, David Orr (2002) speaks of using natural capital sustainably, not exceeding the regenerative capacity of planet Earth. It is a refreshing shift away from the extraction driven language that coined the term, "natural resources;" however, I prefer the deeper notion of "natural relations," which in addition to the physical and mental realms of interdependence, offers humans the emotional and spiritual connection to the Tree of Life, the living waters and the gifts of Mother Earth (Deloria, 2001).

In my community work, I incorporate cultural ethics, the power of ceremony, humor, and multiple voices in dialogue as well as ethnographic tools. Introducing children to the many gifts of the plant world is a multi-layered, multi-sensory, multigenerational, multicultural, multidisciplinary experience that introduces them to the gifts they carry within themselves. Learning to gather and know the medicinal and nutritional benefits of plants is valuable knowledge in and of itself. However, it is a window, perhaps like a fractal, that keeps opening up on itself to reveal deeper layers of significance. . . . waves of significance, embodying the whole as it expresses itself in diverse unpredictable ways. In learning a song to sing before gathering branches and leaves for our wintertime tea, the children become aware of relationships that exist and must be cultivated with other life forms beyond the human scale. Expressions of gratitude and respect, vibrations of energy, change the chemistry in their bodies, in the bodies of the plants, the water and the very air that carries the sound waves of their song. The tea made from plants gathered in such a way is doubly healing and contains the power of love to nurture and nourish whoever drinks from the pot.

Another aspect of the work I've done at the Learning Gardens is to outreach with parent/student communities, the neighborhood, and the local tribes of Portland proper, to explore multicultural food cultures and traditions. Part of the vision for the LGL is to offer several workshops during a six-month period, building relationships, sharing information and teaching skills, whether around gardening, cooking or catching rainwater. In collaboration with the Confederated Tribes of Grand Ronde and Confederated Tribes of Siletz Indians, LGL will host a springtime workshop where I will present, "The Gifts of the Plant World: Creating Healthy People and Healthy Communities." Both tribes have members living in southeast Portland and they recognize the links of restoring our health to restoration of our traditional foods and growing our gardens of veggies and fruits. Food and feasting is central to most cultures' sense of community and the menu is directly linked to a sense of place. The possibilities and dreams that were shared by each of us from the tribal conversations, revealed the common threads and common ground that will serve as the beginning of an urban gathering place for healthy foods and healthy communities . . . a healing for the land and for the people.

The community-based learning experience complements indigenous ways of knowing and being from my perspective. Mother Earth is longing to hear our voices once more. As we gather around the cedar tree under blue skies, Enrique beats the drum, Georgieanne offers sunflower seeds to the earth, and the children begin singing a "thank you" song. Vietnamese, Guatemalan, English, Laotian, African American, Italian, Native American, Chinese, Mexican, Russian, Irish, and so many more, are all voices coming together in thanks. These are the faces; these are the voices of Portland's future, the earth's future.

Sowing Seeds of Social Change Through Multicultural Gardens
Jill Nicola (2007)

It is an overcast spring afternoon and I am working with a group of five middle school students. Our hoes penetrate the rich earth of the Johnson Creek floodplain as we prepare a space for new life to emerge. As we work, we talk. Suddenly, Angela, a 7th grade African-American student, throws down her hoe and says, "If Blacks were meant to work in the fields, then God wouldn't have freed them from slavery." I ask her why she thinks her class is spending two hours of their weekly class time at this educational farm. She shrugs.

"Who picks the food that you eat for dinner?" I subsequently ask. We discuss how most of the food we eat these days is the product of industrial agriculture which employs low-wage workers with no health benefits and inadequate housing, who often live and work in slave-like conditions. . . . Part of the reason we are learning to grow our own food is to ensure that no one must live in slavery to feed us. She nods and returns to hoeing.

Angela's question on that spring afternoon reminded me that gardens have the ability, and perhaps even the obligation, to teach us how to consume in a way that protects and nurtures both land and people. Our mainstream American lifestyle threatens not only the incredible plant and animal diversity that our planet has to offer, but also its rich cultural diversity. For example, while today 7,000 plants are known to be farmed and used for food worldwide, this number is rapidly decreasing as farms enter the global economy and depend on corporations that carry a limited variety of seeds, many of which are genetically modified. Ten corporations control 32 percent of the world's commercial seed market and are quickly claiming intellectual property rights on the abundant diversity of seeds that farmers and peasants have spent centuries cultivating (Shiva, 1999). Similarly, 6,000 languages currently exist, but half of these languages are not being taught to children and teeter on the brink of extinction (Davis, 2005).

This loss is the result of an economic and cultural system based on unbridled consumption and homogenization. Creating a new system that respects bio-cultural diversity starts with the education of our children. Garden-based education is an ideal way to help us move beyond our history of both ecological and human oppression. However, as gardens emerge as a legitimate and powerful educational philosophy it must be shaped by diverse voices, particularly those voices that have traditionally been marginalized in mainstream education. But, what does it really mean to make a school garden multicultural? It is not about adding bok choy and chilies to your planting list. The word "multicultural" implies a deeper, more complex process. I want to explicitly tie multicultural education theory to gardens so that we can sow seeds of social change in this city.

Conclusion

The most fundamental questions that must be addressed have at their core the challenges facing the field of sustainability—predominantly, White middle-class perspectives drive what happens in the United States. Since sustainability is a global issue, it is critical that multiple cultural perspectives inform the discourse. The readings, discussions, and outcomes point students to this need and also provide skills in the community to address this need, as seen clearly in the preceding student reflections. Yet, to practice sustainability, a long-term commitment to place, locale, and communities is necessary. Several of my graduates are continuing to work in the field of food, health, and the learning gardens in the metropolitan region of Portland and in the state of Oregon, helping to continue to tie this work to a new generation of PSU and PPS students.

Note

1. I am grateful to my master's students Jennifer Anderson (2009), Judy Bluehorse Skelton (2008), and Jill Nicola (2007) for their willingness to join me in sharing their reflections from their master's research projects.

References

Anderson, J. (2009). *Tongue-tied no more: Garden-based education and social justice.* Unpublished master's culminating research project, Portland State University, Oregon.

Bluehorse Skelton, J. (2008). *Green paths to healing.* Unpublished master's culminating research project, Portland State University, Oregon.

Collier, P., & Williams, D. R. (2005). Reflection in action: The learning-doing relationship. In C. M. Cress, P. Collier, & V. Reitenauer (Eds.), *Service and learning: A student workbook for community-based experiences across the disciplines* (pp. 83–98). Sterling, VA: Stylus.

Fehrman, M. (2008). *Building community food systems through assessment, projects, and policy: A study of the Lents Example in Southeast Portland, Oregon.* Unpublished master's culminating research project, Portland State University, Oregon.

Gilbert, K. (2010). *Youth voices of bounty and opportunity: High school students' experiences with food and community* (Master's thesis). Available from ProQuest Dissertations and Theses database. (UMI No. 1490971)

Howard, G. (1999). *We can't teach what we don't know: White teachers, multiracial schools.* New York, NY: Teachers College Press.

McIntosh, P. (1988). *White privilege: Unpacking the invisible knapsack.* Wellesley, MA: Wellesley College Center for Research on Women.

Nicola, J. (2007). *Sowing seeds of social change through multicultural gardens: A guide to practices and resources in Portland, Oregon.* Unpublished master's culminating research project, Portland State University, Oregon.

No Child Left Behind Act of 2001, 20 U.S.C. § 1111 *et seq.* (2002).

Orr, D. (2002). *The nature of design: Ecology, culture, and human intention.* New York, NY: Oxford University Press.

Parajuli, P. (2006). Learning suitable to life and livability: Innovations through learning gardens. *Connections: The Journal of the Coalition for Livable Future, 8*(1), 6–7.

Payne, K. (1998). Listening with respect: Issues of class and race in working the land. In J. Kiefer & M. Kemple (Eds.), *Digging deeper: Integrating youth gardens into schools and communities.* Montpelier, VT: Food Works, Common Roots.

Sheets, R. H. (2005). *Diversity pedagogy: Examining the role of culture in the teaching-learning process.* Boston, MA: Pearson.

Williams, D. R., & Bernstine, D. O. (2002). Building capacity for civic engagement at Portland State University: A comprehensive approach. In L. A. K. Simon, M. Kenny, K. Brabeck, & R. M. Lerner (Eds.), *Learning to serve: Promoting civil society through service learning* (pp. 257–276). Norwell, MA: Kluwer Press.

Williams, D. R., & Brown, J. D. (in press). *Learning gardens and sustainability education: Bringing life to schools and schools to life.* London, UK: Routledge.

SECTION THREE

SUSTAINABILITY CONCEPTS IN BUSINESS AND ECONOMICS

9

BUILDING BRIDGES AND SOCIAL CAPITAL THROUGH SERVICE LEARNING

A Blueprint Model

Curtis L. DeBerg

The accrediting association for colleges of business—Association to Advance Collegiate Schools of Business (AACSB, 2006b)—created an International Peace Through Commerce special task force that acknowledged that business schools, like corporations, have missions aimed at producing managers who understand how to make money. Under this worldview, the financial bottom line is paramount. But the task force urged educators to "offer students opportunities to explore the underlying philosophical, nonfinancial aspects of business. By integrating these concepts into the educational experiences of students, schools can produce more globally conscious leaders and heighten understanding—and even prospects for peace" (AACSB 2006b, p. 6).

This chapter addresses how service learning can be a useful strategy in helping educators address nonfinancial aspects of business, such as social capital, civic engagement, social responsibility and sustainability. Business schools can help students envision a more prominent role for international business to contribute to a more peaceful world. Traditional finance theory stipulates that a company's value changes each period as a result of the market's assessment of the amount, timing, and uncertainty of its future cash flows. At issue is the extent to which future cash flows (and, by extension, the company's reputation) are affected by management's environmental and social policies. With environmental regulations becoming more restrictive and terms like *social responsibility* and *sustainability* becoming more than buzzwords, companies like Unilever, Dow Chemical, and Philips Electronics are changing their business practices to maximize corporate profits by becoming better corporate citizens (Engardio, 2007).

Several studies have shown a positive relationship between economic performance and environmental stewardship. One such study was conducted by Russo and Fouts (1997), who examined the economic and environmental performance for a sample of 243 companies over a two-year period. Results showed that environmental performance and economic performance are positively linked, using independently developed environmental ratings. Interface, Inc., one of the world's largest producers of commercial carpet tiles, attributes substantial cost savings to its environmental initiatives. Interface's CEO reported the company saved $222 million through its sustainability program between 1995 and 2003 (Anderson, 2004). Reports such as these have management educators wrestling with how to incorporate topics such as social responsibility and environmental sustainability into business curricula.

First, in this chapter I compare the traditional, financial worldview taught in business schools to an expanded worldview that includes social capital. Knowledge of both worldviews is helpful in contextualizing the recommendations of the AACSB task force and seeing how service learning can play a role. Second, I link the concepts of social capital and social responsibility to the expanded worldview. This worldview provides faculty with rich new areas for course work and teaching methods. Third, I address how service learning can be used in business schools to teach these concepts. Last, I provide an example of how I have used service learning to teach the expanded worldview through a program called Students for the Advancement of Global Entrepreneurship (SAGE).

An Expansion From the Financial Worldview to Include Social Capital

An accounting professor's typical use of the word *capital* is primarily restricted to financial capital, meaning that assets and the sources of assets (e.g., liabilities to creditors and equity to owners) are measured in dollars. Increases in financial net assets during a period, assuming no owner withdrawals or additional contributions, are called *financial net income*. From the worldview perspective offered by Giacalone and Thompson (2006), proponents of the organization-centered worldview (OWV) are concerned primarily with financial capital. Historically, business educators and business professionals have operated from this worldview.

Conversely, proponents of a human-centered worldview (HWV) go beyond economic wealth to where business ethics, social responsibility, and sustainable business practices are part of an organization's core goals. Giacalone and Thompson (2006) espouse a broader business curriculum that is oriented toward broader community good. One problem with this worldview, however—at least from an accounting perspective—is that the value created by a company's commitment to these nonfinancial aspects of business is not easily quantifiable. Nonetheless, proponents of this worldview, such as Kofi Annan and Bill Gates, urge businesses to break away from the OWV. Kofi Annan, in promoting the United Nations' Millennium Development Goals, argued that the United Nation's goals can be achieved only by breaking away from the traditional business model. In his commencement speech at Harvard, Gates (2007) called such a new business model "creative capitalism." According to Gates, one of the challenges for him and his wife, Melinda, was to find an answer to this question: How can we do the most good with the greatest number with the resources we have? Creative capitalism encourages business to make a profit by serving the needs of the poor.

Though the value added to a company's balance sheet by its environmental policies and socially responsible business practices may be difficult to measure—especially in the short run—creative capitalism is an excellent launching point to introduce the HWV to students. Now, with explicit AACSB sanctioning, business educators are encouraged to expand their teaching to include both worldviews.

Because private sector businesses seek new opportunities and markets, they are innovative in finding effective solutions that transcend personal and cultural differences. Creating new value—wealth—"can inspire collaboration between strangers, and sometimes even between those who might have regarded each other as enemies" (AACSB, 2006b, p. 7). The ability to find mutually beneficial opportunities often depends on one's network, and when people of different backgrounds and perspectives decide to work together, they create bridging social capital (Putnam, 2000b, p. 1). Social capital is a function of the networks and associations one belongs to, and such networks and associations lie at the heart of civic engagement.

Middleton (2005) argued that one way business educators can teach the importance of social capital is through service learning. According to Middleton, it is business education's

> responsibility for producing future business leaders with the civil, moral and intellectual service skills needed to effect the social changes that are anticipated. The introduction of service-learning projects in the business classroom can provide the means for linking theory with practice, and for endowing graduates with the necessary skills for addressing the urgent needs of their changing communities. (p. 295)

The AACSB's (2006b) task force concurred: "By integrating these [nonfinancial] concepts into the educational experiences of students, schools can produce more globally conscious leaders and heighten understanding—and even prospects for peace" (p. 6).

Social Capital, Social Responsibility, and Sustainability in an Expanded Worldview

Researchers in sociology and political science have attempted to measure social capital, providing a rich avenue of possible collaborative research exploring how civic engagement contributes to strengthening democracy, promoting peace, and alleviating poverty. For example, Smith (2001) described how transnational social movement organizations (TSMOs) are building social capital globally, linking local problems to global initiatives. Her work has direct implications for the AACSB's peace initiative, in that "the presence of transnational organizations, prepared to organize global campaigns and strategically link local conflicts with global policy processes, enable these global/local links to be made" (p. 200). Given the AACSB's desire for business educators to provide students with greater global sensitivity and awareness, such research would be especially timely. TSMOs create common interests among otherwise diverse members by relating various local problems to common, global problems. With the communication networks in place today, social capital can be created without face-to-face contact. Smith said that "the ability to engage in such transnational dialogue—either face-to-face or via newsletter or via e-mail—is a necessary component for the formation of social capital and for the strengthening of a global civil society" and led her to conclude that "transnational social movement mobilization promises more than any other contemporary trend to help break down rather than reproduce existing global inequalities" (p. 206).

The AACSB, by its standards and with its new task force on peace, encourages faculty to step beyond their comfort zone, an area often characterized by a single-minded focus on helping students acquire the tools and knowledge to help maximize profits. Now that the AACSB openly supports course work and teaching strategies to include civic, social, and moral responsibilities, new incentives for research—within and across disciplines—are possible. With additional course work, teaching methods, and research opportunities, the academic environment may now be more receptive to what Boyer (1990) termed the *scholarship of integration*. In addition to the scholarship of teaching, application, and discovery, Boyer urged professors to integrate their intellectual capital:

> We need creative people who go beyond the isolated facts, who make connections across the disciplines, who help shape a more coherent view of knowledge and a more integrated, more authentic view of life. And in our fragmented academic world this task of integration becomes more urgent every single day. In the days ahead, we urgently need scholars who move beyond the traditional academic boundaries. (p. 88)

Social capital has been the subject of great study and debate, especially since Putnam (2000a) wrote about the decline in America's social capital in the past few decades. Putnam identified three features of social capital—networks, norms, and trust—that enable participants to act together more effectively to pursue shared objectives. According to Putnam, the greater the number of associations one belongs to, the greater the capacity for civic engagement, which is essential for the functioning of a modern democracy.

While Putnam's definition puts emphasis on civic engagement and face-to-face associations, Bourdieu (1986) and Coleman (1990) include financial capital in their definitions. For example, Bourdieu said that "the volume of the social capital possessed by a given agent . . . depends on the size of the network of connections he can effectively mobilize and on the volume of the capital (economic, cultural or symbolic) possessed in his own right by each of those to whom he is connected" (p. 249). For Coleman, social capital is a variety of entities having two characteristics in common: They all consist of some aspect of a social structure, and they facilitate certain actions of individuals who are within the structure. . . . Unlike other forms of capital, social capital inheres in the structure of relations between persons and among persons. It is lodged neither in individuals nor in physical implements of production. (p. 302)

In comparing Bordieu's views with Coleman's, Edwards, Foley, and Diani (2001) indicate that both Bourdieu and Coleman are in agreement that financial and human capital are not necessarily connected to social capital "in the sense in which concrete social relationships can give individuals access to crucial resources not otherwise available, despite ample endowments of human or financial capital" (p. 10).

It is important to note that just because an organization has a large amount of social capital, it does not mean it is committed to social responsibility or sustainability. This is because some voluntary organizations are not committed to the environment (e.g., a political action committee that encourages coal production by dynamiting mountaintops in West Virginia), nor are they socially responsible (e.g., Ku Klux Klan). A sustainable business is one that "creates profit for its shareholders while protecting the environment and improving the lives of those with whom it interacts" (Savitz & Weber, 2006, p. x). Thus, any business that makes a profit (i.e., the financial bottom line), improves the lives of those in its community (i.e., the social bottom line), and protects the environment (i.e., the environmental bottom line) is a sustainable business. Sustainable businesses, the authors argue, have the best chance to remain in business in the long term.

Savitz and Weber (2006) also are careful to differentiate between a sustainable business and one that is socially responsible. Sustainability is more encompassing because a company's officers who believe in sustainability look for the benefits inside *and* outside the business. In other words, sustainability gives equal importance to the internal benefits enjoyed by the corporation itself. On the other hand, a company that is socially responsible primarily emphasizes the benefits to social groups outside the business.

The topics of social capital, civic engagement, social responsibility, and sustainability are often used in similar contexts, or interchangeably, and can be confusing. It is useful to link them together as in Figure 9.1.

Here we see that social capital is a function of networks, trust, and norms possessed by an organization. The greater the networks, trust, and

FIGURE 9.1

The Relationship Among Social Capital, Civic Engagement, Social Responsibility, and Sustainability

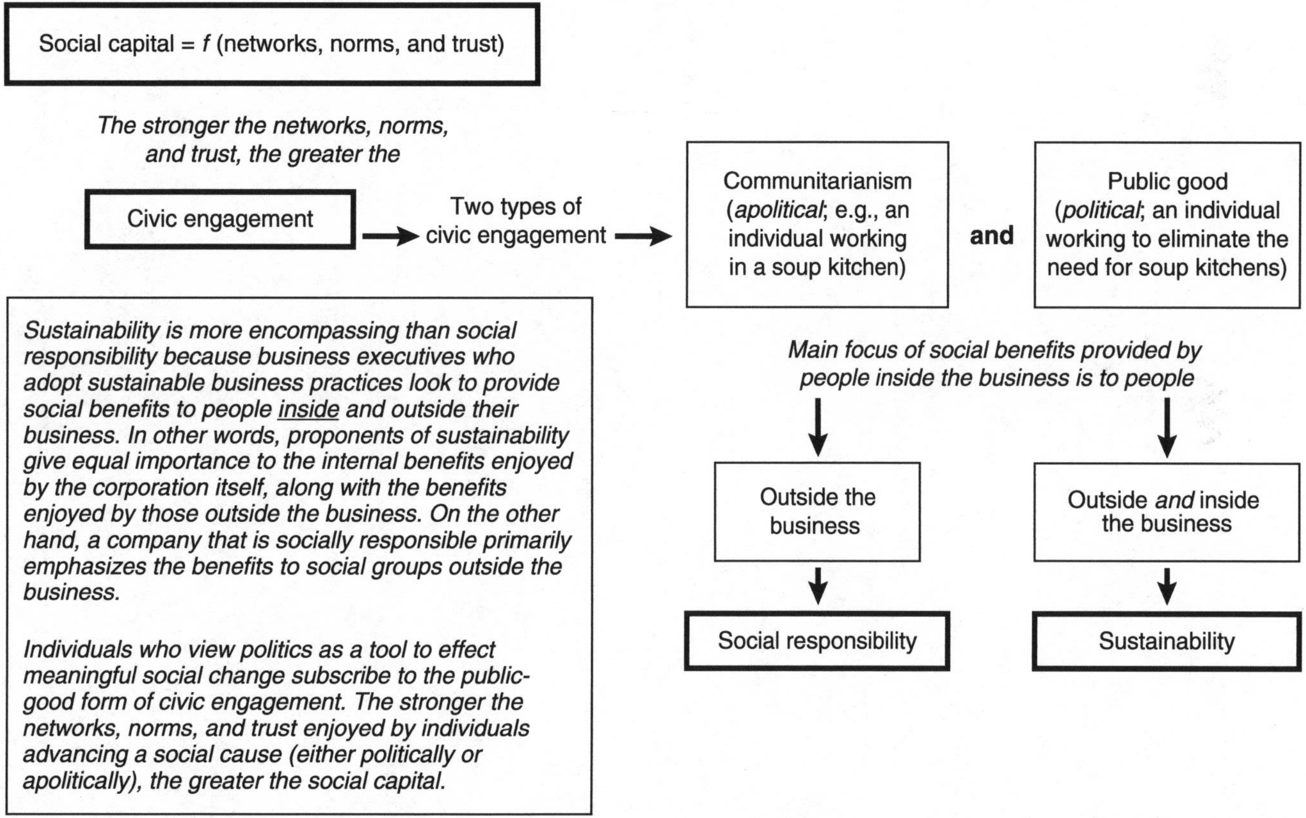

Social capital = f (networks, norms, and trust)

The stronger the networks, norms, and trust, the greater the

Two types of civic engagement →

Civic engagement

Communitarianism (*apolitical;* e.g., an individual working in a soup kitchen)

and

Public good (*political;* an individual working to eliminate the need for soup kitchens)

Main focus of social benefits provided by people inside the business is to people

Outside the business → Social responsibility

Outside *and* inside the business → Sustainability

Sustainability is more encompassing than social responsibility because business executives who adopt sustainable business practices look to provide social benefits to people inside and outside their business. In other words, proponents of sustainability give equal importance to the internal benefits enjoyed by the corporation itself, along with the benefits enjoyed by those outside the business. On the other hand, a company that is socially responsible primarily emphasizes the benefits to social groups outside the business.

Individuals who view politics as a tool to effect meaningful social change subscribe to the public-good form of civic engagement. The stronger the networks, norms, and trust enjoyed by individuals advancing a social cause (either politically or apolitically), the greater the social capital.

norms, the greater the civic engagement. There are two perspectives of civic engagement in the sociology and political science literature: communitarianism and public work. Communitarianism, the prevalent view of service in higher education, sees the service provider as an apolitical volunteer rather than as someone who views service as a way for people of diverse backgrounds to negotiate interests for the sake of solving public problems (Boyte, 2003). Battistoni (2002) provides an example of the communitarian view by citing Chi's (1999) famous story of a student who after completing a service-learning project told her director that the experience was so meaningful she hoped her children would have the opportunity to work in a homeless shelter. Communitarian service providers often narrow their focus on the needs and interests of those being served while adopting a stance of altruism or selflessness. Rather than view political action as an opportunity to solve public problems, those who subscribe to communitarianism remain free of the political process, or they focus on social objectives whose singular focus is on distributive justice.

Under the public work perspective, however, helping individuals is only part of the solution. The public-work view asks why people are homeless in the first place. Boyte (2003) explained that these service providers express their compassion through voluntarism or service by conveying "boldness, intelligence, gritty determination in the face of adversity, courage in fighting injustice, or capacities for sustained work with others outside our 'community' with whom we may have a sharp disagreement" (p. 10). Here citizens embrace politics as a means to solve problems.

Putnam (2000b) noted that communities and organizations can be more productive "when there's a pattern of connectedness, where people trust one another and behave in a responsible way toward one another" (p. 1). How connected one is in a community or an organization alludes to the strength of one's network and the associated norms of reciprocity, which according to Putnam means, "I'll do this for you now without expecting any favor back immediately from you, because down the road you'll do something for me and we'll all be connected anyhow" (p. 1). He also distinguished between two types of social capital: *bonding* social capital, which links you to people like you, and *bridging* social capital, which links you to people unlike you. Whereas the former can be good, or bad (e.g., racist or ethnocentric organizations), social capital's greatest potential in the 21st century is to connect people who are not alike.

Using Service Learning to Teach Sustainability

The AACSB acknowledged that it cannot mandate faculty to change what they teach or how they go about it. However, it sent a powerful signal to faculty by stating that "not all professors are eager to expand their teaching styles and content to include more than the narrow core of disciplinary content. The good news is that many are already doing so and that a host of emerging forces and support systems may help to ensure more" (AACSB, 2006b, p. 11). Business educators have a large role to play in ensuring that students adopt a broader worldview in what Drucker (1994) calls the *knowledge society*. For a knowledge worker to become so, he or she needs specialized education, and thus "education will become the center of the knowledge society, and the school is the key institution" (Drucker, p. 66). This society will be characterized by lifelong learning, and students must acquire more and more knowledge, especially advanced knowledge, to obtain access to the best jobs and social position.

In this chapter I argue that such knowledge includes greater emphasis on nonfinancial aspects of business. With new support from the AACSB, faculty who wish to expand curricula and employ alternative pedagogies now have more leverage. Social capital might even be featured as prominently as financial capital in some courses and, as Figure 9.1 indicates, social capital is a function of civic engagement, social responsibility, and sustainability.

Curriculum

In the AACSB's (2006a) latest standards for accreditation, colleges of business are encouraged to pursue their own diverse missions, with the ultimate goal that business education prepare students to contribute to their organizations and the larger society. The AACSB recognized that challenges for business education are similar to the challenges faced by other organizations, including global economic forces, differences in organizational and cultural values, cultural diversity among employees and customers, and changing technology in products and processes.

Business school administrators can integrate existing courses to teach students about corporate social responsibility, or they can design stand-alone course work. One way to do this is to increase coverage of business ethics (Swanson [2005] criticizes the AACSB for not requiring business colleges to require a self-standing ethics course). Samuelson (2006) calls for a new rigor that replaces a short-term view of profit maximization with a long-term view of profits and an expanded view of assets:

> By rigorous we mean that business school students will need to understand business and society as a complex, dynamic, and interdependent system and to carefully explore theory, use frameworks, and build skills to match. We are seeking a new rigor that replaces *homus economicus* with a professional stance devoted to a larger purpose—where morals, ethical reasoning, and careful judgment truly matter. And where externalities are incorporated and measured as part of a holistic and systems-based analysis. The bottom-line is the need to put the lynch-pin of all business decision rules— short-term financial profit maximizing—into context. Otherwise, it's two-dimensional analysis in a three-dimensional world, and we believe that the business schools are an appropriate—and necessary—venue to rethink the paradigm. (p. 357)

Another way universities are incorporating social capital into their curricula is by creating new course work in social entrepreneurship. During the past 30 years we have seen a dramatic increase in the number of nonprofit organizations dedicated to social causes that the public and private sectors— government and business—have been unable or unwilling to address satisfactorily. Bornstein (2004) calls these "citizen organizations" (p. 3), the types of organizations that make up Drucker's social sector. In essence, it is through the social sector that individuals who create or work for nonprofit companies contribute to the social capital of that organization, but they also contribute to their own social capital as well.

Social entrepreneurs who start their own organizations are not content to work for a company whose main mission is profit, and their organization is usually started by

> one obsessive individual who sees a problem and envisions a new solution, who takes the initiative to act on that vision, who gathers resources and builds organizations to protect and market that vision, who provides the energy and sustained focus to overcome the inevitable resistance, and who—decade after decade—keeps improving, strengthening, and broadening that vision until what was once a marginal idea has become a new norm. (Bornstein, 2004, p. 3)

But social entrepreneurs are not necessarily founders of their own organizations. According to Duke University's Center for the Advancement of Social Entrepreneurship, social entrepreneurship is

> the process of recognizing and resourcefully pursuing opportunities to create social value. Social entrepreneurs are innovative, resourceful, and results oriented. They draw upon the best thinking in both the business and nonprofit worlds to develop strategies that maximize their social impact. These entrepreneurial leaders operate in all kinds of organizations: large and small; new and old; religious and secular; nonprofit, for-profit, and hybrid. These organizations comprise the "social sector." (Duke University, 2007)

Many of the leading U.S. business schools, including Harvard, Stanford, and Wharton, have developed at least one course in social entrepreneurship.

Pedagogy

In addition to curricular changes, faculty can experiment with forms of experiential learning such as service learning. In one of two articles that address how service learning can contribute to civic engagement in a democracy, DiPadova-Stocks (2005) pointed out that peace cannot be addressed without considering poverty. She noted that third world and developing countries may have a hard time taking the United States seriously when

> some of our graduates have amassed immense personal wealth at the expense of health, well-being, and sometimes safety of others. . . . We the educated and the educators in the United States have stood by while poverty in the wealthiest nation on earth continues its dramatic increase. (p. 352)

She added that a well-designed and well-implemented service-learning program "is grounded in the value of the human dignity and the inherent innate worth of the individual. These values are fundamental to democracy and belong to all disciplines" (p. 352).

In the other article, Papamarcos (2005) also viewed civic engagement as a key aspect of service learning, but he also saw how service learning offers much more by providing students with exposure to the vast network of interdependencies of business and society as well as expansive real-world management experience that gives traction to theory—preparing them to be workers in the economy and citizens in a democracy. Properly structured, this new type of service learning creates a state-of-the-art instructional environment wherein teaching theory, applying theory, preparing students for lives of civic engagement, and involving students as voluntary agents of social change happen simultaneously. (p. 326)

Examples

Outstanding examples of what various business faculty are doing to promote peace through commerce can be found in Shinn (2006). According to this article, available through the AACSB website, programs included sponsoring international students, global business ventures, consulting, faculty exchange projects, developing management education programs in war plagued areas, and student-created business plans for communities emerging from conflict.

Teaching an Expanded Worldview Through SAGE

According to Bornstein (2004), "Teenagers are the single most influential group in a low-income community" (pp. 76–177). Moreover, the International Labour Organization (ILO, 2011) reports that

> of the world's estimated 211 million unemployed people in 2009, nearly 40 per cent—or about 81 million—are between 15 and 24 years of age. More youth are poor or underemployed than ever before: some 152 million young people work but live in households that earn less than the equivalent of US$1.25 per day. Millions of young people are trapped in temporary and involuntary part-time or casual work that offers few benefits and limited prospects for advancement at work and in life.

Moreover, according to the ILO, "66 million young people are unemployed and an even higher number are underemployed. A generation without the hope of a stable job is a burden for the whole of society. . . . There is a desperate need to create employment and harness the youth resource" (Haftendorn & Salzana, 2003, p. 3).

High school youth are the primary focal point of a program I founded in summer 2002, because they are the future entrepreneurs, employees, investors, customers, and citizens. The program is called Students for the Advancement of Global Entrepreneurship (SAGE), and its conceptual foundation relies heavily on social entrepreneurship as a discipline and experiential education as a teaching strategy. Three primary outcomes from this program are greater awareness among global youth of the power of socially responsible business and entrepreneurship to improve their lives, greater social capital contributed by the participants and greater social assets enjoyed by the community, and stronger links among local education and business activists to effect meaningful changes in their communities by being linked to the global SAGE network.

The SAGE initiative allowed me to become a social entrepreneur, as well as to introduce social entrepreneurship and integrate civic engagement and social responsibility into my accounting courses through service learning. By encouraging students to complete service-learning activities, we are asking them to provide social capital to organizations in their community, exactly what leaders of many companies are asking of their employees in the name of corporate social responsibility. Moreover, the university business students who are assigned to high schools as business consultants have the opportunity to teach their newly acquired knowledge and skills to a group of highly motivated high school students.

A brief description of the SAGE program is provided here as a practical example of how any member of the business faculty can involve his or her students in service-learning projects.

What Is SAGE?

SAGE is an international nonprofit organization that links secondary school student organizations to mentors from local universities and businesses. Its purpose is to advance youth business and social entrepreneurship in an ethical and socially responsible manner. Youth use their experience as SAGE members to become self-reliant, create wealth, and help others. SAGE provides a new avenue for youth working individually, or in cooperative teams as if they were business partners, and contributing to their communities. Those in SAGE further believe that youth have much untapped potential that could benefit themselves and the adults in their communities. The first goal of the SAGE program is for youth to become self-reliant and better skilled to succeed in life by actually creating real entrepreneurial and social ventures. The second goal is for the communities to benefit directly, because their SAGE students are self-reliant and better skilled. (See http://www.sage global.org for the history, scope, and additional details about the SAGE program.)

SAGE fills an unmet need at the high school level because many young people who want to become entrepreneurs, or entrepreneurial employees, may never be able to realize their dreams. They do not have the necessary knowledge or skills to act on that knowledge, they are missing role models or personal relationships to see what it means to be a successful entrepreneur, and they lack encouragement needed to undertake a new venture (Walstad & Kourilsky, 1998). The program is premised on the compelling usefulness of assisting youth to plan and operate businesses, as a means for them to use their classroom learning and develop self-reliance. Entrepreneurship is a key element according to Prahalad (2005), and companies, academics, and nongovernmental organizations must collaborate. According to Prahalad, "Market development at the bottom of the pyramid will also create millions of new entrepreneurs at the grass roots level—from women working as distributors and entrepreneurs to village-level micro enterprises. . . . Entrepreneurship on a massive scale is the key" (p. 2).

A Blueprint Model

I have created and disseminated a detailed blueprint model containing documents and processes, readily adaptable by others, in the business discipline and in other disciplines such as sociology and political science. For example, from the SAGE website, users can download handbooks, manuals, sample annual reports, sample grant proposal templates, and marketing materials such as PowerPoint presentations introducing SAGE to prospective university hosts and new member high schools. Also, sample syllabi are available explaining how university faculty can implement SAGE as a service-learning activity.

SAGE Structure

Figure 9.2 shows how SAGE is structured.

Although high school youth are the primary focus of the SAGE program, everyone affiliated with SAGE is a benefactor, including high school teachers; business and civic leaders; and, of course, university students. In addition to serving as business advisors, members of the community play a second vital role as evaluators for the competitions. The host for the competition, usually a faculty member from the university business program, recruits a panel of jurists from the local business, civic, and education communities. These jurists are assigned to a "league" consisting of 15 to 20

FIGURE 9.2
The SAGE Model

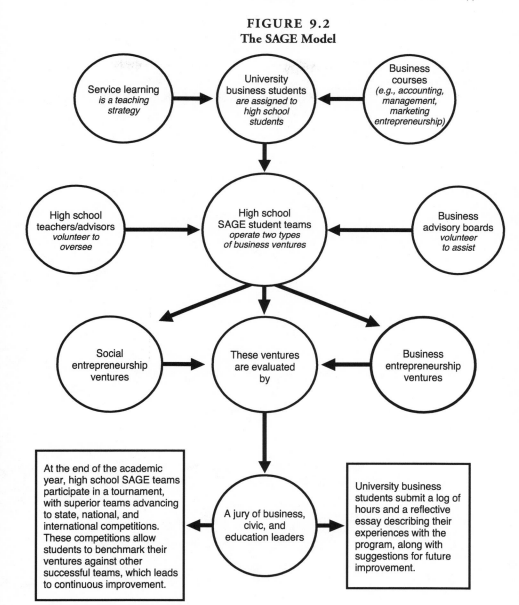

jurists per league, with two or three teams per league. Using a detailed rubric as a guide, jurists are instructed to help determine which teams were the most effective in meeting the criteria. Jurists score the teams based on how well they integrated all four criteria into their action-learning ventures during the year. This structure encourages the community to support the students for their academic accomplishments to the same extent it does for athletics and other cocurricular activities.

Figure 9.3 is an excerpt from the syllabus used in Principles of Accounting I. In the past five years, over 100 university students have participated as SAGE mentors. University students work closely with high school teachers to identify, deliver, and assess the problem-based learning activities completed by the younger students. It is important to note that university students who sign up for the SAGE service-learning project do so voluntarily.

Assessment

University students must keep a log of their time spent on projects, attend weekly meetings, visit their assigned high schools as SAGE mentors, and write a reflective essay at the end of their experience. Other metrics include

- number of new or improved business ventures created by high school students;
- number and quality of annual written reports summarizing each team's activities (e.g., authentic assessment);
- number of business and community leaders directly involved with SAGE; this involvement can be made in two ways: by serving on a high school SAGE team's business advisory board or by serving as a judge at the SAGE competition;
- reflective essays written by university students;
- number and quality of new social ventures created by high school SAGE teams;
- number and quality of verbal presentations made at the SAGE competitions;
- number of university/college mentors who have assisted each SAGE team in identifying, completing, and reporting its projects; and
- feedback from teachers regarding the quality of service provided by participating university students.

FIGURE 9.3
Excerpt From Syllabus Regarding Service Learning

OPTIONAL BONUS POINTS

You may earn bonus points in this class by completing a community ser-vice-learning project. You must *commit* to doing this project *before* the first exam.

Community service learning (CSL) is a powerful process that combines meaningful service to the community with a structured opportunity to learn from the service experience. This learning is most effective when it occurs as part of the academic curriculum. It is both a philosophy of education and a method of teaching that bridge the classroom and the community by engag-ing learners in the application of theory to service.

You may earn 40 bonus points in this class by participating in a community service-learning project called Students for the Advancement of Global En-trepreneurship (SAGE). You will be assigned to make at least one presenta-tion to an area high school, and you will make at least three visits to this high school during the year to become a business consultant for its commer-cial and social ventures. See http://www.csuchico.edu/sage for details about the program.

To earn the bonus, you must

1. Attend a one-hour meeting each week to learn about SAGE and plan logistics for your presentation and site visits, and
2. Write a two-page summary (single-spaced) reflecting on your experi-ence at the end of the semester. The paper should describe the proj-ect; explain what you learned, and offer recommendations to improve the project. This paper must be turned in on final exam day.

Note: You cannot be hurt by NOT doing the service-learning bonus. It can only HELP. In other words, I don't intentionally make my initial curve "harsher" to reflect that some grades will increase slightly due to the bonus.

Sustainability of the SAGE Program

I have incorporated sustainability of the SAGE program in several ways. First, I have exposed introductory business students to service learning by offering them bonus points if they choose to volunteer to serve as a SAGE mentor. After the semester is over, many of these same students continue with the SAGE program as experienced mentors and leaders. This system ensures a continuous supply of new and experienced university mentors. Second, based on the success of the program, the dean of the College of Business made SAGE an integral part of the Center for Entrepreneurship at California State University, Chico. Third, SAGE teams are encouraged to enter the same business venture in the competition for up to three years, demonstrating how it has grown and improved over time. Fourth, sustainability has been achieved through strategic partnerships with such organizations as Youth Venture, the youth branch of the Ashoka Foundation. The Ashoka Foundation is a global association of the world's leading social entrepreneurs, providing its fellows with living stipends, professional support, and access to a global network of peers in 70 countries (Ashoka, 2011). Last, throughout the past nine years, I have enlisted the continued financial support of several companies and private foundations.

Summary

In summary, SAGE challenges students to complete real-world business and social ventures and provides incentives to integrate civic engagement, environmental awareness, and global dimensions in their projects; uses an inter-scholastic competitive model similar to athletics; showcases projects in a tournament that recognizes outstanding high school teams based on their effectiveness and creativity; and motivates and inspires all participants to become active, productive, and inspiring business and community leaders in their communities.

SAGE is not just another service-learning project. It is a new way of thinking about how universities can involve high school educators and students in hands-on, real-world activities. University students can encourage younger students to create social and business ventures under the direction of leaders from the business community. SAGE also provides universities and schools with opportunities to expand networks and make new connections to facilitate such ventures. In short, the SAGE program can be implemented by entrepreneurial educators at the university and high school levels who want their students to become better prepared for a life that will be increasingly more dependent upon interaction with people from other countries.

Conclusion

The time for a new business model, and a new way of teaching business, is now. Free markets are powerful, and they are especially effective at serving the needs of developed countries. But as Prahalad (2005) said, traditional "market-based solutions cannot lead to poverty reduction and economic development" (p. 9). Sachs (2005) agreed:

> Although introductory economics textbooks preach individualism and decentralized markets, our safety and prosperity depend at least as much on collective decisions to fight disease, promote good science and widespread education, provide critical infrastructure, and act in unison to help the poorest of the poor. When the preconditions of basic infrastructure (roads, power, and ports) and human capital (health and education) are in place, markets are powerful engines of development. Without those preconditions, markets can cruelly bypass large parts of the world, leaving them impoverished and suffering without respite. (pp. 2–3)

As noted earlier, Putnam (2000b) distinguished between *bonding* social capital, which links people with similar backgrounds, and *bridging* social capital, which links people from different backgrounds. Gates (2007) suggested that a new business model based on creative capitalism can build bridges across cultures and countries, and the AACSB (2006b) believes that such a model can contribute to world peace.

The big questions addressed in this chapter are the following: Can a new business model be envisioned that balances financial and social capital, one that leads to more sustainable businesses—businesses that might even contribute to world peace? Can business educators create rigorous new courses based on such topics as business ethics, social responsibility, and social entrepreneurship? Can they effectively employ new pedagogies such as service learning to create a new generation of university graduates with a greater sense of social purpose, civic engagement, and social responsibility? Can business educators employ social capital as a topic and service learning as pedagogy to work with educators from other disciplines to address environmental issues and social injustice?

The traditional business model is based on financial capital, individualism, and an organization-centered worldview. But the AACSB's (2006b) task force understood the importance of expanding this model to include social capital when it suggested that "once people work together and learn that people are essentially the same, regardless of their backgrounds, making war is likely to become far less attractive than making money" (p. 7). Poverty, terrorism, and war are political, social, and economic problems.

All people—including the corporate person—have a moral and social responsibility not to do harm or to be evil in their quests for profits and the good life, and one goal of this chapter has been to show that making money and being socially responsible are not mutually incompatible. On the contrary, pursuit of both goals can hasten our consumption of scarce resources and degradation of the environment. Furthermore, pursuit of financial and social capital can alleviate poverty, combat terrorism, and reduce the likelihood of war. To do this, all stakeholders—including business educators—must cooperate and implement a more sustainable way of thinking and acting. This will mean rethinking the 20th-century business model from the organization-centered worldview and moving toward the human-centered worldview.

The new business model will move away from mass production and consumption to one that shows greater concern for the global community. Bridges must be built across nations to ensure that future generations have the same opportunities as previous generations, and business education has a critical role to play. This chapter has shown the time is ideal for business schools to introduce new course work and pedagogy that includes social capital. One such pedagogy is service learning, and one such example is SAGE.

References

Anderson, R. (2004, February). Climbing mount sustainability. *Quality Progress*, *37*(2), 32–37.

Ashoka Foundation. (2011). *Ashoka innovators for the public.* Retrieved from http://www.ashoka.org/

Association to Advance Collegiate Schools of Business. (2006a). *Eligibility procedures and accreditation standards for business accreditation.* Tampa, FL: Author.

Association to Advance Collegiate Schools of Business. (2006b). *A world of good report: Business, business schools and peace.* Tampa, FL: Author.

Battistoni, R. M. (2002). Civic engagement across the curriculum: A resource book for service learning faculty in all disciplines. Providence, RI: Campus Compact.

Bornstein, D. (2004). *How to change the world: Social entrepreneurs and the power of new ideas.* New York, NY: Oxford University Press.

Bourdieu, P. (1986). The forms of capital. In J. Richardson (Ed.), *Handbook of theory and research for the sociology of education* (pp. 241–258). New York, NY: Greenwood Press.

Boyer, E. L. (1992). *Scholarship reconsidered: Priorities of the professoriate.* Princeton, NJ: The Carnegie Foundation for the Advancement of Teaching.

Boyte, H. (2003). A different kind of politics: John Dewey and the meaning of citizenship in the 21st century. *The Good Society, 12*(2), 3–15.

Chi, B. (1999). What's wrong with this picture? Education for democracy. In J. S. Coleman (Ed.) *Foundations of social theory.* Cambridge, MA: Harvard University Press.

DiPadova-Stocks, L. N. (2005). Two major concerns about service-learning: What if we don't do it? And what if we do? *Academy of Management Learning & Education, 4*(3), 345–353.

Drucker, P. F. (1994, November). The age of social transformation. *Atlantic Monthly, 274*(5), 53–80.

Duke University. (2007). *What is social entrepreneurship?* Retrieved from http://www.caseatduke.org/about/whatissocialentrepreneurship/

Edwards, B., Foley, M. W., & Diani, M. (Eds.). (2001). *Beyond Tocqueville: Civil society and the social capital debate in comparative perspective.* Hanover, NH: University Press of New England.

Engardio, P. (2007, January 29). Beyond the green corporation. *Business Week,* 50–64.

Gates, B. (2007, June 7). *Remarks of Bill Gates, Harvard Commencement 2007.* Retrieved from http://www.networkworld.com/news/2007/060807-gates-commencement.html.

Giacalone, R. A., & Thompson, K. R. (2006). Business ethics and social responsibility: Shifting the worldview. *Academy of Management Learning & Education, 5*(3), 266–277.

Haftendorn, K., & Salzana, C. (2003). *Facilitating youth entrepreneurship, part I: An analysis of awareness and promotion programmes in formal and non-formal education.* (Small Enterprise Development, Job Creation and Enterprise Department working paper No. 59). Geneva, Switzerland: International Labor Organization.

International Labour Organization. (2011). *Youth employment.* Retrieved from http://www.ilo.org/employment/areas/youth-employment/lang--en/index.htm

Middleton, K. L. (2005). The service-learning project as a supportive context for charismatic leadership emergence in nascent leaders. *Academy of Management Learning & Education, 4*(3), 295–308.

Papamarcos, S. D. (2005). Giving traction to management theory: Today's service-learning. *Academy of Management Learning & Education, 4*(3), 325–335.

Prahalad, C. K. (2005). *The fortune at the bottom of the pyramid: Eradicating poverty through profits.* Upper Saddle River, NJ: Wharton School Publishing.

Putnam, R. D. (2000a). *Bowling alone: The collapse and revival of American community.* New York, NY: Simon & Schuster.

Putnam, R. D. (2000b). *Bowling alone: Living alone and liking it.* Speech presented at the Commonwealth Club of California, San Francisco.

Russo, M. V., & Fouts, P. A. (1997). A resource-based perspective on corporate environmental performance and profitability. *Academy of Management Journal, 40*(3), 534–559.

Sachs, J. (2005). *The end of poverty: Economic possibilities for our time.* New York, NY: Penguin.

Samuelson, J. (2006). The new rigor: Beyond the right answer. *Academy of Management Learning & Education, 5*(3), 356–365.

Savitz, A. W., & Weber, K. (2006). The triple bottom line: How today's best-run companies are achieving economic, social, and environmental success—and how you can too. San Francisco, CA: Wiley.

Shinn, S. (2006, May–June). The dimensions of peace. *BizEd,* 24–31.

Smith, J. (2001). Global civil society? Transnational social movement organizations and social capital. In B. Edwards, M. W. Foley, & M. Diani (Eds.), *Beyond Tocqueville: Civil society and the social capital debate in comparative perspective* (pp. 194–206). Hanover, NH: University Press of New England.

Swanson, D. L. (2005). Business ethics education at bay: Addressing a crisis of legitimacy. *Issues in Accounting Education, 20*(3), 247–253.

Walstad, W., & Kourilsky, M. L. (1998). Entrepreneurial attitudes and knowledge of black youth. *Entrepreneurship Theory & Practice, 23*(2), 5–18.

SUSTAINABLE DESIGN PRACTICES FOR THE SOCIAL ENTREPRENEURIAL BUSINESS

Connie Ulasewicz

A primary component of the definition of sustainable design and development requires that the needs of the current generation be met without compromising the needs of future generations (World Commission on Environment and Development, 1987). My belief is that most of us desire to be socially and environmentally conscious but find it difficult to assess and analyze the various choices we face on a daily basis. Frequently, colleagues, students, or community partners ask educators for assistance in determining how to become greener or more sustainable. Without standards or frameworks, determining which sustainable business practices among many are better for people and the environment can be daunting; it is challenging for us to make informed decisions and move forward thoughtfully. To understand sustainability, an appreciation and recognition of the connections among people, business, and social innovation are critical, for without an understanding of this interdependency, neither business nor society can thrive.

Students are integral participants in business and society. As future designers, marketers, and managers of sustainable products and services, many are eager for the opportunity to learn how to engage with real businesses in the creation and assessment of sustainable business choices. This chapter describes the pleasure I have had working with students while teaching a new graduate course, Social Entrepreneurship. Rich McCline and I developed this cross-listed course to foster a link between the entrepreneurship program in the management department in the College of Business and the apparel design and merchandising program in the consumer and family studies/dietetics department in the College of Health and Human Services. As social entrepreneurs and supporters of community-engaged learning, McCline and I are inspired to join the minds of creative design students with those of the more analytical business students to craft social change. Entrepreneurs think creatively and develop new solutions that dramatically alter existing ones with a motive of profit; social entrepreneurs neither anticipate nor organize to create profit (Martin & Osberg, 2007). The catalogue description for our course states, "Exploration of how entrepreneurial individuals and companies find innovative methods to leverage scarce resources in the pursuit of social values. Special focus on socially responsible business practices used in the apparel industry" (see http://www.sfsu.edu/~bulletin/courses/34944.htm). Of the seven objectives developed for the course, two are pertinent to this chapter:

1. to understand and define relationships between sustainable business practices, green business practices, and social entrepreneurship; and
2. to participate, as directed by community service-learning requirements, with local community agencies and businesses that engage in socially responsible business practices.

The typical mix of students in a multidisciplinary graduate-level class is considerable, with much diversity in majors, such as apparel and interior design, accounting, management, business practices, and other fields such as art, education, social science, or environmental science where a course such as this counts as an elective.

Social entrepreneurship applies the principles of business entrepreneurship to societal problems. Many apparel businesses are now at the forefront of developing practices that are socially responsible because the fashion process is the design and creation of material objects or clothing that have a direct link to the environment and the people who create and wear them (Hethorn & Ulasewicz, 2008). A socially responsible business may be defined as one "encompassing the roles companies take in addressing individuals' concerns and societal needs in ways that go beyond the bottom line" (Dickson, Rudd, & Leonard, 2006, p. 175). One example of social responsibility is sustainability, which is about seeking solutions while maintaining healthy economies and solving social inequities; it is not about taking resources from future generations and not about behaving in a way that causes harm to the planet but sustains it. The special focus of our course is the apparel industry, since everyone participates in and can relate to the purchasing, wearing, and disposing of clothing. The idea is that creating and consuming clothing uses resources, some of which are renewable or reusable, and some of which are not renewable and are considered wasteful. The U.S. Environmental Protection Agency (2008) reports that in 2008, U.S. residents, businesses, and institutions produced more than 250 million tons of trash. Of that, 8.0% came from rubber, leather, and textiles—all basic components used in the creation of clothing. The clothing, footwear, and textile industries are second only to agriculture in consuming the most water and in contaminating waterways with chemicals for bleaching, dyeing, and finishing fashion products (Stockinger, 2006). Using apparel design and merchandising as the platform for class discussion and the catalyst for exploring other industries, students have great opportunities to explore and define the relationships between sustainable business practices, green business practices, and social entrepreneurship.

To meet San Francisco State's requirements for a service-learning course, a student is required to complete a minimum of 20 hours of service during the semester. In addition,

- students are involved in activities at the community site that provide meaningful experience related to the content of the course; and
- students must engage in critical reflection on their community experience as part of their classroom activities.

As educators, we are charged with inspiring students to become agents of change. This chapter, segmented by weeks in a college semester, addresses the power of the service-learning pedagogy for teaching civic engagement as it relates to the curricular content of sustainability and social entrepreneurship. Examples of how students can connect in the community and engage in socially responsible business practices in areas of design are provided. Student community learning sites and critical reflections of their experiences are highlighted in the following pages, as well as the grading strategy for student evaluation. Each week purposely builds on the previous week and takes students deeper into the subject matter. The grading strategy is based on the philosophy that the interaction of the students in the community and in the class is essential. A suggested assessment scale is

Project journals and service learning	25%
Attendance and class discussions	20%
Assignments and tests	30%
Final paper and presentation	25%

Week 1: Who Is a Social Entrepreneur? A Case Study Approach

Most students are familiar with the term *entrepreneurship*; when it is used in combination with the word *social*, it raises a question. From the first day of class, the definitions of social entrepreneurship we explore come from our basic text for the class, *How to Change the World*, by David Bornstein (2007). Bornstein views social entrepreneurs as transformative forces: people with new ideas to address major problems who are relentless in the pursuit of their visions, people who simply will not take no for an answer, who will not give up until they have spread their ideas as far as they possibly can. My objective is for students to truly identify with and understand the process of change by working with sustainable organizations in the community and learning from the visions of those who directed them. The class focuses on real people doing real things. My goal is for students to have the opportunity to internalize the concept that important social change can begin with a single entrepreneur who "sees a problem and envisions a new solution, who takes the initiative to act on that vision, who provides the energy and sustained focus to overcome the inevitable resistance" (Bornstein, p. 3). The case study methodology is used to achieve this outcome.

Cases are commonly used in teaching to illustrate a point, a category, a condition, or something important for the instruction (Denzin & Lincoln, 2000). In this course, cases provide students with the ability to analyze and appreciate sustainability and socially entrepreneurial business practices they have not had the opportunity to experience firsthand. From the first day of class, students participate in detailed contextual case analysis of business events or conditions and their relationship to social entrepreneurship and sustainability, in either full-class discussions, pairs, or small groups. Case studies selected for inquiry initially come from the texts, other readings, or presentations made by guest speakers from the community. As the class progresses, each community organization in which the students will be engaged functions as a live case. Our class uses the following explanation of the case study, which is fully discussed in class and is in the syllabus:

> In this course, we use a variety of approaches to establish and reinforce the key principles involved in understanding the nature of social entrepreneurs and social entrepreneurism. One approach, case analysis, is designed to put you at the scene of the action and familiarize you with the situation as it unfolds in a real organization. The essence of your role in case analysis is to diagnose and evaluate the situation described in the case. Based upon the information presented in the case (and, sometimes, other appropriate outside information), you are expected to immerse yourself in the case situation.

The first homework assignments (see Appendix A) are designed to ensure students understand this methodology. My intent is to inspire and encourage students by assigning cases or stories of successful international social enterprises, especially since "large parts of the population feel that business has become detached from society—that business interests are no longer aligned to societal interests" (Paine, 2003, p. 95). Students need to be presented with case studies identifying someone or some company that has taken the lead and repositioned the business to be socially conscious. In class, my approach is for the students, in pairs or teams, to review their understanding of the case, the challenges facing the company, and make their recommendations for sustainable practice. The discussion is then opened to the entire class, and students are given the opportunity to explain their ideas. Through such discussions, they experience how to convey their ideas effectively and gain confidence, and a community of support develops in the classroom.

This case study methodology and approach also fosters the exploration of civic engagement, a goal of most social entrepreneurial ventures focusing on sustainability (Bornstein, 2007). The basic question for discussion is, What leads people to act on their beliefs? As students explore the cases, they begin exploring their own values and beliefs and question what would lead them to act in a socially responsible manner. My goal is to provide students with the opportunity to become active citizens; to become aware of issues in the community; to be motivated to engage in and promote change; and to reflect on their decisions, actions, and work.

Week 4: Class Participation and Choosing Sites for Community Partnerships

To many students, the task of choosing a suitable community site that partic-ipates in sustainable design seems overwhelming. A possible approach to make them feel more confident in matching their needs with the needs of the community is to invite guest speakers from community organizations to share their visions and the missions of their companies. Because my objective is for the students to analyze and appreciate the business practices of organi-zations regarding sustainability and social entrepreneurship, we enlist the case study methodology when the guest from the community organization visits the classroom. This methodology allows the students and the commu-nity participants to interact in dynamic conversations and to reflect on their missions and develop partnerships.

Community sites willing to employ students in meaningful service vary by location. The aim is to have students participate in a practice-oriented concept of civic education (Casey, Davidson, Billig, & Springer, 2006) that includes dialogue, setting agendas and action recommendations, and when possible, implementation. Reading the mission and vision statements of our partner organizations is an effective way to start the site search process. One guest speaker from Golden Gate Community (see http://www.ggci.org) gen-erated excitement about its mission of helping at-risk youth and young adults through Ashbury Images (see http://www.ashburyimages.org), a silk-screen business that uses the slogan "Rebuilding lives one shirt at a time." The youth employed by Ashbury Images often have recovered from sub-stance abuse and homelessness. With the help of this organization, they gain job skills and build their self-esteem. Another guest speaker from Urban So-lutions (see http://www.urbansolutionssf.org) described the organization as a nonprofit economic development corporation that helps neighborhoods at-tract, retain, and expand community-serving and job-creating businesses. Urban Solutions enhances opportunities for underrepresented businesses by providing business services (sales training, promotional activities, and visual merchandising) to many retail stores in one of San Francisco's redevelop-ment areas. One such store, Re-Runs Thrift Boutique, is an affordable sec-ondhand clothing outlet whose slogan is "If you don't look good, we don't feel good." Managers of these types of organizations are eager to connect with students skilled in social entrepreneurship and design. Because they are often too occupied with day-to-day tasks, or because they are overwhelmed with new ideas they want to put into action, these managers are willing to brainstorm new ideas with students.

Exploring the use of the case study methodology in class with community organizations provides an opportunity, beyond the textbook, for students to understand how design practices and skills are integrated into socially responsible business practices. As their understanding is enhanced, so is their confidence to delve into their community. As one student explained,

> There is always a gap between what one learns in the classroom and what is happening where the rubber meets the road. By getting into the community and applying ourselves in a dynamic environment, all the while knowing you have school to process your experiences, [it] makes the experience surmountable.

Week 8: Reflection Logs and Sharing Experiences

As the semester progresses, the students who are most involved at their community sites seem to be those most involved in class. Weekly check-ins provide an open forum for students to discuss their experiences and their increased understanding of socially responsible management and business practices. The classroom energy is contagious as classmates share their personal insights and learning. The variety and locations of community business sites and the depth of student engagement with their projects vary. Some examples are

- development of a Girl Scout badge focused on social entrepreneurship and design projects that represent the local community;
- a website that illustrates best practices for photographing children with special needs;
- a business survey on design specifications for a new sustainable product for a nonprofit business; and
- design and development of a nonprofit clothing closet, a space where men and women returning to work can select clothes and accessories.

Another component of the class is the reflective journal (see Appendix B). Reflection is a substantial element of the community engagement learning pedagogy and a useful tool to transform raw experiences into personal and intellectual growth (Pinzon & Arceo, 2006). Students are required to make an entry each time they participate at their community site, with a minimum of five entries (most students volunteer for four-hour shifts.) Students bring journals to class and use them to document their activities. As a group, we continually ask the following questions:

- How does this organization practice social entrepreneurship?
- What makes this organization socially responsible?
- How is your engagement contributing to social change?

The following passages from student journals reflect what they learned about themselves through their service-learning experiences:

> This learning experience [Urban Solutions] reaffirms that as an interior designer, I can offer my professional knowledge to anyone who needs it, no matter their status in society. Many professionals have donated hundreds of hours to this community, providing affordable housing and training to low-income families.

> I am learning that I can make a difference in the lives of others and that is one of the reasons I want to teach someday, because through serving others I grow more compassionate and wise. I have learned so much about the Girls Scouts [sic] organization that I did not know before and that information makes me want to continue to support what they do for young girls.

> I learned that although my expertise was outside the boundary of a particular organization's focus, I was still relevant. By meeting with the organization's leaders, [Golden Gate Community] we bridged the gap and I became a valued individual who contributed to [a] specific goal.

> I am learning how to be a coordinator, which requires one to facilitate a project [starting a clothing closet] from the brainstorming phase until its completion, as well as how to motivate both the client and those who are working on a project. In addition, after my initial timeline was created, I discovered that a coordinator often has to go into a situation and learn as he goes along, while trusting his own instincts in the creative process of decision making.

Week 10: The Final Case Study Project

Since a significant portion of the class is devoted to using a case study methodology to understand sustainable business practices, students have the opportunity to share their understanding of concepts that underpin social entrepreneurship and to guide systematic analyses that are important to a successful venture creation. An important objective of the final project is to give students the opportunity to write a case study analysis of their community site. The final projects follow the guidelines for case study analysis (see Appendix A) and are further enhanced by two additional requirements: a six-to eight-page paper and an oral/visual presentation. The papers and presentations are due at the last two class sessions. After each final presentation, fellow class members give immediate, unsigned, written feedback to the presenters. Students are instructed to provide feedback by answering the following questions:

- What are several points/key ideas you gained from this presentation?
- What was the strongest aspect of the entire presentation? How/why?
- What part of the presentation/project needs more clarification or improvement? Why?
- Is this community service project an example of social entrepreneurship? Why/why not?

This written feedback proves to be an excellent tool to keep all students focused on the presentations. It also provides thoughtful comments from each member of the class community, not just the instructor, for the individual presenter.

When students turn in their final written projects, they are asked to provide an example of how their experiences of learning in this course are different from their learning experiences in a traditional classroom without the community learning requirement. Their responses speak for themselves:

> There is no better learning experience than practicing in the field. Hunger has to be solved with action, poverty has to be solved with action; if we do not go out and see that hundreds of children go to school without having breakfast every morning, or cannot go to a doctor because they do not have health insurance, how will students solve social problems? What can they do sitting at school if they do not know what is going on?

I learned that these people needed a clothing closet, a place to have direct on site assistance in putting together a professional interview and working wardrobe, because many of the residents did not know how to dress for these occasions. Furthermore, I learned that they needed to go to a place that did not resemble a thrift store, but in fact resembled a small upscale boutique where personalized service was part of the experience. They needed to have an environment that treated them with dignity and thus would give them the psychological confidence going forward into the job interview process.

In a traditional classroom setting, I would only be reading about the experiences of social entrepreneurs from a textbook. However, in this service learning experience, I found myself comparing what I was going through in my social venture to the characters in David Bornstein's book, *How to Change the World*, which provided me with a thorough understanding of the process of being a social entrepreneur.

In the classroom, I was surrounded by students and teaching professionals; in the field, I encountered youth whose lives have been shaped not by the promise of an education, but by the complexities of the urban street. By simply being one more adult, bettering myself through school, but someone who was willing to give my time to them, we all prospered.

Getting out of the classroom helped me to develop skills in a different environment with people who had needs different from my own. This experience taught me how to apply what I learned in school to the real world.

Week 16: The Final Test and Personal Evaluation

The only test of the semester, given the last day of class, is open note, and study questions are given in advance for guidance. My objective for the test is not to produce fear but rather to allow students an opportunity to integrate their learning experiences with the process of studying. For the actual test, students are given an hour, instructed to answer questions 1 and 2, and one more question from 3 to 6 of their choosing. A majority of students will be very well prepared; the first time I taught this course, over 80% earned a B or better on the test. The questions are

1. Choose and explain three different variations on the definition of what a social entrepreneur is that we have discussed and referenced this semester.

2. List and define six qualities of social entrepreneurs. Choose and explain how someone, a class speaker, classmate, or an entrepreneur described in our text, embraces each quality. You may choose six different examples. Clearly cite your reference.

Additionally, students are instructed to respond to one of the following questions:

3. List and define four qualities of sustainable organizations. Choose and describe in depth a sustainable organization that exemplifies these qualities.
4. Explain and define the similarities and differences between nonprofit organizations, philanthropic organizations, and social entrepreneurs.
5. What is the Skoll Foundation? Define its mission and focus and explain a project it has funded.
6. Explain the similarities and differences between social entrepreneurs and entrepreneurs. Give an example of each and explain.

On the day of the final, I have an appointment with each student to review and return his or her papers, projects, and tests. This final allows the instructor and student further reflection and insight into what they have discovered regarding civic engagement, sustainable business practices, the community, and themselves. I am humbled at the end of the semester and inspired by the experiences of all students. One graduating senior business student said, "This experience has changed my life path. Being a business major, I always thought profit and making money were the real reasons to go into business, and I struggled with these motives." This student embodies the civic learning outcomes, the combination of knowledge, skills, and disposition (Eisman, 2007) that are the objectives of the class, and she will make a difference in the civic life of our communities, along with the other members of the class. Why am I sure these students will make a difference? A majority of class members voluntarily double the university-required 20 hours per semester for community service learning, and several continue to work on their original or new projects in their community organizations. Together we step outside the traditional structure of disciplinary learning, and the transformation for all of us is contagious.

Conclusion

As an educator, I continually face the task of letting go of students at the end of a semester. At the end of this nontraditional class I wonder if students will continue to practice and inspire others to be agents of change as they continue to volunteer and enter or reenter the workforce? Are the course objectives beneficial for lifelong learning? Is the case study methodology an effective tool for engagement? In the spring of 2008, the effectiveness of the class was solidified. Our university president presented a former class member with the Graduate Award for Community and Civic Engagement for his continuing work with a clothing closet project initiated in my class (see examples in Week 8: Reflection Logs and Sharing Experiences, p. 193). What a thrill it was listening to him describe his connections between our social entrepreneurship class and his community engagement.

References

Bornstein, D. (2004). *How to change the world: Social entrepreneurs and the power of new ideas.* Oxford, UK: Oxford University Press.

Casey, K. M., Davidson, G., Billig, S. H., & Springer, N. C. (Eds.). (2006). *Advancing knowledge in service-learning: Research to transform the field.* Greenwich, CT: Information Age Publishing.

Denzin, N. K., & Lincoln, Y. S. (2000). *Handbook of qualitative research.* Thousand Oaks, CA: Sage.

Dickson, M. A., Rudd, N. A., & Leonard, S. J. (2006). Focused social responsibility: Part 1. *Clothing and Textiles Research Journal, 24*(3), 175–177.

Eisman, G. (2007). About the series. In G. Stahly (Ed.), *Gender identity, equity, and violence: Multidisciplinary perspectives through service learning* (pp. xv–xxvi). Sterling, VA: Stylus.

Hethorn, J., & Ulasewicz C. (2008). *Sustainable fashion: Why now?* New York, NY: Fairchild Press.

Martin, R., & Osberg, S. (2007). Social entrepreneurship: The case for definition. *Stanford Social Innovation Review, 5*(2), 29–39.

Paine, L. S. (2003). *Value shift: Why companies must merge social and financial imperatives to achieve superior performance.* New York, NY: McGraw-Hill.

Pinzon, D. P., & Arceo, F. D. B. (2006). Critical thinking in a higher education service learning program. In K. M. Casey, G. Davidson, S. H. Billig, N. C. Springer (Eds.) *Advancing knowledge in service learning: Research to transform the field* (pp. 89–110). Greenwich, CT: Information Age Publishing.

Stockinger, B. (2006, May–June). The fairest of them all. *Sportswear International.* Retrieved from http://www.katharinehamnett.com/Press/oos/Sportswear+International/

World Commission on Environment and Development. (1987). *Our common future.* Oxford, UK: Oxford University Press.

U.S. Environmental Protection Agency. (2008). *Municipal solid waste generation, recycling and disposal in the United States: Facts and figures for 2008.* Retrieved from http://www.epa.gov/wastes/nonhaz/municipal/pubs/msw2008rpt.pdf

U.S. Environmental Protection Agency. (2011). *Wastes.* Retrieved from http://www.epa.gov/osw

Appendix A

Learning Activity I

Understanding the Case Study Methodology

The purpose of this activity is to analyze and appreciate business practices regarding sustainability and social entrepreneurship. Please write your responses to the statements below and bring them to class, where you will share them to stimulate more thought and discussion.

1. What is the mission of the company? Identify the key people and the interests they represent.
2. How/why did the company/business develop? What is the history?
3. What is the structure of the company?
4. What aspect of the business is representative of a social entrepreneur or social entrepreneurship?
5. What are the company goals? What challenges is it facing in meeting these goals?
6. How/why is its business model sustainable?

What are the obstacles for success? What recommendations do you have to help them succeed?

Appendix B

Learning Activity 2

Project Journals—The Reflection Component

Project journals are required as a method for you to reflect on your community service experiences. You are asked to respond to three separate issues in *each* of your daily journal entries. Entries do not need to be typed; they may include sketches or clippings from magazines.

1. Describe what happened in your creative service experience, including what was accomplished, some of the events that puzzled or confused you, interactions you had, decisions you made, and plans that you developed. Include pictures and sketches of projects to aid in descriptions.

2. Analyze how the course content relates to the service experience, including key concepts that can be used to understand events and guide future interactions.

3. Apply the course materials and the service experience to you and your personal life, including your goals, values, and beliefs.

TEACHING SUSTAINABLE RURAL ECONOMIC DEVELOPMENT USING SERVICE-LEARNING PEDAGOGY

Beth Wilson

T eaching a service-learning course is an extremely rewarding experience for the students and the professor. Students master the course material at a deeper level because they are able to make connections between theory and reality. According to the National Youth Leadership Council (n.d.), "Service-learning is a philosophy, pedagogy, and model for community development that is used as an instructional strategy to meet learning goals and/or content standards."

In this chapter I describe the pedagogy I use for a service-learning course I developed titled Sustainable Rural Economic Development. First, I discuss the course goals in terms of content and service. Second, I explain how I developed this course. Third, I discuss how I attempt to meet the course goals through the course format. Fourth, I highlight how I handle the service component of the course. Fifth, I discuss how I assess whether I am successful at meeting the course goals. Finally, I highlight some of the challenges I have faced. Please see the appendix for a course syllabus.

Course Goals

The content goal of this course is for students to understand the challenges of rural community development from an economic perspective, focusing on

Humboldt County, our local region. A key challenge is how a community balances the need for a vibrant business environment that creates jobs and opportunities while maintaining a rural quality of life. Humboldt County is a natural amenity-rich region plentiful in forests, rivers, coastlands, wetlands, mountains, and clean air. In the past, the regional economy was heavily dependent on extraction industries in forestry and fisheries. Today the regional economy has diversified into tourism, specialty agriculture, and niche manufacturing, among other sectors. In class I highlight the importance of natural amenities as a resource for nonextraction types of economic activity, such as tourism and the attraction of business owners and retirees seeking the quality of life Humboldt County has to offer. Finding the right balance between natural resource extraction and maintaining natural resources for these alternative uses is a challenge. In this context, the students and I explore issues of land planning and environmental sustainability.

We also discuss the importance of base industries and the multiplier effect. Base industries export products and bring new money into the region.[1] The multiplier effect means that this new money is multiplied through the economy so the total boost to the local economy is larger than the initial injection. The multiplier effect occurs because base industry firms create new income for locals as they purchase local inputs (supplies, materials, inventory, machinery, etc.) and pay their workers. These local suppliers in turn buy some of their inputs locally, and the workers spend a portion of their income on local products, thus creating additional new income for locals. This process continues and the initial influx of new money is multiplied through the local economy. For example, if a local manufacturer sells $1 million outside the area, and the multiplier is two, the total boost to the local economy is $2 million. The larger the tendency to buy locally, the larger the multiplier effect; thus, we discuss the importance of a vibrant local economy that supports the base industries.

We explore theoretical models of how owners and managers decide where to locate their business, how they choose their workforce, their financial capital needs, and so on. We discuss how a community makes decisions about economic development plans and the importance of social values and culture in this process. Through these models, we consider a number of ways economic development professionals can facilitate and encourage the type of economic activity the community deems desirable.

The service goals are to help students learn about their role as community members, realize the importance of social networks in creating sustainable development for their community, and inspire them to become thoughtful, caring, committed, and contributing members of society. Most of the students are working with economic development professionals, governmental agencies, or nonprofit organizations. This experience gives them firsthand knowledge of the complications associated with reaching development goals. They quickly see how the material learned in class is relevant to the projects they are involved in in the community. They see the challenges businesses face in our region and start to understand the conflicts between different factions in the community (land developers vs. conservationists, loggers vs. environmentalists, pro-growth/business vs. anti-growth/business, etc.). They see how important it is to build relationships among community members, because this creates the social capital so necessary to achieve change. Many students start thinking about how to solve these problems and how to find a compromise that will allow the various factions to work together toward a common community goal.

It is my hope and belief that service learning helps students think critically about what they learn in the classroom and make connections they would otherwise miss. This richer understanding about how communities organize, make decisions, and achieve their goals helps better prepare students for jobs in development planning and graduate study in development. In addition, because many of the ideas discussed in class apply to less-developed countries, students are also better prepared to pursue international development interests.

Course Development

In the spring of 2003, I created this course with the support of a service-learning fellowship awarded by the Humboldt State University Service Learning Center. The fellowship included financial support for my time, training workshops on how to incorporate service learning into a course and how to use reflection techniques, and information on support services for service-learning courses. This fellowship was essential to the development of this nontraditional course for three key reasons: unique course content, the variety of majors enrolled, and developing the service-learning component.

Unique Course Content

While it is common for economics programs to offer undergraduate courses on economic development in the third world, courses on rural economic development in the United States are less widespread. Thus, there are very few textbooks on this topic, and those in print are primarily geared toward economic development professionals. Consequently, I had to develop all my own pedagogical tools including homework questions, exam questions, lecture notes, and discussion notes. I also had to find additional sources for case studies and applications.

I chose a textbook (Shaffer, Deller, & Marcouiller, 2004) that provides a strong theoretical background in neoclassical economics, while explaining the strengths and weaknesses of our market-based system. Because the market system is the environment where an economic development professional in the United States operates, it is crucial students understand this system. It is also important to understand how and why the market fails. Thus, much of the course focuses on market failures and what a community can do to improve market outcomes. For example, in the land-planning chapter of the text, the theoretical land-rent models of David Ricardo and Johann Heinrich von Thunen are discussed. From these models students can better understand why market failure is associated with land use (i.e., fewer open lands, wetlands, agricultural lands, etc., than socially optimal). The text then discusses the pros and cons of zoning, urban growth boundaries, conservation easements, and other government policies geared toward correcting this market failure.

I supplement the textbook with a reader composed of case studies (Schaeffer & Loveridge, 2000). These cases cover topics such as building industrial parks to attract industry, the importance of community leadership to revitalize a downtown area, the economic and fiscal impacts of a planned retirement community, the benefits of expanding an agricultural base into value-added activities (i.e., food processing), and the benefits of agricultural/ nature-based tourism. I have also used newspaper and journal articles on the economic impact of a theater renovation (Wilson, 2007), land-planning alternatives for population growth (Steinberg, Smith, & Gough, 2007), agglomeration economies from coffee shops locating close to each other (Clark, 2007), and the effect of Walmart on the social capital of a local community (Goetz & Rupasingha, 2006), among others.

Variety of Majors Enrolled

Humboldt State University has a relatively small number of economics majors. To offer a variety of economics electives each semester, administrators of the economics department found it necessary to offer some electives accessible to noneconomics majors. Consequently, I designed this service-learning course as a seminar-style course with no prerequisites. With the hope of attracting more serious and mature students, I restrict enrollment to juniors, seniors, and graduate students and limit the class size to 15–17 students. Historically, most of the undergraduates have been business and economics majors, but French, sociology, geography, and environmental sciences majors have enrolled in the course. The graduate students are mostly from the interdisciplinary environment and community master's program, with a few from the environmental systems master's program.

Thus, some students have a solid background in economic theory, while others have never taken an economics course at the university level. Although I designed the course for students with little or no economics background, the textbook and many of the additional readings assume students have some background in economics. Consequently, I have had to make a number of adjustments that would not have been necessary if a prerequisite were in place. For example, I use vocabulary lists and lecture on a few of the more technically oriented models to ensure that everyone understands the models intuitively rather than mathematically, and so they can see how they apply to rural economic development in the modern day.

Furthermore, graduate students have different pedagogical expectations than undergraduates. For example, they prefer a variety of readings rather than a textbook, and papers rather than exams. The breakdown in the past has been about 85% undergraduate and 15% graduate students. Thus, it was essentially an undergraduate course taken by a handful of graduate students. However, I am working to integrate this course into the core curriculum for the environment and community master's program. Because of this, the breakdown has shifted to 50% undergraduate and 50% graduate students. To meet the different expectations of these two groups of students, the economics department will offer the graduate course separately in the future.

Developing the Service-Learning Component

Developing a service-learning component for the first time was a challenge for me. My fellowship was instrumental in helping me understand what service learning is and how it differs from volunteerism or internships. It also helped me design reflection techniques I use to help students make connections between their service activities and class material. Although the Humboldt State University Service Learning Center staff was very helpful with general information on service-learning pedagogy, I had to spend quite a bit of time making connections with economic development professionals in the community. Before each semester begins, I contact a number of people in the community to let them know I am teaching this course and may have students interested in working with them. They send me descriptions of projects they have in mind. I make it very clear that I may not have a student for them if nobody shows interest in their project. I make a list of these service-learning options, and I hand them out on the first day of class. Staff at our campus Office for Economic and Community Development has also helped me make these connections. Every semester I need community input for service sites, class speakers, and a field trip.

Course Format

The course is a four-unit course. We meet in the classroom for three hours per week, and the fourth hour is for the students' service obligations. In class we discuss textbook and case/article readings, listen to guest speakers from the community, reflect on our service experiences in discussion format, and take exams. We also have one field trip where we tour two local manufacturing firms. Outside class, students meet with their community partner supervisor, and together they decide what tasks the student is to complete.

I primarily use a discussion format for this class, lecturing on only the more technically advanced theories. Students are required to have read the assigned readings. A typical assignment includes a textbook chapter and either a case study or an article. In addition, I assign open-ended discussion questions as homework. Students are required to write responses to these questions before class, and their responses form the basis for our discussion in class.

Some of these questions are geared toward understanding the main theoretical points of the chapter. An example of such a question from the land-planning chapter is: "Intuitively explain the Ricardian land-rent model. Intuitively explain the von Thunen land-rent model. How do they relate to modern-day reality?" Answering this multipart question requires the student to summarize the two theories in layperson's terms and discuss how they relate to the land issues of today. Because the text uses mathematics and graphs to explain each theory, students without an economics background will often have difficulty picking out the main points of the theories on their own. Thus, we spend class time making sure everyone understands the main assumptions and implications of each theory. As mentioned, some theories are so technically advanced I have found it necessary to give a short lecture on them. But for most theories we can unveil the main points through discussion.

Other assigned questions are geared toward applications of the theory. An example from the land-planning chapter is: "Explain what is meant by urban sprawl. Explain the economic basis for urban sprawl. Explain how urban growth boundaries (UGBs), transfer of development rights (TDRs), and purchase of development rights (PDRs) help to reduce sprawl." To answer this multipart question, students apply the Ricardian and von Thunen theories to the modern day by using them to explain why agricultural and open lands are undervalued by our market system and how urban sprawl is a result of this market failure. Since UGBs, TDRs, and PDRs are three of the many tools a government can use to correct this market failure, students gain a practical understanding of how these strategies work.

I also use questions that link an article or a case to the chapter material. One article (Steinberg et al., 2007), used in conjunction with the land-planning chapter, explores how McKinleyville, a large unincorporated area just north of Arcata in Humboldt County, can meet the housing needs of its expected population growth through 2025. The article presents a geographic information systems (GIS) model that is used to explore the look and feel of different density options in each of the three levels of zoning currently in place in McKinleyville. One option is similar to the UGBs discussed in class, while other options allow for more sprawl. The article allows students to explore issues of affordable housing, exurbanization of rural areas, and quality of life. In addition, I often use case studies that illustrate rural development issues in other parts of the United States, and we discuss the lessons Humboldt County can learn from them.

Finally, once students have started their service projects, about one month into the semester, I begin asking a reflection question for each chapter. An example from the land-planning chapter is: "Reflect on your service project and make connections between what you are observing and the land issues discussed in this chapter." I ask two or three students to briefly tell the class about their project and highlight the connections they are making. Students working on affordable housing, carbon credits, and agricultural projects are able to make the strongest connections to this chapter. Other students make stronger connections with other chapters but still have some connection to make with land issues. This part of our class discussion is informative and fun. Students enjoy hearing about other students' projects, and the discussion often allows students to look at their own projects in a new way.

To enhance the application-oriented nature of a service-learning course, I invite speakers from the local community to talk about their experiences with economic development. Generally, we hear from three speakers each semester. I invite speakers who are community development professionals from a variety of organizations. Speakers are asked to give a presentation on how their organization contributes to economic development in the region and allow plenty of time for questions. I always have someone from the Humboldt County Economic Development Office, because it is directly involved with Prosperity! the economic development plan for Humboldt County. This plan is based on many of the theories we discuss in class, and we refer to this plan repeatedly throughout the course.

In the past I have also used speakers from the Small Business Development Center, an organization that provides management assistance to small businesses. For example, the center staff helps with writing business plans and providing information on how to get funding. We have also heard from the Arcata Economic Development Corporation, a local nonprofit that makes loans to entrepreneurs who cannot get loans through banks. An entire chapter is devoted to financial capital, so students understand how important debt and equity financing are for economic growth. The director of our campus Office for Economic and Community Development has also spoken to my class. His office creates linkages between the university and private, public, and nonprofit sectors of the community, an issue integrated throughout the semester. The Center for Environmental Economic Development, a nonprofit organization working for environmentally sustainable economic development, has also sent representatives to speak to the class. Staff at the center has worked on a variety of projects, including carbon credit programs and the development of an eco-hostel that would be energy self-sufficient and provide a location for environmental conferences.

At midsemester, I start emphasizing the connections between the students' service projects and class material. At this stage, we have had one or two speakers, and each student is engrossed in his or her project. Students begin to have a greater depth of understanding about the difficulties of translating theory into practice. Again, this is a good opportunity for students to learn from each other.

Finally, the last section of the course is exclusively application oriented. Students have a solid theoretical foundation, and they have made strong connections between their service projects and the course material. The final section encourages students to think about the challenges an economic development professional faces when trying to instigate change. At this stage of the course we have our field trip.

The field trip, organized with the help of our campus Office for Economic and Community Development, consists of a tour of two local manufacturing plants. In class we emphasize the importance of export industries and entrepreneurship. Our local manufacturers provide an example of the various issues involved. Because Humboldt County is so remote, our manufacturing sector is small but vibrant. Manufacturing is also a sector of the economy that is less visible to the average citizen, compared to retail establishments, restaurants, and the logging industry. Over the past few years, my classes have visited a variety of local manufacturers, including the Tofu Shop (artisan organic tofu products), Holly Yashi (jewelry), Cypress Grove (artisan goat cheese), American Hydroponics (hydroponics equipment), Yakima (car racks), Kokatat (high-end clothing and dry suits for water sports and the military), and J. R. Stevens (furniture for institutions like hospitals and schools).

The field trip to local businesses is the highlight of the semester for most students. It is, of course, interesting to see how a product is made, but students are more interested in the business side of things. Each tour is usually conducted by the owner of the firm, allowing students to ask in-depth questions. Students are interested in how the business got started, how funding and technical assistance were obtained, where and how the business obtains its raw materials, and how the finished product is transported to its final destination. Other areas of interest are the number of workers the business employs, whether benefits are offered to workers, what challenges the business has faced regarding workers' compensation, and the business's stance toward unions. The owners are quite appreciative of the interest the students show.

Service-Learning Component

The fourth unit of the course is the service component. On the first day of the semester, I hand out a list of service site options from the information I obtained before the semester started. Many students, especially graduate students who wish to link their service project with their thesis research, have their own projects in mind. I ask them to discuss their ideas with me so I can determine whether their proposed project fits the definition of service learning and relates to the course content. I use the following criteria for determining whether a particular project is an appropriate service-learning opportunity:

- The student cannot be paid for his or her work. It is not an internship. Some students work with their current employer, but the service project has to be clearly defined and separate from their normal duties.
- The outcome of the project cannot be solely for profit but must include general benefits for the community as a whole. For example, one student worked with a local developer on affordable housing. The developer was interested in the feasibility of including affordable housing in his development. This benefits the developer, but it also has general benefits to the community because there is an affordable housing shortage in Humboldt County.
- The project must be related to community economic development so that the student is able to make connections to class material. Service learning is based on the idea of reciprocal learning (Sigmon, 1979). The student and the community partner must benefit from the experience, which is what separates service learning from pure volunteerism and pure internships. Service learning is a balance between these two concepts (Furco, 1996).

Once the student has chosen a project, he or she contacts the service site supervisor and discusses the details. The goals of the project and the responsibilities of each party are formally communicated through the service-learning agreement and the learning plan. These forms are provided by our campus service-learning center and are available online (http://www.hum boldt.edu/servicelearning/handbooks_forms.html). The service-learning agreement lists the expectations of the student, the site supervisor, and the faculty member, and all three parties sign the agreement. The learning plan, the most important document, is essentially a contract the student makes with his or her supervisor. Each party describes expectations and agrees on the learning objectives and the service objectives. The learning objectives are what the student hopes to learn from the experience; the service objectives are the specific tasks the student will undertake. The interaction required to complete these forms highlights and clarifies the reciprocal nature of the service-learning experience.

Students are required to make a 25- to 30-hour time commitment to their service partner and are required to fill out the service learner time log as they work on their projects and accumulate their hours. Their site supervisor signs this form at the end of the semester. In addition, the supervisor completes an evaluation on each student.

Reflection

Students reflect on their service experiences through a journal assignment and class activities. The journal requires that they describe the work they did that week and reflect on challenges, frustrations, rewards, and connections they are making with the course material. I read the journals two to three times during the semester and make comments to encourage thought and deepen reflection. I grade this assignment based on the frequency of entries and improvement in the depth of the students' reflection over the semester. Usually students who are writing regularly show improvement and find value in the exercise.

There are multiple purposes for requiring each student to keep a journal. First, journaling helps students reflect on their service experience and make connections between the course material and their real-world experience. Second, the activity helps students gather their thoughts when preparing their final project or paper. Finally, keeping a journal helps improve writing skills.

During class discussions, as students reflect on the connections between the course material and their service experience, it becomes apparent that certain service site challenges occur with some frequency. For example, it is often difficult for students to find meeting times with busy people in the community. Sometimes, business owners or managers are reluctant to talk to students about controversial issues. Sometimes the community partner is so busy, it is a challenge to get started. Oftentimes, the original project is too large for the 25- to 30-hour time requirement and needs to be pared down. The reflection process brings these issues to light and allows students to find solutions together.

Project Outcome

Because each project is different, outcomes will differ. However, every student presents his or her work to the class and delivers some tangible item that can be evaluated. Most of the service experiences are project based. In these cases, students hand in a copy of the final product created for their service partner with a two- to three-page executive summary. Often the final product is a paper, but sometimes it is a survey, data collected, a poster, a game, or something else. Occasionally, a students do time-based service in which they write a paper discussing their experiences, highlighting how they relate to economic development and perhaps making some policy recommendations.

Service Sites

Most students work on an independent project with a service partner. Occasionally, students work in pairs. Tables 11.1–11.4 present examples of the types of service sites where students gain their experiences. In general, students have worked with economic development organizations (Table 11.1), government entities (Table 11.2), nonprofit organizations (Table 11.3), and for-profit organizations (Table 11.4).

Assessment

In general, I think I am successful at meeting the course objectives. I base this on student feedback, feedback from community partners, students' final projects, exam results, and class discussion. Nevertheless, I do think there is room for improvement.

Student Feedback

Feedback comes from course evaluations, student assessment forms, and informal comments from students months (or years) after the course. My evaluations are generally very high for this course, which shows that students

TABLE 11.1
Service With Economic Development Organizations

Service Site	Type of Organization	Project	Student Role in Project	Benefit to Community
California Center for Rural Policy	University research center	Latino Health Study	Create an annotated medical bibliography for the study	Understand health care challenges faced by Latinos
Humboldt County Office of Economic Development	Economic development for the county	Community outreach	Create board game to show linkages between community groups	Builds social capital, facilitates development
North Coast Small Business Development Center	Provider of technical assistance to firms	Mentor program	Develop outreach letter and mentor questionnaire	Entrepreneurs can help other entrepreneurs to be successful
Office for Economic and Community Development (OECD)	University link to community	1. Marketing 2. Nonprofit status for film commission	1. Pull together multimedia stories 2. Customize paperwork	1. Shows impact of OECD on community 2. Encourages film/ads to be produced in Humboldt
Small Business Development Lead Center	Provider of technical assistance to firms	Discovers needs of local businesses	Survey local businesses about transportation needs	Provides information that can be used to meet business needs

TABLE 11.2
Service With Government Entities

Service Site	Type of Organization	Project	Student Role in Project	Benefit to Community
1st District Assembly	State government	Wastewater issues	Create survey to determine wastewater plant conditions; pilot test survey	Promotes understanding of problems facing community wastewater treatment facilities
Arcata Chamber of Commerce	City government	Green business program	Develop a plan to establish a green business program	Encourages firms to adopt green business practices
City of Fortuna	City government	General plan update	Research economic components of city general plans	Provides community development planning

TABLE 11.3
Service With Nonprofit Organizations

Service Site	Type of Organization	Project	Student Role in Project	Benefit to Community
Arcata Economic Development Corporation (AEDC)	Lender and provider of technical assistance	1. Evaluate Individual Development Account program 2. Marketing research	1. Surveyed participants; compiled results 2. Prepared timeline of AEDC history	1. Helps low-income entrepreneurs 2. Highlights impact of organization on community
Arcata Educational Farm	Agricultural cooperative	Time based	Weeded and harvested; built tables	Sustainable agriculture
Arcata Endeavor	Day shelter/crisis center	Time based	Helped with food boxes and clothing boxes	Aids the poor
Center for Environmental Economic Development	Environmental advocacy firm	1. Eco-hostel 2. Carbon-credits	1. Completed various research projects 2. Looked at viability of using program in Humboldt County	1. Encourages ecotourism 2. Increases environmental sustainability
Democracy Unlimited	Advocacy organization	1. Independent business directory 2. Job density study for Arcata	1. Developed business plan for producing directory; created prototype of directory 2. Surveyed firms on Plaza and in West End	1. Facilitates consumers' ability to buy locally 2. Illustrates differences between outside chains and locally owned firms
Healthy Humboldt Coalition	Advocacy organization	1. Education on rural development basics 2. Job density study for Eureka	1. Created PowerPoint and notes 2. Surveyed firms in Mall and Old Town	1. Educates locals on sustainable rural development 2. Illustrates differences between outside chains and locally owned firms
North Coast Growers Association	Sponsors of farmers markets	Time based	Helped prepare for season	Increases viability of local agriculture

TABLE 11.4
Service With For-Profit Organizations

Service Site	Type of Organization	Project	Student Role in Project	Benefit to Community
AlgaRhythms	Fertilizer company	Harvesting algae from wastewater ponds	Set up a dissolved air flotation system	Uses side effects of city's wastewater system
Security National	Property management company	Brownfield development	Researched viability of including affordable housing in developments	Promotes more affordable housing

enjoy it and find it to be a valuable experience. The student assessment form, provided by our service-learning center, specifically evaluates the service-learning component. Students say they like the new perspective they get. They like the hands-on learning, and they think service learning helps them better understand the class material. Table 11.5 lists some of the responses to the key objective questions.

Informally, many students say the class is the best experience they have had in school. When I ask why, they say they feel like they learned so much more because of the real-world applications. I have the sense that my students view their role in the community differently after taking my class. Some students go on to work for nonprofits, and others think about how their for-profit activities affect their community. Unfortunately, I do not have a formal measurement of whether I am meeting the goal of creating better citizens. This would be extremely difficult but worthwhile to do.

Community Partner Feedback

The feedback from the community partners has also been very positive. Supervisors fill out the evaluation by site supervisor form obtained from our service-learning center. I also receive informal comments from site supervisors. The vast majority of students do an exceptionally good job, and the community partners are satisfied with the students' work. Because of the importance of community partner satisfaction, this is an area I continually try to improve. Table 11.6 lists some of the responses to the key objective questions on the evaluation form.

TABLE 11.5
Responses to Key Student Assessment Questions

Question	Rank 1–5 With 5 Being Very Satisfied
Overall, I am satisfied with the service-learning experience in this course.	71% marked 5 29% marked 4
I was able to apply the concepts I learned in class to the service-learning experience.	50% marked 5 36% marked 4 14% marked 3
Service learning in this course strengthened the learning experience.	71.5% marked 5 21.5% marked 4 7% marked 3

TABLE 11.6
Responses to Key Evaluation by Site Supervisor Questions

Rate the Service Learner's Performance in	*Rank 1–5 Where 5 = Excellent and 3 = Satisfactory*
Fulfillment of learning plan objectives	58.3% marked 5 25% marked 4 16.7% marked 3
Quality of performance of service activities	58.3% marked 5 25% marked 4 16.7% marked 3
Benefit of service provided by agency	58.3% marked 5 33.3% marked 4 8.3% marked 3

Final Project

Students hand in their final projects for evaluation and present their work to the class. This is one of the most enjoyable parts of the course. It is extremely rewarding for me and the other students to formally hear about the projects we have been discussing all semester. The vast majority of students do an exceptionally good job on these projects.

Exam Results and Class Discussion

I evaluate course content learning primarily through the essay exam results. The essay questions come from the homework questions. Often I incorporate two related homework questions into one essay question. I also design a question asking students to connect their service experience to the course material. What I notice is that by the last exam, the students' depth of thought and their synthesis of ideas have improved significantly. I see a similar improvement in our class discussions. Students are able to integrate past chapters, case studies, articles, other students' service projects, their own projects, guest speakers, and our field trip. I attribute this depth of understanding to the service-learning nature of the course. The real-world experience makes the course material more relevant to the students than it might otherwise be.

218 SUSTAINABILITY CONCEPTS IN BUSINESS AND ECONOMICS

Challenges

Quality control for the service project is the most important challenge I face. I believe the standard must be higher than it would be in a regular course because the output is for a community partner. As mentioned previously, the vast majority of students do an exceptional job on their projects. The challenge is to make sure *all* students do an exceptional job. In the past, a couple of students merely did a satisfactory job, and in one case a student did an unsatisfactory job. Fortunately, these instances are the exception rather than the rule. Yet, improving the quality of the service projects is an area I pay constant attention to. Each semester I have made modifications that I hope improve the likelihood of obtaining high-quality projects from all students. Currently, I closely monitor students through their journals and class discussion. I emphasize the learning plans and make sure each student is clear about the expectations of his or her site supervisor. I require each student to hand in a rough draft of his or her project prior to giving it to his or her supervisor. This allows me to make comments and if necessary help the student deliver an exceptional final product to the community partner. All this monitoring also helps ensure that projects are completed on time. Of course, nothing is foolproof, but I believe my modifications have made a positive difference.

Another challenge is that the format of the final product can be difficult to evaluate. For example, one student was to provide his site supervisor with raw data from a survey he created and administered. The raw data was his deliverable, and that is all he handed in to me. To avoid this problem, I now require all students to write a two- to three-page executive summary to accompany the final product they hand in to their supervisor. This summary briefly describes the project, highlights the work the student has done, includes any conclusions and results from the student's work, and makes connections to class material. This is also helpful for grading projects completed in pairs. Since each student is required to hand in an executive summary to accompany the joint final project, it allows me to better assess the quality of work from each student.

With a discussion-oriented course, it is crucial that students come to class prepared. They must have read the assigned material and answered the homework questions. It can be a challenge to inspire students to take on this responsibility. However, I have not had too many problems with unprepared students. This could be for a variety of reasons. It is a small class, and students know they will stand out if they are unprepared. They probably recognize that the small seminar style requires more responsibility on their part. Enrollment is restricted to upperclassmen and graduate students, who tend to be more mature and motivated. Finally, students take this course out of interest rather than as a requirement. Because this has not been a problem, I have not implemented a hefty process for checking their preparedness. I simply walk around the room and glance at their homework. If they have not attempted the homework at all, they get a zero for the day.

Even the field trip poses its challenges, the first being logistics. Fortunately, I have a university organization that helps me with this. The Office for Economic and Community Development staff contacts various firms and makes the arrangements. Then I contact each firm to let management know what my course is about and the emphasis the tour should take. The second challenge is making sure every student attends. Because the field trip takes place outside regularly scheduled class, I discuss the timing of the trip with my students well in advance, and together we choose a date and time that works for everyone. Some students need to get permission to miss another class and I help them with that. I also send an e-mail reminder the day before the field trip. Nevertheless, at the last minute, there is always one student who cannot go for one reason or another. If a student is ill or has a family emergency, it is an excused absence, and I make an exception. If a student simply forgets, I reduce his or her class participation grade. I allow no exceptions.

Some Final Thoughts

I have found teaching a service-learning course to be extremely rewarding. I believe the depth of understanding and synthesis of ideas I observe in my students would not be possible without the service-learning component. Students see a relevance to the material they do not get in an ordinary course. It is a very powerful experience for most students. The course requires more work for the student and the teacher than a regular course does, but it seems worth the extra effort. Student learning appears to be much higher.

In addition, it is a good opportunity to create valuable linkages between the community and the university. I feel strongly that it is important for a university to be a good citizen in its community. Fostering university-community relationships creates social capital, which helps to increase the productivity of the region and is important for achieving economic development. Service-learning courses help students and faculty better understand the needs of the community. This can have a number of spillover effects in terms of faculty research, student projects, and graduating community-minded students. It is exciting to be part of something so relevant.

However, getting started can be challenging. As stated previously, I am fortunate to have several university resources that are extremely helpful in developing and maintaining a service-learning course. With a few years' experience, I have developed a strong list of community partners and potential speakers. Community participants and our students look forward to this course offering each year. I strongly believe the benefits of developing and offering a service-learning course far outweigh the challenges and extra work. A service-learning course would be a valuable addition to most programs.

Note

1. In Humboldt County we have identified nine base industries: forest products, education/research, tourism, niche manufacturing, dairy, specialty agriculture, fisheries, information technology, and arts and culture.

References

Clark, T. (2007). Don't Fear Starbucks. *Slate.* http://www.slate.com/id/2180301/

Furco, A. (1996). Service learning: A balanced approach to experiential education. In B. Taylor (Ed.), *Expanding boundaries: Service and learning* (pp. 2–6). Washington, DC: Corporation for National Service.

Goetz, S. J., & Rupasingha, A. (2006). Wal-Mart and social capital. *American Journal of Agricultural Economics, 88*(5), 1304–1310.

National Youth Leadership Council. (n.d.). *Discover service learning.* Retrieved from http://www.nylc.org

Schaeffer, P. V., & Loveridge, S. (2000). *Small town and rural economic development.* Westport, CT: Praeger.

Shaffer, R., Deller, S., & Marcouiller, D. (2004). *Community economics: Linking theory and practice* (2nd ed.). Ames, IA: Blackwell.

Sigmon, R. (1979). Service-learning: Three principles. *Synergist, 8*(1), 9–11.

Steinberg, S., Smith, M., & Gough, M. (2007). *McKinleyville community planning area residential development analysis.* Arcata, CA: Humboldt State University, Department of Environmental and Natural Resources Sciences.

Wilson, B. (2007). *Economic impact study of the Ingomar theatre.* Eureka, CA: Northern California Indian Development Council.

Appendix

Syllabus: Sustainable Rural Economic Development—
ECON 470/570—Spring 2008

Professor: Dr. Beth Wilson   Phone: (707) 826-5302   E-mail: bwilson@humboldt.edu

Office: 206-D SH   Office Hours: TR: 1:00–1:50pm, or by appointment.

Required:	*Community Economics: Linking Theory and Practice*, 2nd ed, by Shaffer, Deller, & Marcouiller. Moodle: (http://learn.humboldt.edu user id=axe id, password=HSU password). You are required to check Moodle regularly for a schedule of class activities, assigned readings, dates of interest (ie., exam dates, due dates, etc), and links to some assigned readings. E-mail—You are expected to check e-mail regularly. Your classmates or I may contact you via e-mail.
Goal of Course:	The primary goal of this course is for students to learn to analyze the challenges of rural economic development from an economic perspective. A secondary goal is to help the student to become a better citizen. This is a service-learning course, thus you will have the opportunity to experience the reality that our economic theories are trying to explain while providing a valuable service to the community. You will engage in continuous reflection about your experiences through oral discussion in class and also by keeping a journal. Throughout the course, you will learn to think critically about development issues and your role as a member of society. You will recognize that there are both costs and benefits to any development plan and that there are no easy solutions. Please notice that this course requires substantial reading and thinking about economic issues. To accomplish the course goals you should expect to work hard over the next few months.
Course Units:	This is a 4-unit course. We will meet in class for 3 units, where we will discuss readings, listen to guest speakers, reflect on our service experiences, and take exams. In addition, we will have at least one "field trip" to local firms. The 4th unit is your service. You are expected to spend at least 25–30 hours at your service site or doing work for your "client." In addition, you will spend time writing in your journal and preparing a final "product" to present to the class at the end of the semester.
Goal of SL:	To help students to learn about their role as community members, to help them realize the importance of "social capital" in creating sustainable development for their community, and to inspire them to become thoughtful, caring, committed, and contributing members of society. In addition, service learning helps students to think critically about what they learn in the classroom and make connections that they may otherwise miss.

Course Requirements: Your grade will be based on the following:

Participation & Homework	10%
Service & Journal	10%

Exams	51%
Final Service Project	29%
Total	100%

Part/Hmwk: The course format is seminar-style discussion. The homework questions are used as the basis of our discussions. Therefore, it is crucial that you attend every class and that you read the assigned materials and complete the weekly homework questions. I also expect you to arrive on time. As a service learning course, we will often discuss reflection questions to help you make connections between your service experience and the theory in the text. We will also have a number of guest speakers. If you must miss class, it is your responsibility to let me know why. Your grade will be reduced with each unexcused absence and each incomplete homework assignment. I do not accept late homework for any reason.

Service/Journal: You are required to make a 25–30-hour commitment to your service partner and you are expected to take your work seriously. You will also keep a journal to help you to reflect on your service experience.

Exams: There are three exams throughout the semester (see following page [or Moodle] for dates and mark your calendar now). Each covers material from the text, extra readings/cases, and class discussions. Each exam is worth 17% of your grade. The exam format is short essay.

Project: Some service experiences are project-based. In this case, you will give a brief presentation to the class about your service experience and what you learned and you will hand in a copy of the final product with a brief introductory summary about what you did, what you learned and how it relates to class. Other service experiences are service-oriented. In these cases, you will write a paper discussing your experiences and how they relate to economic development and perhaps make some policy recommendations. You will present your ideas to the class.

Grade Scale: I round up to the half point, then use the following scale:

100–92.5:	A
92–90:	A–
89.5–88.5:	B+
88–82.5:	B
82–80:	B–
79.5–78.5:	C+
78–72.5:	C
72–70:	C–
69.5–68:	D+
67.5–60:	D
59.5–0:	F

Make-Ups: Make-up exams are only available if you have proof of an excused absence. Examples of excused absences include illness (only with evidence of a doctor visit), family emergencies, job interviews, etc. Sleeping through an exam or leaving for vacation are NOT excused absences. Based on the information that you provide, I will determine whether or not your absence is excused. My decision is final.

Responsibilities and Classroom Etiquette:

Professor responsibility: I am responsible for facilitating the learning process for students who are committed to learning. I am responsible for determining the extent to which students have met the stated goals in this course. I am expected to be fair, courteous and respectful, to be responsive to student needs, and not to discriminate based on race, gender, ethnicity, or sexual or religious preference. Grades are assigned based on my professional judgment of the quality of your work and are not subject to negotiation.

Student responsibility: You are responsible for your learning outcomes and your performance on all assignments. You are responsible for contacting the professor or a tutor if you are strug-gling with the material. You are expected to attend class regularly and on time, to be active learners who contribute to the classroom discussion/activities, and to be courteous and re-spectful of the other students and the professor. This includes arriving on time, turning off cell phones/pagers/alarms, refraining from talking (or whispering) to your neighbor if the professor or another student is addressing the class, refraining from packing up your bags prior to the end of class, etc. Cheating is taken very seriously and will not be tolerated. Please refer to the university's Academic Dishonesty Policy in your Catalog to inform yourself of the consequences of such actions.

Please help me to create a classroom culture that is friendly, supportive, and encourages learning.

General Outline of Course

The class format is seminar-style discussion. To maximize the effectiveness of this methodol-ogy, it is crucial that you read the assigned chapters and articles, and complete the related homework assignment, prior to class.

NOTE: This text is technical, but the course is not. You are responsible for understanding the material in an intuitive, non-mathematical manner. The target audience for this text is BOTH economics majors and those without an economics background. If you are an eco-nomics major, you may find the equations and graphs helpful to understanding the theories and ideas. If you are new to economics, simply ignore the technical aspects and develop an intuitive understanding of the theories and ideas. When necessary, I will create a list of eco-nomic vocabulary words to help you better understand the terminology used in the text (see homework).

The following is a brief list of topics to be covered and related textbook reading assignments. In addition, I will often ask you to read extra materials and case studies. Please check Moodle for the most recent information on class activities and reading assignments.

Material Covered:	Assigned Textbook Readings:
What is Service Learning?	Handouts
Defining Community Economic Development	Chapter 1
Growth Theory	Chapter 2

Space and Community Economics	Chapter 3
Concepts of Community Markets	Chapter 4

Exam #1—Thursday, February 21st

Land Markets	Chapter 5
Labor Markets	Chapter 6
Financial Capital Markets	Chapter 7
Amenities & Services	Chapter 9

Exam #2—Thursday, April 3rd

Institutions and Society	Chapter 11
Policy Modeling and Decision Making	Chapter 12
The Practice of Community Economic Development	Chapter 13

Exam #3—Thursday, May 1st

Project presentations are on May 6 & 8 during class time, and May 13 during final time (3–4:50pm). Attendance is required.

I reserve the right to alter the above schedule if necessary. You are required to check Moodle regularly for changes.

AACSB. *See* Association to Advance Collegiate Schools of Business
AACU. *See* Association of American Colleges and Universities
activism, and environmental awareness, 116–134
advocacy, in ecosystem course, 139, 141
American Association of State Colleges and Universities (AASCU), 64, 135
American College & University Presidents' Climate Commitment, 72
American Democracy Project (ADP), 64, 135
Anderson, Jennifer, 154–156
Andersonville Development Corporation, 85
Anielski, Mark, 12
Annan, Kofi, 167
apparel industry, sustainable design and, 188–189, 192–193
Arcata Economic Development Corporation, 209
Ashbury Images, 192
assessment
    in economics course, 213–218, 216*t*
    in ecosystem course, 141
    in environmental science course, 123–124
    in PACSE program, 12–15
    in SAGE program, 180
    in science and sustainability curriculum, 31–32
    in sustainable design course, 196–198
    See also evaluation
Association of American Colleges and Universities (AACU), xi
Association to Advance Collegiate Schools of Business (AACSB), 165, 167, 169, 173
Augustana College, 3–20, 19n7

Barbier, E. B., 78, 94
base industries, 203, 220n1

Berdon, T. J., 43
Berry, Wendell, 4
Berthold, Laura, 50
biodiesel, STEP program on, 39–45
blueprint model, for SAGE program, 178–180, 179*f*
bonding social capital, 172
Bornstein, D., 174, 176, 190
Bourdieu, Pierre, 169
Boyer, E. L., 169
bridging social capital, 172
Brooks, Jeremy, 78–115
Brown, Lester, 35–36
brucellosis, 136
Brundtland Commission, 78
buffer zone, 24
business
    social entrepreneurial, sustainable design and, 187–201
    socially responsible, definition of, 188–189
    and sustainability, 74–75
business course, service learning in, 165–186
    syllabus for, 180, 181*f*
Butte Community College (BCC), 72–73

California State University (CSU), xv
    Chico, 61–77
    and service learning, 63
campesinos, 9
campus sustainability efforts
    CSU Chico and, 66, 70–72
    Green Mountain College and, 22
    Loyola University Chicago and, 45, 79, 92, 94
    Whittier College and, 118, 124–125, 128
Canada World Youth (CWY), 7, 188n1
capital
    term, 166
    See also social capital

Carnegie Foundation, 64
case studies
    in social entrepreneurship, 190–192, 195–
        196, 200
    in sustainable rural development, 205
CAVE. *See* Community Action Volunteers in
    Education
citizen organizations, 174
civic engagement, xv–xvi
    and environmental awareness, 116–134
    and environmental stewardship, 135–145
    infrastructure and, 68–75
    Loyola and, 79
    projects in, 110
    social capital and, 168–174, 171*t*
    and sustainability, 61–77
    types of, 171*f*
CLIC. *See* Community Legal Information
    Center
climate change
    environmental science course on, 120
    McDonald on, xxiii–xxv
Coffman, Elizabeth, 47–48
Coleman, J. S., 169–170
Collins, Jim, 67
communitarianism, 171*t*, 172
community
    environmental sustainability course and,
        92–94
    Loyola University Chicago and, 80–81
    PACSE program and, 9
    STEP program and, 50
    term, xxiv, 80
    See also rural communities; urban
        communities
Community Action Volunteers in Education
    (CAVE), 63
community-based learning
    and learning gardens, 146–161
    term, 147
    See also service learning
Community Legal Information Center
    (CLIC), 69
community partners
    and assessment, 32
    and campus sustainability efforts, 69–70,
        72

economics course and, 214*t*–215*t*, 216–217,
    217*t*
ecosystem course and, 142–143
environmental sustainability course and,
    85–88
and learning gardens, 146–161
science and sustainability curriculum and,
    27–29
STEP program and, 46
sustainable design course and, 192–193
community service learning. *See* service
    learning
compact fluorescent bulbs, 28–29
conferences, on sustainability, 71–73
core commitments, AACU on, xi
core instructors, 18
Corrigan, Robert A., xi–xiii
Cortese, Anthony, 72
Cow Power, 22
Crace, Jim, 120
creative capitalism, Gates on, 167
creativity, service learning and, 25
critical pedagogy, of place, 6, 8, 11–12
critical thinking
    environmental sustainability course and,
        94–95
    learning gardens and, 148–149, 154
cross-disciplinary learning. *See* interdisciplin-
    ary service learning
CSU. *See* California State University
cultural contexts, and learning gardens, 148
cultural relativism, 12
curriculum
    business, 173–175
    environmental liberal arts, 22
    science and sustainability, 21–34, 78–115
CWY. *See* Canada World Youth

Dakota Digital Network (DDN), 137
DeBerg, Curtis L., 165–186
democracy, problems with, civic engagement
    and, 61–77
development studies program, 15
diaries. *See* journals
dinámicas, 11
DiPadova-Stocks, L. N., 175

Drucker, P., 173
Duke University, 175

Eames, J. Marshall, 78–115
ecological crisis, Berry on, 4
economics
    business course, 165–186
    and learning gardens, 148–150
    PACSE program and, 11
    and sustainability, 69–70
    sustainable rural development, 202–225
economics course, 202–225
    challenge in, 218–219
    development of, 204–207
    format of, 207–211
    goals of, 202–204
    service sites in, 213, 214*t*–215*t*
    syllabus for, 222–225
ecosystem course, 135–145
    development of, 137–138
    future directions for, 144–145
    requirements in, 139
    structure of, 138
Edgewater, IL, 79–81, 85, 92
Eisman, Gerald, xv–xvi
ELA. *See* environmental liberal arts
    curriculum
elementary school, learning gardens and, 146,
    150
engagement
    science and, 117
    See also civic engagement
entrepreneurship
    term, 190
    See also social entrepreneurship
environment, STEP program and, 50–51
environmental awareness, service learning
    and, 116–134
environmental liberal arts (ELA) curriculum,
    22
environmental literacy, 70
Environmental Protection Agency, 148, 189
environmental science course, 116–134
    learning objectifes for, 123
    student demographics in, 119*t*
    syllabus for, 120*t*, 133–134

environmental stewardship, 88
    economics and, 166
    service learning and, 135–145
environmental sustainability course, 78–115
    future of, 97
    goals and structure, 81–82
    objectives for, 83*t*, 106–107
    projects in, 84–89, 86*f*–87*f*
    reading lists for, 101–102, 109
    syllabus for, 99–113
    topics in, 82–84
Epp, Roger, 5
Erlich, Tom, 64
essays. *See* papers
ethics, business, 173
evaluation
    of civic engagement, 75–76
    in economics course, 216
    in environmental sustainability course,
        89–92
    in science and sustainability curriculum,
        31–32
    in STEP program, 44–45
    in sustainable design course, 196–198
    See also assessment

faculty
    and PACSE program, 8, 16–18
    STEP program and, 47–48
    and sustainability, recommendations for,
        95–97
    and transformation, 173
Faith in Place, 88
field experience
    in economics course, 210–211
    in ecosystem course, 137
    in PACSE program, 6–8, 19n7
    in science and sustainability curriculum,
        24
Field Museum, 44, 49
finance theory, traditional, 165–166
    expansion of, 166–168, 176–183
financial net income, 166
first-year link, 116
flexibility, service learning and, 25
food gardens, 146–161
fossil fuels, 40

Freire, Paulo, 6, 10, 17
freshman writing seminar (FWS), 116–134
    syllabus for, 121*t*, 133–134
Fromm, Erich, 5

Gates, Bill, 167
generational partnerships, learning gardens
    and, 148, 150
Golden Gate Community, 192
GOLum. *See* Green Organic Literacy Forum
graduate-level service learning, and learning
    gardens, 146–161
Greater Yellowstone Ecosystem (GYE), 136
Green Campus, 66, 72
green chemistry, 33
Green Mountain College, 21–34
Green Organic Literacy Forum (GOLum),
    31
grizzlies, 136–137
group projects, in environmental sustainabil-
    ity course, 102–103
growth economics, questioning assumptions
    of, 3, 5, 165–168
GYE. *See* Greater Yellowstone Ecosystem

Helling, Mary Kay, 135–145
high school, SAGE program and, 176–183
hortalizas, 9
human-centered worldview (HCW), 167
Humboldt State University, 202–225
hunger, learning gardens and, 150
Hutterites, 9
hybrid model, for service-learning sustain-
    ability course, 78–115

immersion learning, 17
Institute for Sustainable Development, 74
integration, scholarship of, 169
interdisciplinary service learning
    and environmental awareness, 116–134
    and environmental stewardship, 135–145
    PACSE program as, 15
    sustainability and, xxv, 69
    and sustainability education, 35–58
    and sustainable development, 206
International Labor Organization, 176

International Peace Through Commerce
    task force, 165, 168
Ishiguro, Kazuo, 120

johnston, sal, 116–134
journals
    in ecosystem course, 139
    in sustainable design course, 194–195, 201

Kiley, Maeve, 48
knowledge society, 173
Korten, David, 5
Koulentes, Tom, 50

learning communities
    and learning outcomes, 128–129
    science and, 117, 122
learning gardens, 146–161
    goals of, 150
Learning Gardens Laboratory (LGLab), 151–
    152, 156–157
learning outcomes. *See* student learning
    outcomes
lessons learned
    ecosystem course and, 143–144
    PACSE program and, 16–18
Levy, Irv, 31
liberal education, characteristics of, xii–xiii
Lishawa, Shane C., 35–58
listening, faculty and, 16
Loyola University Chicago (LUC), 35–58,
    78–115
    characteristics of, 37
    STEP program and, 48–49

McCline, Rich, 187
McDonald, Tracy, xxiii–xxxii
McKibben, Bill, xxv
McNall, Scott G., 61–77
mentors
    environmental sustainability course and,
    85
    STEP program and, 41, 44–45
methodology
    in STEP program, 40–42
    in sustainable design course, 190–192, 200
Mexico, service learning in, 3–20

Middleton, K. L., 168
midterm exams, in environmental sustainability course, 90, 114–115
moral education, xi
multiculturalism, and sustainability education, 146–161
multiplier effect, 203
Mündel, Hans-Dittmar, 3–20
Mündel, Karsten, 3–20

Naditz, A., 29
National Park Service, 135
National Wildlife Federation, 74
National Youth Leadership Council, 202
Native Americans, and learning gardens, 157–158
Nature Conservancy, 24
Nicola, Jill, 154, 158–159

organization-centered worldview (OWV), 167
Ornelas Lizardi, Arturo, 6, 17
Orr, David, 65, 157

PACSE. *See* Puebla-Alberta Community Service Exchange
papers
    in ecosystem course, 139
    in environmental science course, 120
    in environmental sustainability course, 91–92
    in learning gardens project, 153–154
    in sustainable design course, 195–196
    topic selection for, 143
Parajuli, Pramod, 148
participant observation, in ecosystem course, 142
participatory democracy, and service learning, 118
participatory research, in PACSE program, 14
Payne, Kara, 156
pedagogical strategies, in environmental science course, 117–118, 121–122
pedagogy
    in business course, 175–176
    in PACSE program, 10–12

in STEP program, 39
and sustainable development, 202–225
place, critical pedagogy of, 6, 8, 11–12
podcasts, in PACSE program, 14–15
policy analysis, ecosystem course and, 140–142
popular education, 11, 19n6
portfolios
    in environmental sustainability course, 91, 103
    in PACSE program, 14
Portland State University (PSU), 96, 146–161
poverty
    business ethics and, 175
    learning gardens and, 150
Power Shift 2009, 46–47
Prahalad, C. K., 178, 183
problem-based learning, in ecosystem course, 141–142
project proposals, in STEP program, 41–42
projects
    in environmental science course, 118–123
    in STEP program, 42–44
PSU. *See* Portland State University
public good, 171*t*, 172
public opinion, on climate change, xxiv
public schools, in urban communities, 151–152
Puebla-Alberta Community Service Exchange (PACSE), 3–20
    course objectives of, 7
    program components, 8–10
    teaching modalities in, 10–12
    theoretical framework of, 4–6
Pushnik, Jim, 70
Putnam, R. D., 169, 172, 183
Pyles, Jesse, 21–34

Ramaley, Judith, 147
Rawlins, Jack, 70
readings, on sustainability, 101–102, 109
reflection
    in economics course, 208–209, 212–213
    in environmental science course, 124
    in environmental sustainability course, 91
    in learning garden project, 149
    in learning gardens project, 153–159

in PACSE program, 10, 13
and SSPs, 24–27
in STEP program, 48
in sustainable design course, 193–195, 201
reports. *See* papers
Re-Runs Thrift Boutique, 192–193
research
in PACSE program, 14
subjects, community partners as, 88
rural communities
PACSE program and, 5–6, 8
sustainable development in, 202–225

Sachs, J., 183
SAGE. *See* Students for the Advancement of Global Entrepreneurship
SALG. *See* Student Assessment of Learning Gains
Samuelson, J., 174
San Francisco State University (SFSU), 187–201
scholarship of integration, 169
school gardens, 146–161
science courses
environmental science course, 116–134
and environmental stewardship, 135–145
future of, 33
sustainability and, 21–34, 78–115
service learning, xi–xiii
and civic engagement, xv–xvi
definition of, 118
and environmental awareness, 116–134
and environmental stewardship, 135–145
quality control and, 218
in science curriculum, 21–34
and sustainability, 78–115, 173–176
and sustainability education, 35–58
and sustainable development, 202–225
SFSU. *See* San Francisco State University
simple short projects (SSPs), 21, 23–25
Skelton, Judy Bluehorse, 154, 156–158
small group research, in PACSE program, 14
Smith, J., 168–169
social capital
definition of, 169–170
service learning and, 165–186
and sustainability, 168–174, 171*t*

traditional finance theory and, 166–168
types of, 172
social entrepreneurship, 174–175
SAGE program and, 176–183
sustainable design and, 187–201
term, 190
social justice
and learning gardens, 149
and service learning, 118
social responsibility, 168–174, 171*t*, 188–189
Solutions to Environmental Problems (STEP), 35–58
challenges in, 51–52
future directions for, 52
program, 37–39
syllabus for, 54–58
South Dakota, ecosystem projects in, 139–141
SSPs. *See* simple short projects
staff, STEP program and, 47–48
stewardship. *See* environmental stewardship
student(s)
as educators, 9, 29–31
environmental science course and, 126–128, 127*t*
environmental sustainability course and, 93–94
STEP program and, 46–51
and sustainability, xxiv–xxv
Student Assessment of Learning Gains (SALG), 32
student-directed learning, 39
in ecosystem course, 140, 142
student learning outcomes
in ecosystem course, 138
in environmental science course, 123–128, 125*t*–127*t*
learning communities and, 128–129
in learning gardens project, 152–153
in PACSE program, 13
service learning and, 124–126
in STEP program, 38, 45–46
Students for the Advancement of Global Entrepreneurship (SAGE), 166, 176–183
structure of, 178–180, 179*f*
syllabus for, 180, 181*f*
sustainability
and business, 170

civic engagement and, 61–77
importance of, xxiii
infrastructure and, 68–75
and science curriculum, 21–34
service learning and, 78–115, 173–176
social capital and, 168–174, 171*t*
students as educators on, 29–31
term, xxiii–xxiv, 78, 118
sustainability education
conceptual framework for, 148–149
issues in, 3
multiculturalism and, 146–161
PACSE program, 3–20
recommendations for, 95–97
service learning and, 35–58
sustainability movement, 77n5
sustainable design
definition of, 187
and social entrepreneurship, 187–201
sustainable development
community partners and, 69–70
definition of, 65, 187
in rural communities, 202–225
Sutheimer, Susan, 21–34
Swift, Cheryl, 116–134

traditional finance theory, 165–166
expansion of, 166–168, 176–183
transformation
ecological crisis and, 5–6
social entrepreneurship and, 190
STEP program and, 47
transnational social movement organizations
(TSMOs), 168–169
tree of life exercise, 11–12
Tuchman, Nancy, 35–58

Ulasewicz, Connie, 187–201
Uncommon Ground Rooftop Farm, 46, 49

unemployment, 176
Universidad Autonóma del Estado de Morelos (UAEM), 6–7, 15
Universidad de las Americas, Puebla
(UDLAP), 8, 15
urban communities
gardens in, 146–161
public schools in, 151–152
Urban Solutions, 192

value-based organizations, 67–68
Varty, Alison K., 35–58
Voss, Courtney, 71

water consumption, 126–127, 126*t*
Weber, Max, 68
Weisman, Alan, 120, 124
Welch, Michael, 48
Whitehead, Karen, 135–145
White privilege, 155
Whittier College, 116–134
Williams, Dilafruz R., 146–161
Wilson, Beth, 202–225
wind power, 140–141
wolves, 65, 136
World Commission on Environment and
Development, xxiii–xxiv
writing
in environmental sustainability course, 89
freshman writing seminar, 116–134
See also journals; reflection

Yellowstone National Park (YNP), 64–65,
135–145
youth, and unemployment, 176
YouTube, 14

Zingg, Paul J., 64, 66, 68, 72

Service Learning for Civic Engagement Series

Series Editor: Gerald Eisman

To stimulate the adaptation of the approaches described in these books, each volume includes an Activity / Methodology table that summarizes key elements of each example, such as class size, pedagogy, and other potential disciplinary applications

Race, Poverty, and Social Justice
Multidisciplinary Perspectives Through Service Learning
Edited by José Calderón

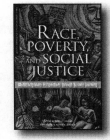

"Calderón compiles a collection designed to advance service learning 'beyond volunteerism (or charity) to a level of civic engagements that advances social justice in our institutions and a democratic culture in a civil society.' With topics ranging from day laborer centers and homelessness to preparing the student for life in a diverse global society, the collection provides practical strategies for achieving transformative learning in multiple contexts." —*Diversity & Democracy (AAC&U)*

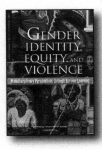

Gender Identity, Equity, and Violence
Multidisciplinary Perspectives Through Service Learning
Edited by Geraldine B. Stahly

The authors of the thirteen chapters in this volume bring excitement and innovations to teaching about gender from a wide range of theoretical and discipline perspectives. They exhibit the inclusiveness that is central to feminist pedagogy—a perspective that centers the educational enterprise in the analysis of the interconnectedness of social categories that have traditionally divided and given root to inequality and oppression and aims for no less than social transformation. Empowerment is a core value in gender education and the experiential approach nurtures that goal.

Research, Advocacy, and Political Engagement
Multidisciplinary Perspectives Through Service Learning
Edited by Sally Cahill Tannenbaum

"The examples in the book offer something for professors of all fields, and make this book an indispensable resource for those interested in adding a service learning component to their courses. Summing Up: Highly recommended."—*Choice*

The chapters in this book describe how teachers in Politics, Education, Urban and Regional Planning, Business, Communications, Sociology, Mathematics, Economics, and Women's Studies have created effective activities that advance disciplinary knowledge, develop collaboration with communities, and engage students in the political process.

Promoting Health and Wellness in Underserved Communities
Multidisciplinary Perspectives Through Service Learning
Edited by Anabel Pelham and Elizabeth Sills

Starting from the premise that our health status, vulnerability to accidents and disease, and life spans—as individuals and communities— are determined by the organization, delivery, and financing (or lack thereof) of health care, this book explores how educators and community caretakers teach the complex web of inter-connection between the micro level of individual health and well-being and the macro level of larger social structures.

Through the lenses of courses in anthropology, ESL, gerontology, management information systems, nursing, nutrition, psychology, public health, and sociology, the contributors offer examples of intergenerational and interdisciplinary practice, and share cutting-edge academic creativity to model how to employ community service learning to promote social change.

Sty/us

22883 Quicksilver Drive
Sterling, VA 20166-2102

Subscribe to our e-mail alerts: www.Styluspub.com